CHINA TO CHINATOWN

GLOBALITIES
Series editor: Jeremy Black

GLOBALITIES is a series which reinterprets world history in a
concise yet thoughtful way, looking at major issues over large
time-spans and political spaces; such issues can be political,
ecological, scientific, technological or intellectual. Rather than
adopting a narrow chronological or geographical approach,
books in the series are conceptual in focus yet present an array of
historical data to justify their arguments. They often involve a
multi-disciplinary approach, juxtaposing different subject-areas
such as economics and religion or literature and politics.

In the same series

Why Wars Happen
Jeremy Black

A History of Language
Steven Roger Fischer

The Nemesis of Power
Harald Kleinschmidt

*Geopolitics and Globalization
in the Twentieth Century*
Brian W. Blouet

Monarchies 1000–2000
W. M. Spellman

A History of Writing
Steven Roger Fischer

*The Global Financial System
1750 to 2000*
Larry Allen

Mining in World History
Martin Lynch

*Landscape and History
c. 1500–2000*
Ian D. Whyte

China to Chinatown

Chinese Food in the West

J.A.G.ROBERTS

REAKTION BOOKS

For my wife Jan,
for her love and forbearance

Published by Reaktion Books Ltd
79 Farringdon Road, London EC1M 3JU, UK

www.reaktionbooks.co.uk

First published 2002

Printed and bound in Great Britain by
Biddles Ltd, Guildford and King's Lynn

British Library Cataloguing in Publication Data

Roberts, J.A.G (John Anthony George), 1935–
    China to Chinatown: Chinese Food in the West. – (Globalities)
    1. Cookery, Chinese 2. Food habits – China 2. Civilization,
    Western – Chinese influences
    I. Title
    641.5'951

ISBN 1 86189 133 4

Contents

Acknowledgements

My thanks are due to the friends and colleagues who have helped in many ways with the ideas which have gone into this study. At an early stage in my research, I was much encouraged to come across Professor Jack Goody's chapter on the globalization of Chinese food in his wide-ranging study *Food and Love: A Cultural History of East and West* (London, 1998), and I enjoyed the opportunity to discuss some matters with him. I was urged to go ahead with the topic by Professor Steven I. Levine of the University of Montana, and it was he who referred me to the on-line web-based Asian history discussion group E-Asia, from whose subscribers I received very useful information. I must thank staff at several libraries who have helped me, notably Huddersfield University Library, the John Rylands University Library of Manchester, Leeds University Library, the British Library Newspaper Library, the Wellcome Library for the History and Understanding of Medicine and the BBC Written Archives Centre, Reading. I received many helpful suggestions from subscribers to *Saga Magazine* and from readers of the *Huddersfield Examiner.* Special thanks are due to Raymond Wong of Maxi's Restaurant, Leeds, to Beth Mallinson whose recent dissertation gave me a glimpse of what today's English students think of ethnic food, and to Aimée Laycock who worked as a waitress in a Chinese restaurant and shared her reflections on British attitudes to Chinese food.

The author and publishers wish to express their thanks to the following sources of photographic material and/or permission to reproduce it: The Glenbow-Alberta Institute (ND-2-211), p. 153; Hulton Getty, p. 158; Bernard Llewellyn, on behalf of the late Jack Skeel, p. 98; The Manchester Chamber of Commerce, p. 183; Peters Fraser and Dunlop Ltd, p. 182; Mr Stanley T. Smith,

Introduction

We the Chinese conquered the world – through our food.
                                          Chinese saying

This book is concerned with one of the most remarkable social changes of modern times: the radical alteration in the eating habits of the Western world. This subject is so extensive and so little researched that I have confined my discussion to a single aspect of that transformation: the changing attitudes of the West towards Chinese food, which in recent years has led to the opening of a Chinese restaurant or takeaway in almost every Western town, and to the adoption, in a modified form, of many Chinese cooking techniques. As material on this theme is vast and scattered, the main emphasis here is restricted, in terms of literature, to the ways these changes have been perceived by Westerners writing in English and, in geographical terms, to the introduction of aspects of Chinese food culture to North America and to the United Kingdom.[1]

The book is divided into two main sections, a division which reflects the distinction made by the food writer Kenneth Lo between 'Chinese cooking in China' and 'Chinese food abroad'. Lo remarked that Chinese food, like everything else 'suffers a sea change when removed from its native shores'. The same observation applies to attitudes to food, whether it is viewed through strangers' eyes as an aspect of a foreign culture, or whether it is perceived from the vantage point of home as an exotic or perhaps suspect addition to one's own foodways.[2] Part I investigates the attitudes of Westerners encountering Chinese food in China from the earliest records to the present day. At first Westerners – chiefly missionaries and merchants – regarded Chinese food as a curiosity and treated it as an aspect of the exotic character of the country. From the late eighteenth century Westerners' descriptions of Chinese food became more hostile, and the Chinese list of foodstuffs, and their methods of preparing them, were sometimes dismissed with contempt or even disgust. By the twentieth century a more subtle range of attitudes had emerged: some Westerners recognized the achievements of Chinese gastronomy, some continued to find grounds for criticism and rejection, and others, heedless of personal taste, ate the food of the common people of China to demonstrate political support for their cause.

Part II looks at the reception of Chinese food in North America and the United Kingdom. It traces the opening of the first Chinese restaurants catering for foreigners, and the beginning of the appreciation of Chinese cuisine in the West. It then examines the phenomenon of the mass acceptance of Chinese food, with the proliferation of Chinese restaurants and takeaways in the cities and towns of the Western world, the increased availability of Chinese foodstuffs in shops and supermarkets, the injection of capital into the ethnic food market, the publication of recipe books for Chinese food and the use of the media to popularize its consumption. The final chapter sets these changes in the wider context of how eating habits have evolved and relates these changes to the globalization of food in general.

Two broad themes recur. The first relates to the analysis of images of other cultures and of attitudes towards other races. Harold T. Isaacs, struck by the contradictory notions of China and the Chinese shared by generations of Americans, once suggested the following sequence of attitudes: the Age of Respect (Eighteenth Century); the Age of Contempt (1840–1905); the Age of Benevolence (1905–1937); the Age of Admiration (1937–1944); the Age of Disenchantment (1944–1949) and the Age of Hostility (1949–). Isaacs was quick to admit that these descriptions were crude, that expressions from different ages coexisted, and that the views of individuals might vary. It would be presumptuous to suggest that this study answers the question how images of another society are formed and perpetuated. However, by concentrating on a single theme, that of food, it does reveal the complexity of attitudes towards what is perceived as foreign. Present-day attitudes to Chinese food may be manipulated by advertising and the forces of international capitalism, but the fundamentals of those attitudes were established over centuries of Western contact with China; it is for this reason that a study of the range of those attitudes and of the factors that shaped them remains relevant today.[3]

The second theme concerns how, when and why the eating habits of the inhabitants of the West have changed to incorporate Chinese food. This change is characterized by two qualities: it is cultural and comparatively recent. Although many books have been written about changes in American and British diets, their emphasis has been on gastronomical and medical developments rather than cultural change. However, the worldwide acceptance of ethnic foods is the outcome of a variety of influences of which gastronomical preferences and health considerations are only two. In Britain the most dramatic example of the incorporation of ethnic foods is the acculturation of Indian food – in 1997 a Gallup poll estimated that over 25 per cent of the British population ate curry at least once a week. This popularity must be attributed as much to cost and convenience rather as to aesthetic appreciation, and the same is true for much of the consumption of Chinese food, though other factors encourage the trend – to identify some of these factors I make a brief comparison between the assimilation of Indian and of Chinese food in Britain. My main theme, however, is that of tracing how Chinese food came to achieve widespread acceptance in North America and Britain. This has involved tracking down examples of moments when Chinese restaurants and Chinese food stores began to attract Western customers, when Chinese food and Chinese cooking methods began to be welcome in Western kitchens and on Western tables and when Westerners began to cook a version of Chinese food to eat in their own homes. In its early stages this change was the product of Chinese enterprise and a modification on both sides: Chinese dishes adapted to suit Western taste-buds and, later, the gradual alteration of American and British eating habits. The change accelerated when the media began to popularize Chinese food and when publishers began to include ethnic cookbooks on their lists. Recently heavy investment in the industrial production of ethnic foods and in the operation of up-market restaurants has initiated a new stage in the consumption of

Chinese food. To continue Isaacs's sequence of attitudes listed above, we are now perhaps living in an Age of Acceptance.

Whereas in the past the eating habits of a people or of a nation appear (perhaps misleadingly) to have been relatively fixed, in the modern world eating habits in the affluent West are subject to rapid and continuous change. This book considers one example of how that transformation has taken place.

Part I: West to East

ONE

Chinese Food[1]

Which foodstuffs should be described as 'Chinese'? The range of foodstuffs consumed in China at present is much greater than that of the past. Much of this extension has come through the introduction of foodstuffs from America and the West in the late Ming dynasty and their dissemination in the Qing period. Maize, sweet potatoes, Irish potatoes and peanuts became basic crops, and other introductions, for example the capsicum and the tomato, have also been cultivated. Many of these plants were described as *fan*, meaning foreign or barbarous. More recently Western foodstuffs, for example field mushrooms, have been grown commercially on Taiwan.

The basic food most closely connected with China in the Western mind is rice. Rice has been an important element in the Chinese diet for a long time. The plant *oryza sativa* may have been domesticated first in South China. The consumption of rice is so much part of the Chinese diet that a proverb states that 'even a clever wife can't cook without rice'. Of course rice is consumed throughout East and South Asia, and to label rice a Chinese food requires further definition. The preferred rice for main meals is the long-grained variety, whereas glutinous rice is used mainly for confectionery. Until recently the rice consumed by the great mass of the Chinese people was only lightly milled, thereby preserving a high proportion of its nutritional value. In modern times polished rice has been preferred by those Chinese who can afford it, and is eaten exclusively by Chinese overseas.

Much of North China is too cold, or too dry, to support rice, and there the main crop is wheat. Some Chinese minority groups, for example the Uighur, use wheat to make bread, but most Chinese use wheat flour to make steamed dumplings and noodles. Steamed dumplings are filled with either a savoury or a sweet concoction. Noodles are made either by forcing the dough through a type of colander, or by manipulating the dough until it falls into strands, a technique sometimes demonstrated in Chinese restaurants. The provenance of noodles has been much debated. There is little evidence to support the legend that Marco Polo brought pasta, including spaghetti and ravioli, from China to Europe. Egg noodles are probably Chinese in origin, but meat-filled dumplings are more likely to derive from Central Asia.[2] Other grains, for example kaoliang (sorghum), millet and maize form an important part of the diet of northern Chinese. Neither sorghum or maize are indigenous crops, the former having been domesticated first in Africa, while maize, which is made into corn meal cakes, was introduced into China from America early in the sixteenth century. Sweet potatoes, which were also introduced from America, are counted as grain in statistics. They are grown on poor soils in the south and have usually been regarded as a human food of last resort, being ordinarily used as animal feed. These grain crops are also used to produce alcohol. Chinese wine is made from rice and spirits from kaoliang or millet. The fiery spirit *maotai*, named after the city of that name in Guizhou, is distilled from a liquor made from kaoliang and wheat.

Several pulses are important in Chinese food. The best known in the West is the soya bean, which was domesticated in Zhou times. The raw soya bean contains substances which inhibit digestion of its protein and so it requires considerable preparation before it is edible. When prepared it contains more protein than other common cultivated plants. Soya beans may be cooked down to a sort of porridge, but its better-known products are bean curd, soy sauce and black bean sauce. Bean curd, *doufu* (also known in the West by its Japanese name *tofu*) is produced by boiling the soya bean and then coagulating the liquid produced with gypsum, so creating a soft curd which can be used either fresh or dried. Soy sauce is made by fermenting a mixture of soya beans, flour, salt and strains of fungi. Black bean sauce was originally made from boiled soya beans which were then fermented with a fungus. The sauce sold commercially also contains vegetables, ginger and other ingredients. Yellow soya beans are the main ingredient of Hoisin sauce, which is widely used when cooking poultry and prawns. Other beans widely used as food in China include the mung bean, which can be made into bean curd, but is better known as the source of bean sprouts, and the red bean which is used in soups and sweet-meats.

Chinese food, taken as a whole, uses a very wide selection of vegetables. In the context of Western acceptance of Chinese food, however, only some of these have a particular significance. The best-known green vegetable is the Chinese cabbage, *Brassica chinensis*, known in the West as bok choy. Other vegetables identified as Chinese food include water chestnuts, bamboo shoots and lotus root. The water chestnut, *Eleocharis dulcis*, known in China as *mati* or horse's hoof, is the corm of a bulrush. It was first grown for food in South-east Asia, but the best Chinese water chestnuts are grown in Guilin. Bamboo shoots come from several varieties of bamboo, the best from the genus *Phyllostachys*. The shoots come from buds growing from the base of older canes, which may be covered up as celery is in the West, or from underground rhizomes. In China they are usually used fresh, and in winter, when they are considered as at their best. Chinese cooking makes considerable use of members of the onion family, most commonly the *Allium fistulosum*, the Welsh or bunching onion, the onion referred to as scallion in Chinese cookery books.

Four other plants used in Chinese food may be mentioned: the lotus, the lily, seaweed and varieties of fungi. Lotus leaves are used to wrap food and the lotus root is commonly used around Guangzhou as a food medicine, said to promote fertility. Lily buds, known otherwise as 'golden needles', which have an unusual musty taste, are used in some meat dishes. Several varieties of seaweed are eaten, including the red algae called purple laver, *Porphyra*, sometimes served crisp as an hors d'oeuvre, and the large brown algae, *Laminaria japonica*, from which the gelatinous extract known as agar-agar is derived, which is sometimes used as a cheap substitute for birds' nests. As for fungi, three of the most common used in Chinese cooking are padi-straw mushrooms, and those known as wooden ear and monkey head. Wooden ear is a type of bracket mushroom which grows on fallen trees. Monkey head, also known as hedgehog fungus because of its strange appearance, is a delicacy found in the forests of the north-east. All these fungi are now cultivated.

Some fruit may be considered as Chinese food, the most typical being the lychee and the longan. The lychee was probably first domesticated in South China and it is now cultivated extensively in Guangdong and Tonkin. The longan, that is the *longyan* or dragon's eye, which occurs widely throughout Southeast Asia, also has a long history of cultivation in China.

Some spices have a strong connection with Chinese food. Star anise was probably first domesticated in South China or South-east Asia and it is now cultivated around Nanning in Guangxi province. It is either used whole or in the form of anise-seed oil. Fagara is a peppery fruit used in Sichuan peppery hot sauce. Cinnamon is native to a large part of Asia, but *Cinnamomum cassia*, which produces the best bark, is found in Guangdong and Guangxi. Guilin, the provincial capital of Guangxi province, means 'cassia forest'. Cassia also has a wide range of medicinal uses, in particular to check nausea and diarrhoea, and is also said to prolong life. Baopuze, a Daoist alchemist living in the fourth century AD, was said to have eaten cassia and toads' brains for seven years, and thereby could walk on water and avoid ageing and death. Ginger, although not native to China, was already known in Zhou times and has since been widely cultivated. 'Five-spice powder', a combination of star anise, fennel, cinnamon, cloves, ginger and cardamom, and sometimes fagara, is used to season red-cooked meats and poultry. Ginseng may be mentioned in this context, although it is used more as a medicine than as a spice or flavouring, for it is believed to add *qi* or vital essence. The use of monosodium glutamate or MSG, although now ubiquitous in some forms of Chinese cooking, is a recent additive, for it only came into large-scale production in Japan in the early twentieth century.

The first item of Chinese food to be consumed in quantity in the West was tea. The tea plant, *Camellia sinensis*, is indigenous to the China-India-Burma border region and the habit of drinking tea is believed to have been introduced from India to China in about the fifth century AD, its original purpose being medicinal.

Only in the late eighth century, with the publication of the *Classic of Tea* by Li Yu, did the aesthetic cult associated with the drinking of tea begin to develop, and thereafter tea drinking became widespread in China. At first tea was drunk with salt and milk or butter, a practice continued at the Manchu court of the Qing dynasty, but in modern times it is drunk as a simple infusion. Tea is processed into five main forms: black or fermented tea, oolong (*wulong* or black dragon) semi-fermented tea, green or unfermented tea, scented teas such as jasmine tea, and brick tea. Tea is used in cooking, to flavour foods such as eggs, chicken and shrimps, and is also made into a pickle.

Turning now to animal products, first it must be said that economic conditions in China, and the Buddhist aversion to killing animals, have ensured that the consumption of large quantities of animal products has never been typical of the Chinese diet. In 1931–7 the United States annual per capita consumption of meat was about 150 kilograms, whereas consumption in China was less than 13 kilograms. The most important meat has always been pork, followed by mutton and goat meat, which is more popular among Chinese Muslims. Beef, either from the cow or the water buffalo, has rarely been eaten, partly on religious grounds derived from India and partly on economic grounds. Fresh milk and cheese, whether from cows or from goats and sheep, have never formed a significant part of the Chinese diet. Several reasons have been put forward to explain this, two of which may be cited. The Chinese, like most Asian people, cease to produce the enzyme lactase at about the age of six, and as a consequence have difficulty in digesting lactose, that is milk sugar. This is not an absolute prohibition as many Central Asian people do depend on dairy products for much of their animal protein. The second explanation is that dairy foods were associated in the Chinese mind with Central Asian peoples, for example the Mongols. Consequently, either because of prejudice against the customs of such peoples, or because of an unwillingness to increase economic dependence on them, the Chinese rejected these foods.

Chickens were reared in China as early as 5,000 BC and ducks and geese were being kept soon after that date. As chickens and ducks are so much part of the Chinese menu which is now familiar in the West, one might suppose that poultry has long been an important element in Chinese food. As in the West, however, before the introduction of battery rearing, chickens and ducks were festival fare. The former were always eaten fresh, but various methods of preserving ducks have been developed. Eggs are used extensively in Chinese cooking, although peasant families traditionally sold their eggs rather than consumed them. Various methods of cooking eggs have been popular, including boiling them in tea. From the Western viewpoint the most notorious form of preparation is the 100-year old (or 1,000-year old) egg, this being a duck egg which has been coated in a mixture of salt, pine-ash and lime and placed in an earthenware jar for 45 days.

It has long been observed by Westerners that the Chinese, particularly in the south, are omnivorous. In part this may be attributed to a rational approach to the food value of animals and insects, and in part to a highly developed set of concepts relating food to health, a matter dealt with at greater length below. The animals eaten as food which have drawn particular comment among Westerners are dogs, cats, rats, snakes, other more exotic animals and some varieties of insect.

The eating of dogs in China has a long history. Dogs were one of the 'five domesticated animals' of ancient China, and the breeding of dogs for food was mentioned by Mencius.[3] In the past dog meat was eaten throughout China, but in modern times its consumption has largely been limited to the south. The consumption of dog meat is closely linked with the belief that it provides winter warmth. Cats have also been eaten, but more rarely, and usually for medicinal reasons. The aversion to the eating of dogs and cats has been expressed so loudly by Westerners that it is important to point out that dog-eating was certainly practised in Germany until early in the twentieth century, and that the killing and eating of cats, as an ingredient in spells or for medicinal purposes, was common in France in the eighteenth century.[4]

Supposed medicinal benefits explain the consumption of other animals and insects. Snakes are regarded as a tonic and heating food, and like dog meat, snake meat is eaten in preparation for the winter. Rats may be offered for sale as a sovereign remedy for baldness in women. Some insects, notably grasshoppers and caterpillars, are consumed in times of famine. Other insects are eaten as a delicacy or because of their ascribed therapeutic value. Stinkbugs, for example, are the main ingredient of 'blue-dragon pills', an aphrodisiac preparation.

Marine fish and freshwater fish and many varieties of crustaceans may be regarded as Chinese food. Particular mention should be made of carp, which have been pond-reared since the Zhou dynasty, and marine products, in particular crabs and prawns. Oysters feature in a variety of Chinese dishes, and oyster sauce, made from oysters and soy sauce, is a commonly used ingredient.

Particular mention should be made of the 'four Chinese delicacies': birds' nests, sharks' fins, bears' paws and the sea cucumber. Birds' nests are composed of nest cement, a form of salivary secretion from swiftlets which nest in caves in Southeast Asia. Western travellers' reports suggest that the consumption of birds' nests only became common from the mid-fifteenth century. Birds' nests are regarded as a strengthening food and as a medicine. Black nests, which contain quantities of feathers before they are cleaned, are expensive, but white nests of the top quality may sell for 25 times the price of black nests. Sharks' fins, which first gained favour in Song times, are obtained from tiger sharks, shark-like guitar fishes, and from rays. Bears' paws, which have also been regarded as a delicacy in Europe, were highly esteemed by Mencius. Nowadays the shortage of bears means that fortunately bears' paws rarely appear on a menu. The sea cucumber or sea slug, otherwise known as the trepang or bêche-de-mer, is one of several varieties of *Holothuria* which are dried and used in combination with other seafoods. A delicacy which appears on the menu of important banquets, it is sometimes described as 'sea ginseng' and is claimed to be a strengthening food.

Of the many cooking methods employed by Chinese cooks, five may be described as characteristic of Chinese cooking. These are stir-frying, red-cooking, clear-simmering, steaming and cooking drunken foods.[5] Stir-frying is economical of heat, which has always been a consideration in a country where fuel is scarce. The food to be cooked is shredded or sliced and cooked rapidly thereby preserving flavour. Red-cooking involves the cooking of meat in a broth of water, soy sauce, sugar and other ingredients, which gives it a deep brownish colour. Clear-simmering is similar to red-cooking, but soy sauce is not used, and the meat is only lightly seasoned. Steaming is used not only for meat and vegetable dishes, but also for pastries and desserts, in which case it may replace baking. As with stir-frying, steaming is economical of fuel and the food retains its flavour. Drunken foods are meat or fish cuts which after cooking are steeped in wine or sherry for several days.

These cooking methods call for the use of a variety of tools and utensils. The most important tool is the knife or cleaver, which has a rectangular blade and a wooden or bamboo handle. Originally made of iron, it is now available in stainless steel. The blade of the cleaver is used for chopping and slicing, the back for pounding or crushing and the side to pick up food. Certain techniques for using the cleaver are characteristic of Chinese cooking, for example diagonal cutting which is used for meat and vegetables to be cooked rapidly. To chop a chicken with a cleaver, the legs and wings are severed, the legs cut into three pieces and the wings into two. The carcass is then cut across the breastbone three times and each cut is divided into two, giving sixteen portions in all. The other two indispensable utensils in the Chinese kitchen are the wok and the steamer. The wok, which is typically made of cast iron, which conducts heat rapidly and evenly, is ideal for stir-frying, but can be used for many other forms of Chinese cooking. Basket steamers, traditionally made of bamboo, can be stacked as high as three or even five layers and may be large enough to cook several dishes in one basket.

As for eating implements, the most important are spoons, usually of porcelain, though now commonly made of plastic, chopsticks and a bowl. The Chinese term for chopsticks is *kuaizi*, sometimes literally, and perhaps absurdly, translated as 'quick little ones'. Chopsticks may be made of a variety of materials, the best being made of ivory, while those in everyday use are made of bamboo, and increasingly, of plastic. The use of chopsticks goes back to the Shang dynasty and has acquired a deep cultural significance, as explained by Raymond Dawson:

no line so definitely divided civilized people from barbarians as that which separated men who consume their food with chopsticks from those who used their fingers or in later times such inferior instruments as knives and forks.[6]

The typical dish from which Chinese eat is the bowl, which is usually quite small, having a diameter of approximately 10–12 cms. A larger, shallower bowl is used for noodle dishes. The bowls in common use carry a variety of standard designs including dragons and flowers and may have a pattern of rice grains pressed into them. Large shallow bowls for noodle dishes are usually decorated with a picture of a carp.

'Chinese food' denotes not a single cuisine, but a number of regional cuisines. These are usually defined as the northern cuisine, centred on Beijing (Peking) and Shandong province, the eastern cuisine of Shanghai and the lower Yangzi valley, the western cuisine, in particular associated with Sichuan province, and the southern cuisine, often described as Cantonese, from Guangzhou (Canton). Sometimes the food of Fujian province, in the south-east, is considered to amount to a separate cuisine. The northern cuisine tends to use wheat or millet rather than rice – Beijing duck is traditionally served with pancakes made from wheat flour. Another northern dish, Mongolian hot-pot, indicates that mutton is more commonly eaten in the north. The eastern cuisine has a reputation for gourmet cooking, with red-cooked dishes and delicacies such as Nanjing pressed duck. Sichuan cooking is often spicy. Typical dishes include hot and sour soup, smoked dishes and food cooked in sesame oil. Southern cooking is very varied, with fish an important ingredient. This region is also famous for dim sum (*dianxin*), snack foods composed of a filling of chopped meat, fish or vegetables in a dough or thin wrapping and steamed or deep fried. The term 'Chinese food' also embraces the food styles of different economic classes and ranges from banquets of ten or more courses, to the 'usual five dishes' of chicken, shrimps, pork, eggs and soup, and to famine foods: 'flour of ground leaves, sawdust, thistles, cotton seeds, peanut hulls, ground pumice.'[7]

Jack Goody has suggested that in Eurasia (but not in Africa) societies that were 'stratified culturally as well as politically'

Food shops and restaurants in Beijing, 1717.

developed a 'truly differentiated cuisine'. The differentiation was apparent in the types of food eaten by the rich and by the poor, in practices relating to the public consumption of food, and in the aesthetic appreciation of rich and rare food, an appreciation which was countered by a degree of resentment against culinary extravagance and by themes of denial, restraint and asceticism. Chinese food, because of different concepts of what is acceptable as food, how it should be cooked and how it should be served, has often been regarded as the antithesis of Western food. Goody's comparison of the food practices of the East and West suggests that they also had important features in common. He includes among these the use of literacy to develop ideas about food and eating; the attachment of prestige to the consumption of foods derived from 'outside' – for example, the use of exotic spices in European cooking and the consumption of birds' nests in China; and the similarity in patterns of familial eating, which contrasted with the usual practice in Africa of men and women eating in separate places. He identified as a salient feature of the culinary cultures of Europe and China their association with hierarchical man. There was a great gulf between the frugal diet of peasants and the elaborate tables of the ruling classes and this was epitomized by the wide variety of foods offered at the latter, and the consumption there of dishes which were largely the invention of specialists. This differentiation between high and low cuisine can be traced back to ancient China and to the Roman world and is still relevant in modern times.[8] These similarities may have facilitated the later globalization of Chinese food.

The term 'Chinese food' may be extended to refer to habits relating to serving and eating food. When considering the composition of meals, Chinese make a distinction between *fan*, literally 'cooked rice', but comprising all starchy foods, and *cai*, meaning vegetables. At every meal suitable quantities of both *fan* and *cai* should be consumed, and this balance is achieved in individual dishes and in wonton, dumplings filled with a variety of mixtures, which are then boiled or steamed or, more commonly in the West, deep fried. The same parallelism is evident in the matter of utensils, with the rice cooker used to cook the *fan* part of the meal and the wok the *cai*.

The well-known chef and television personality Ken Hom, addressing a Western audience and speaking for generations of Chinese, wrote 'For us food is more than a passion, it is an obsession, and good eating is believed to be essential to good living.'[9] Whereas Westerners usually entertain at home, much of Chinese entertaining takes place in restaurants, where parties often eat in private rooms. Attention is paid to the selection of appropriate dishes and the presentation of food. A variety of foodstuffs is selected, with dishes composed of pork, beef, chicken, fish and vegetables. Balance is achieved by including dishes representing the five flavours, which are defined as salty, bitter, sour, acrid and sweet. For family-style meals the number of dishes is usually limited to one per person and soup. The dishes appear at the same time and rice is served through the meal. Chinese banquets consist of ten or more courses, starting with appetizers and quick-fried dishes, followed by heavier dishes and then rice-accompanied dishes. Soup may be served at the conclusion of each stage of the banquet. The Chinese meal table is round, not rectangular as in the West, so it has no head which the host might occupy. Nevertheless social conventions dictate how people should be seated. The most distinguished guests are persuaded to take the seats against the wall, with the hosts on the opposite side of the table near the door. Less important guests sit in the intermediate places. When the food is served, each guest helps himself or herself. Alcohol, usually in the form of rice wine drunk hot, may be served. At the end of the meal guests are provided with hot towels and bowls of tea. Tea drinking has developed its own etiquette. At a formal meeting 'guest tea' not intended for consumption is served, its arrival signalling the end of the meeting.

K. C. Chang stressed that the overriding idea about food in China is that the kind and amount of food one takes is intimately relevant to one's health. This is not just a general principle: the selection of the right food is dependent on one's health condition at that time. 'Food,' he remarked, 'is also medicine.'[10] Chinese attitudes to food have been influenced by the concept of the complementary forces of *yin* and *yang* and the need to maintain these in balance. Food is regarded as supplying *qi*, that is energy, and something more than energy, to the body. Foods are divided into categories of hot and cold and, less significantly, categories of wet and dry. Some foods, for example fatty meat, chillies, ginger, and high calorie foods like bread, are considered heating, whereas others, such as water-cress and sea-weed, are regarded as cooling. Shellfish are wetting, whereas dry-roasted peanuts are typically dry. There is no unanimity of view on these divisions, and many foodstuffs are categorized as neutral. For a body to remain healthy, or to return to health, it must remain in, or achieve, balance in terms of heat, cold, wetness and dryness. Heating foods may be prescribed to counter wasting illnesses, whereas cooling foods are appropriate for treating fevers and rashes.

Another important concept concerning Chinese food is *bu*, defined in the dictionary as 'to repair, patch, mend'. Many foods, usually in the form of easily digestible, high-quality protein are said to be *bu*, and by eating them one may enhance one's *qi*. Many of these foods are also exotic and expensive. Birds' nests, sea slugs and sharks' fins are strengthening foods. Ginseng, which may either be eaten mixed with other food, or taken in powder form, is also considered a tonic. Some items, like the genitalia and antlers of deer and rhinoceros horn, are reputed to enhance male sexual performance.

No description of Chinese food and eating habits would be complete without reference to the pleasure which Chinese through the ages have associated with preparing food and with eating. In the words of Doreen Yen Hung Feng, compiler of one of the first Chinese cookery books intended for the use of Westerners,

> The joy of eating is given great importance in China; and cooking, through the decades, has been dreamed and fussed over, in times of want as well as in times of plenty, until it has ceased to be plain cooking, but has grown and developed into an art. Food has been represented through other mediums of art, especially poetry, literature and folklore; and these tales and food beliefs have been handed down, from generation to generation, with ever-increasing glamour. Every aspect of food is analyzed, from its palatableness to its texture, and from its fragrance to its colourfulness; until, as in other works of art, proportion and balance are instilled in every dish.[11]

TWO

The Western Discovery of Chinese Food

Marco Polo's *Travels*, based on his experiences in China between 1275 and 1292, provided the first eye-witness report of Chinese food and eating habits. His failure to refer to the practice of drinking tea is one of a number of omissions which have cast doubt on whether he reached China, but other evidence points conclusively to his having been there. His references to food and eating habits are scattered and incomplete, but in them may be found the origins of some of the Western stereotypes of Chinese food. He recognized the importance of rice, millet and panic (a type of millet) in the Chinese diet. He noted that 'Wheat in their country does not yield such an increase; but such of it as they harvest they eat only in the form of noodles or other pasty foods.' His description of Hangzhou contained a catalogue of the amazing plentifulness and variety of foodstuffs available in the markets, including wild game and fowl, many sorts of vegetables and fruit, including huge pears 'weighing 10 lb apiece, white as dough inside and very fragrant'. He remarked on the vast quantities of fish offered for sale, both ocean fish and lake fish. Of the latter he commented, apparently without irony, 'Thanks to the refuse from the city, these fish are plump and tasty.' His other references to food emphasized the exotic and unattractive aspects of Chinese eating habits. In Kunming the inhabitants ate their flesh raw with garlic sauce, and they also ate huge snakes and serpents (perhaps crocodiles). In Hangzhou, 'They eat all sorts of flesh, including that of dogs and other brute beasts and animals of every kind which Christians would not touch for anything in the world.' In Fuzhou, 'You must know that the natives eat all sorts of brute beast. They even relish human flesh. They do not touch the flesh of those that have died a natural death; but they all eat the flesh of those who have died of a wound and consider it a delicacy,' even though 'they are amply provided with the means of life.' On a more positive note, referring to Chinese beverages, he declared that the inhabitants of Cathay, that is North China, 'make a drink of rice and an assortment of excellent spices, prepared in such a way that it is better to drink than any other wine'. Occasionally Polo mentioned extravagant feasts, but he did not describe the Chinese at table, nor did he refer to the use of chopsticks. He noticed that the Chinese preferred to entertain at a restaurant rather than at home. On an island on the West Lake of Hangzhou there was a building as magnificent as an imperial palace, which was used for wedding parties and feasts. The restaurant supplied all the necessary crockery, napery and plate and could cater for 100 clients at once.[1]

Odoric of Pordenone, a Franciscan friar who spent three years in China in the 1320s, also noted that the Chinese ate serpents, adding, 'These serpents [have quite a fragrant odour and] form a dish so fashionable that if a man were to give a dinner and not have one of these serpents on his table, he would be thought to have done nothing.' He repeated Polo's observation on Chinese entertainment, suggesting that a person wishing to entertain his friends might say to the host of the restaurant, 'Make me a dinner for such a number of my friends, and I propose to expend such and such a sum upon it.'[2]

The Mongol empire collapsed in the fourteenth century and the land route from Europe to China became impassable. It was not until the opening of the sea route in the sixteenth century that Westerners again reached China and fresh observations were made about Chinese food. By now greater awareness had developed in Europe concerning personal habits including table manners and the use of forks rather than fingers when eating.

In 1549 the Portuguese adventurer Galeote Pereira, who had previously visited India, was captured off the South China coast and taken as a prisoner to Quanzhou, Fuzhou and thence overland to Guilin, from where he contrived to escape. His narrative, which was published in Italian in 1565 and in English in 1577, contained a number of references to the growing and consumption of food in China. He recorded that the Chinese practice of collecting human excrement to use as manure was very good for keeping the city clean, his comparison being with contemporary practice in Lisbon. Whereas in India the people ate neither hens, beef, nor pork, the Chinese 'are the greatest eaters in all the world, they do feed upon all things, specially on pork, the fatter that is, unto them the less loathsome'. When the Chinese ate formal meals, they were 'wont to eat their meat sitting on stools at high tables as we do, although they use neither table-cloths or napkins'. The food was carved before being brought to the table, and then 'they feed with two sticks, refraining from touching their meat with their hands, even as we do with forks.'

Gaspar da Cruz, a Dominican friar, spent some months in China in 1556, visiting Guangzhou and travelling along the south coast. He drew on Pereira's account, but also added his own observations on aspects of Chinese life. He too recorded the Chinese practice of using human excrement as manure, noting that 'they say with it the vegetables can be seen to grow'. He tasted a lychee and declared: 'None can have his fill of it, for always it leaveth a desire for more.' Yet his description of Chinese food practices was not entirely complimentary. He alleged than when selling hens the Chinese made them weigh more by filling their bodies with water and their crops with sand. Although he was impressed by the number of eating places in Guangzhou and the cleanliness of the food they had to offer, he added that near the city wall there was a street of vict-ualling houses where,

> they sell dogs cut in quarters, roasted, boiled and raw, with the heads pulled, and with their ears, for they scald them all like pigs. It is a meat which the base people do eat, and they sell them alive about the city in cages.[3]

In 1575 Martin de Rada, a scholarly Augustinian missionary and a member of a Spanish diplomatic delegation, spent a few months in Fujian province and attended an event described as the 'first meeting on equal terms between educated Europeans and high officials of the Ming Empire'. De Rada's account of his visit contained a section entitled 'Of their manner of eating and of their banquets.' The 'chief bread' of the Chinese, he wrote, was cooked rice and they even made a wine from it which was 'comparable with a reasonable grape wine and might even be mistaken for it'. They did not touch their food with their fingers but used 'two long little sticks', and were 'so expert in this, that they can take anything, however small, and carry it to their mouth, even if it is round, like plums and other such fruits'. At the start of the meal they ate meat without bread, and at the end they ate three or four dishes of cooked rice, 'which they likewise eat with their chopsticks, even though somewhat hoggishly'.

The banquets given to the delegates were formal occasions. The Spanish clergy and laymen were seated separately. Opposite the clergy, at the far end of the hall, were the Chinese officials who had invited them, while opposite the laymen sat the Chinese officials who had accompanied them. The cooked food, to be consumed on that occasion, was set out on three tables, but on other tables uncooked food was set out 'for grandeur and display'. All this food belonged to the guests, and was carried to their lodgings after the meal.

De Rada compared the food habits of the Chinese with those of Europeans. He noted that the Chinese were not great meat-eaters, their food consisting principally of fish, eggs, vegetables, broths and fruits. Many of these products were similar to those of Europe, but many others were different. He singled out the black-fleshed fowl of Fujian, which were more tasty than European hens, a point also noted by Marco Polo previously. He cited the wide variety of fruit and vegetables available, and noted that there was much sugar and 'very good conserves'. He also described the drinking of tea, though he did not refer to it by name. He wrote that when one visited a household a servant came forward with cups of hot water

This water is boiled with certain somewhat bitter herbs, and with a little morsel of conserve in the water. They eat the morsel and sip the hot water. Although at first we did not much care for that hot boiled water, yet we soon became accustomed to it and got to like it, for this is always the first thing which is served on any visit.[4]

This was not the first Western reference to tea. In about 1550 Giovanni Battista Ramusio, Marco Polo's editor and biographer, was told by Haji Mahomed how the Chinese

> take of that herb whether dry or fresh, and boil it well in water. One or two cups of this decoction taken on an empty stomach removes fever, head-ache, stomach-ache, pain in the side or in the joints, and it should be taken as hot as you can bear it.[5]

ADVENTURERS AND MISSIONARIES

By the early seventeenth century English adventurers had reached the South China coast. Among them was Peter Mundy who arrived at Macau (Aomen) in 1637 and who kept an illustrated journal of his observations there. Like earlier travellers, Mundy was quick to note exotic features of Chinese food. In a market he saw a snake 'aboutt 4 or 5 Foote long, alive, his Mouth sowed uppe For biting' which was considered to be good meat, and 'Dogge Flesh' regarded as a main dish. He tried 'a certaine Drinke called Chaa, which is only water with a kind of herbe boyled in itt' which was to be drunk warm and which was accounted wholesome. In a temple some priests offered him chicken and pork cut into small pieces and provided him with chopsticks 'butt wee knew not how to use them, soe employed our Fingers'. Chopsticks so intrigued Mundy that he gave an extended description of their use and accompanied this with a drawing. Other illustrations in his journal included 'Fat Hogges', 'Pretty Oranges', 'Strange Crabbes' and 'An Invention to Cast Accompts', that is an abacus.[6]

In 1583 Father Matteo Ricci of the Society of Jesus reached Macau, and from that time onwards Westerners began to acquire a command of the Chinese language and a greater familiarity with Chinese food. While the Jesuits were establishing themselves at the Ming court, from 1633 various orders of mendicant friars penetrated southern China. Perhaps the most lively Western account of China and of Chinese food was penned in the seventeenth century by Friar Domingo

Navarrete, a Dominican friar who first encountered Chinese food when working in the Philippines. There he came across 'Swallows Nests', made by swallows who swam on the sea and built their nests in the rocks of the shore.

> Those birds make them of the foam of the Sea; when dry they look like a piece of ashcolour'd Clay, but being boil'd with flesh they are excellent meat, and very nourishing and substantial, as they all say. When boil'd they look like large Macaroni, as Father Colin rightly says. Those that have week Stomachs use it; and so do Marry'd Men; but it is not good Food for those who are dedicated to God's Service.

The last remark implied that the nests were reputed to be an aphrodisiac.

Navarrete lived in China from 1658 to 1669. Like other Westerners who had visited China, he portrayed the country as a land of plenty. He quoted the book of *Deuteronomy* on the promised land, 'A Land of Wheat and Barley, and Vines, and Fig-trees, and Pomegranates, a Land of Oil and Honey: A Land wherein thou shalt eat Bread without scarceness . . .' China had much more than all this for although it had neither olive trees nor vineyards, it abounded in several sorts of oil, it had plenty of grapes, and 'thousands of things we do not know among us'.

> There is great abundance of Beef, Pork all the Year about, Mutton, Goats-Flesh, Hens, Capons, Geese, Pheasants, tame and wild Ducks, Pigeons, Turtle-Doves, small Birds, and all very good; there is no want of Horse-flesh: Dogs-flesh is looked upon as a dainty, and all over China fresh-water Fish enough in Rivers and Ponds . . . There are infinite quantities of Hen and Goose-Eggs, which latter the Chineses are fond of. In some places there is Milk and little Cheeses, excellent Ham, choice of Olives, Eels, Trouts, Oysters, and Salt-fish . . . great variety of Greens, Beans, infinite Vetches; abundance of excellent Fruit, Rice, Wheat . . .

Whereas the Jesuits, to earn the respect of the Chinese, wore silk robes and travelled in sedan chairs, the friars adopted a simpler lifestyle. Navarrete wished that the friars 'ate as well as even the Jesuits' servants'. When travelling through Fujian in 1659, after crossing 'seven hellish Mountains that day' he saw a Chinese eating cold boiled rice. 'I took a good parcel from him and did eat it without leaving a grain and methought I never did eat anything more dainty in all my lifetime.' He described 'the most usual, common and cheap' sort of food available, namely 'Teu Fu, that is Paste of Kidney Beans'. Eaten alone this was insipid, but it was excellent fried with butter and best of all dried and smoked and mixed with caraway seeds. He added that a Chinese who had bean curd, herbs and rice needed no other sustenance to work, that a pound of it could be obtained for a halfpenny, and that it was made by the Chinese in Manila, but no Europeans ate it because they had not tried it.

On several occasions Navarrete remarked on Chinese enjoyment of food and on the good food which was available. When in Zhejiang, he received a surprise visit from the city magistrate, a man of above 70 years of age who, he was told, every morning ate for his breakfast '30 Eggs, and a Dogs Leg, and drank two Quartillos of hot Wine'. Navarrete commented, 'The good old Fellow look'd so fat and fair, it did a Man good to see him.' The quality of the rice wine of Jinhua was such that he did not miss the wine of Europe. The gammons of bacon were not inferior to the choicest from Estremadura and Galicia. The ducks, either wild ones caught by men swimming with calabashes on their heads, or tame ones, were very good roasted, but when salted and dried were better even than gammon. Navarrete noted that the Chinese did not use tablecloths and napkins, thereby saving a great deal of washing. The tables they used were beautiful, many of them varnished as fine as looking-glasses. Instead of cutlery they used chopsticks, made of various materials including glass, a Dutch invention now copied by the Chinese out of curiosity.[7]

Jesuit missionaries presented China in a positive light to deflect criticism of their decision to allow Chinese converts to continue to practise the 'rites', that is the ceremonies associated with a family's ancestors and Confucius. They sent to Europe well-informed reports on many aspects of Chinese life, including references to Chinese habits relating to food. Selections from their correspondence, under the title *Lettres édifiantes et curieuses*, were published between 1702 and 1773. These letters were the main source for the most influential book on China published in the eighteenth century, Jean-Baptiste du Halde's *Description géographique*, published in French in 1736 and two years later in English as *A Description of the Empire of China and Chinese-Tartary*.

Du Halde's description of Chinese food, although generally positive, emphasized exotic and distasteful elements. He noted that of the flesh of animals, it was the flesh of hogs which was reckoned the most delicious by the Chinese, adding 'especially the Rich, who love their appetites'. There was no finer eating than a Chinese ham. Other meat eaten by the Chinese included 'Wild-Mare's Flesh', 'Stags-pizzles', 'Bears-Paws and the feet of diverse Wild Creatures'. These were 'Dainties fit for the Tables of Great Lords'. The ordinary people, however,

> Are very well pleas'd with the Flesh of Horses and Dogs, even tho they dye of Age of Sickness; nay they do not scruple eating Cats, Rats, and such like Animals, which are openly sold in the Streets.

Of fish, there was scarcely any sort found in Europe which was not also to be found in China and there were other fish unknown in Europe, which had an excellent taste. Among them was the 'Armour-fish', so named because it had scales like tiles on the roof of a house, which tasted like veal. Another fish, which was very plentiful and cheap, resembled the Newfoundland cod. In the Yangzi there was the *'Whang-yu'*, the yellow fish, that is the Yangzi sturgeon, weighing as much as 800 pounds, which had an exquisite taste. The fruit of China could not compare with that of Europe, because the Chinese were not so skilful in cultivating the trees. However, their peaches were as good as, and one sort better than, those of Europe, and there were some excellent oranges.

Du Halde noted the use of human excrement in the manuring of fields, adding that whereas elsewhere this would burn up the plants, in China 'they have an Art of tempering it with Water before they use it.' He noted that they 'even make a sale of Ordure'. The sight of its regular collection 'is very surprizing to an *European*; but in this Country it may be properly said, *Lucri bonus Odor ex re qualibet. Gain has a good Smell let it come out of what it will.*'

In a chapter headed 'Ceremonies of the Chinese' du Halde described several Chinese foodstuffs, including what was probably soy sauce, saying that the Chinese had several sorts of Herbs, as well as pulse, from the seeds of which they made an oil much used in sauces. He then remarked:

> The *French* Cooks, who have refin'd so much in every thing which concerns the Palate, would be surpriz'd to find that the *Chinese* can outdo them far in this Branch of their Business, and at a great deal less Expence. They will hardly be persuaded to believe that, with nothing but the Beans that grow in their Country, particularly those of the Province of *Shantong*, and with Meal made of Rice and Corn, they can prepare a great many Dishes quite different from each other, both to the Sight and Taste.

Du Halde then described some Chinese delicacies. The most delicious were 'Staggs-Pizzles and Birds-Nests'. The pizzles were sun-dried and rolled in pepper and nutmeg. Before cooking they were soaked in rice-water and then boiled in the gravy of a kid, seasoned with various spices. His description of the origin of birds' nests was similarly fanciful. The nests, he claimed, were found on rocks along the coasts of Tongking, Java and Cochin China and were made by a bird resembling a swallow, possibly using little fish which it caught in the sea. More probably the birds distilled a viscous juice from their beaks to make their nests, but they had also been seen using the froth which floats on the sea to cement their nests together.

Du Halde noted that, although the Chinese generally lived upon rice, they also had corn, from which they made small loaves in less than fifteen minutes using a '*Balneo Mariae*', that is a *bain-marie*. These steamed buns, as they would now be called, were very soft, so '*Europeans* bake them a little at the Fire, and they are very light and delicious'. As for wines and spirits, the rice wine which came from Shaoxing was preferred as it was regarded as more wholesome. He mentioned a kind of spirit said to be 'drawn from the Flesh of Mutton', which was mainly drunk by the Manchus. It had a disagreeable taste and soon went to the head. Another very extraordinary sort of wine came from the province of Shaanxi. It was known as 'Lambs' Wine', (*gaoyangjiu*) and was very strong, with a disagreeable smell, but among the Chinese, or rather among the Manchus, it passed as an exquisite wine.

Du Halde paraphrased an account written by Joachim Bouvet of an elaborate, day-long feast given for him by the Governor-General of Guangdong and Guangxi prior to Bouvet's departure for Europe. The guests were seated at square, japanned tables, covered with violet-coloured satin embroidered with golden dragons. On another table, at the more formal, evening entertainment, 'Pyramids of Flesh, other sorts of Meat and Fruit &c.' were placed. Each pyramid was a foot and a half high and adorned with painting and flowers. This display was 'for State-sake', meaning that it was for show. It was distributed later to the guests' servants and to the chairmen and under-servants of the officials attending. On the other tables were set out perfuming pans and their impedimenta, a japanned board with some lines of poetry on it, and small china plates full of herbs, pulses and pickles to procure an appetite. As was usual on these occasions, a play was to be performed during the meal, and Bouvet was asked to choose one from a repertoire of 50 or 60 works the company had by heart. Bouvet, who knew little Chinese, declined on the grounds that a Chinese play might contain something which was not fit for a Christian to hear. Instead a concert was given, with the music regulating the time of each course. This led Bouvet to exclaim:

> During the Feast, all the Motions and Words, as well of the Servants as the rest of the Company, were so very formal and affected, that were it not for the Gravity of the Company, an *European* at first sight wou'd be apter to take it for a Play than a Feast, and have much ado to refrain from laughing.

Before each course of the meal the guests were invited to drink small cups of wine, and as each dish was placed on the table the masters of the ceremony invited them to take up their chopsticks and taste the food. The principal dishes consisted of 'Ragous, Meats hash'd or boil'd (with divers sort of Herbs or Pulse,) and served up with the Broth, in fine *China* vessels almost as deep as wide'. There were 20 such dishes, and after every fourth dish a particular type of broth was served, accompanied by 'a plate of Mazarine Tarts', and the feast was concluded with a dish of tea. In the morning, in accordance with etiquette, Bouvet sent a 'Billet of Thanks' to the Governor-General.[8]

Du Halde's *Description* was an important source for the information on China included in the most famous work of the French Enlightenment and of the *philosophes*, the *Encyclopédie, ou dictionnaire raisonné des sciences, des arts et des métiers*, published between 1751 and 1765 and distributed to libraries throughout Europe. The *Encyclopédie* claimed to provide up-to-date and accurate information on a wide variety of subjects. It contained several articles by the Chevalier de Jaucourt concerning Chinese plants which had a supposed therapeutic value. For the article *GIN-SENG* Jaucourt had used a letter written by Father Jartoux, which had appeared in the *Lettres édifiantes et curieuses*. He had also consulted an article by Dr Jacques Vandermonde, who had translated a Chinese source lauding the efficacy of the root as a cure for a wide variety of disorders, and as a tonic for those exhausted by the pleasures of love. De Jartoux had claimed that ginseng had revived him after a journey through Tartary, but Jaucourt, relying on the opinion of such eminent doctors as Hermann Boerhaave, was much more sceptical of its value, likening its effects to those of angelica. He suggested ironically that ginseng might act more powerfully on a Chinese body than on that of an European, or it might lose some of its properties when transported to Europe. He noted that the importation of ginseng into Europe was effectively the monopoly of the Dutch East India Company, causing an undesirably large debit on the European account. In the article *RHUBARBE* Jaucourt described Chinese rhubarb, the root of which was exported to Europe in a dried form and was made into pills. According to the Chevalier it had two uses, as a purgative and to settle the stomach. Jaucourt also wrote the article *SQUINE* or

China root, which supposedly cured gout, venereal disease, and many other ailments. The Emperor Charles V of Spain tried using it, but failed to consult his doctors and was forced to combine its use with that of lignum-vitae.

Two articles, *JOUI* and *SOUI ou SOI* compounded the existing confusion about soy sauce. Both referred to a sauce made in Japan which had excellent keeping properties. The first article suggested that the sauce was made from semi-roasted beef to which was added a variety of ingredients which the Japanese kept secret. The second article declared that the sauce was made from all sorts of meat, and in particular from partridge and ham. To this was added the juice of mushrooms, salt, pepper, ginger and other spices. Small quantities of the sauce were used to improve the flavour of dishes. The article added that the Chinese also made soy sauce, but it was considered inferior to that made in Japan, apparently because meat in Japan was more succulent than meat in China.

In the long article *RIZ* Jaucourt pointed out that the cultivation of rice in China illustrated the admirable determination of the Chinese to use every square inch of land to produce food rather than to waste it on flower gardens. Chinese industry in terracing mountain sides was praised and the ingenuity of Chinese irrigation systems was lauded. The physiocratic drift of the article then became apparent: rice cultivation could provide employment for, and could feed, large numbers of people in France. To demonstrate this Jaucourt appended two 'recipes'. For the first, ten pounds of rice should be cooked for three hours in 60 pints of water and then ten pounds of bread and ten pints of milk should be added and perhaps a dozen bay leaves to give the resulting food a pleasant taste. This would provide complete nourishment for 60 people for 24 hours. The other recipe used six pounds of rice and half a pound of butter to produce soup for 50 persons, two quarter-pint measures for an adult, one for a child.

Finally, Jaucourt's article *THÉ* should be mentioned. Much of the article summarized information on the characteristics of the tea-plant and how it was cultivated in China and Japan. The final two paragraphs discussed how tea should be drunk and debated its effects on health. In France tea was prepared in the

A European merchant buying tea, *c.* 1780-90.

same way as in China, that is to say boiling water was poured over the leaves which had been placed in a special pot. Cold water was added to reduce the bitterness, and the tea was then drunk hot. Usually the Chinese took a piece of sugar in their mouths as they drank, which was not the custom of the Japanese. More water was added which produced a weaker tincture, and the leaves were then thrown away. As for the benefits to be obtained, Jaucourt noted that both the Chinese and Japanese attributed marvellous qualities to tea as a pleasant way of relieving all forms of suffering. In his opinion, if tea did bring benefits, it was mainly due to the hot water. The volatile elements in tea might serve to dilute the lymph, if that was too thick, and assist perspiration. On the other hand the excessive use of tea could attack the nerves and cause trembling. Jaucourt suggested that it was best to use tea as a remedy, rather than as a pleasant drink. Moreover, he noted, it was certainly addictive, witness the European consumption in excess of ten million pounds of tea a year.[9]

Whereas Jesuit and *Encyclopédie* references to China were predominately positive, Western merchants and adventurers who reached the South China coast adopted an increasingly carping view, particularly of Chinese officials, whom they regarded as obstructive. This critical attitude, which was extended to Chinese food, was given wide currency by Daniel Defoe in *The Farther Adventures of Robinson Crusoe: Being the Second and Last Part of His Life*, first published in 1719. According to Defoe, China was inferior to Europe in every respect other than in the quality of its roads, and the Chinese were a miserable people oppressed by grasping mandarins. He described one such mandarin as a 'greasy Don' who was 'a most exquisite sloven' in his personal habits. Crusoe saw him eating a meal, 'lolling back in a great elbow-chair, being a heavy corpulent man'. His meat was brought him by two women slaves 'one fed the squire with a spoon, and the other held the dish with one hand, and scraped off what he let fall upon his worship's beard and taffeta vest'.[10]

Captain Alexander Hamilton, who travelled in the East Indies between 1688 and 1723, endorsed this hostile view. In an account similar to that of earlier travellers, Hamilton described how the Chinese reared ducks, but then added:

> The abominable Sin of *Sodomy* is tolerated here, and all over *China*, and so is *Buggery*, which they use both with Beasts and Fowls, in so much that *Europeans* do not care to eat Duck, except what they bring up themselves, either from the Egg, or from small Ducklings.[11]

The same hostility may be found in Lord Anson's description of dealings with the Chinese during his circumnavigation of the globe between 1740 and 1744. Anson stopped twice at Macau to refit his ships and was infuriated by what he regarded as obstruction by Chinese officials. For most of his time in Chinese waters Anson remained aboard ship and obtained food from the shore. On his first visit he was supplied with 'plenty of greens', and a variety of daily provisions, but on the second visit, following a contretemps over the payment of dues, the Chinese authorities stopped his supplies. Anson protested that it was not the practice between friendly nations to permit the ships of their friends to 'starve and sink'. His men would not accept starvation in the midst of plenty and he added 'though perhaps with a less serious air,' that this might lead his men to turn cannibal and that they would then 'in point of luxury, prefer well fed *Chinese* to their own immaciated [*sic*] shipmates'.

Anson also criticized the Chinese food suppliers, whom he found to be excessively deceitful. Many of the fowls bought for his ships died quickly, which caused his men to fear the birds had been poisoned. However, when they opened them up they discovered they had been force-fed with gravel to increase their weight. When his men bought dead hogs they discovered that they had had water injected into them. They bought live ones instead, only to find that the animals had been given salt to make them drink a great quantity of water and then had been stopped from discharging urine. When his ships left Macau on the first occasion, the suppliers contrived that the animals taken on board should die quickly. When they were thrown overboard the Chinese, who 'never object to the eating of any food that dies of itself', picked up the carrion. 'These instances', the writer stated, 'may serve as a specimen of the manners of this celebrated Nation, which is often recommended to the rest of the world as a pattern of all kinds of laudable qualities.'[12]

This negative British view of the Chinese was reinforced in John Lockman's edition of the *Lettres édifiantes* published between 1743 and 1762. For example, after quoting Father de Prémare's description of Guangzhou in 1699, Lockman added the following note:

> The *Chinese* eat any kind of Meat; Beasts that die in Ditches, as willingly as those which died by the Butcher's Hand. They eat Frogs, which appear loathsome to an European Eye, but are well-tasted. 'Tis said their Rats don't eat amiss; and that Snake-Broth is in Reputation there. The common people are great Gluttons, and eat four Times a Day, they cramming down the Rice (their principal Food) so greedily with their Chopsticks, that they frequently almost choak themselves.

Lockman translated a description of a Chinese feast by the French Jesuit Father Jachard, but added,

> As all the Guests are obliged to taste of every Thing; and as a great deal of Ceremony is used on these Occasions, it consequently must be troublesome to an *European*, and especially to a *Frenchman*, there being no country, (I believe) where so little Ceremony is used at Table, as among the French; for which Reason I am not surprised that Father *Jachard* should be tired at one of these *Chineze* feasts.[13]

LORD MACARTNEY'S EMBASSY

In the late eighteenth century the admiration for China fostered by the *philosophes* faded. Britain's main concern in China was to extend commercial access beyond the limited trade permitted at the southern port of Guangzhou, a concern which led to the despatch to China in 1793 of an embassy headed by Lord Macartney. Although Macartney refused to perform the ceremonial kowtow, the embassy was received by the Qianlong emperor at his summer residence at Rehe. However, Macartney's requests, which included the opening of additional ports to foreign trade and the accreditation of an ambassador to the Chinese court, were politely but categorically refused. Several members of the embassy published their accounts of the visit and Macartney himself kept a journal. From these sources a range of perspectives on Western attitudes to Chinese food may be extracted.

Macartney's journal offered the most immediate insight into the embassy's reaction to Chinese food. It also provided an interesting example of what might be termed the diplomacy of food, as the Chinese exerted pressure on the embassy either by offering it extremely generous hospitality, or by denying it supplies. Throughout the visit, despite Macartney's entreaties that the embassy should be allowed to provide for itself, all food was supplied by the Chinese court. While the embassy was still on board ship off the north China coast, the Chinese delivered large quantities of fresh food, starting with '20 bullocks, 120 sheep, 120 hogs', which led Macartney to exclaim that the hospitality, attention, and respect he had received 'are such as strangers meet with only in the Eastern parts of the world'. In return Macartney entertained to dinner the two senior Chinese officials attached to the embassy. He wrote that although they were 'at first a little embarrassed by our knives and forks, [but] soon got over the difficulty, and handled them with notable dexterity and execution upon some of the good things which they had brought us'. The officials also sampled a wide variety of wines and spirits, showing their preference for cherry brandy. As the embassy proceeded upriver to Tianjin, the Governor-General of the province twice sent elaborate meals. On one occasion the food brought to the embassy was found to be tainted – Macartney thought this not surprising as the temperature was 88 degrees – but nevertheless those found responsible were punished instantly.

On 14 September 1793 Macartney and members of his embassy were received in audience by the Qianlong emperor. They were entertained to a 'sumptuous banquet', with the emperor sending them several dishes from his own table, and summoning Macartney and the secretary of the embassy to receive from his own hands a cup of warm wine, a drink which Macartney described as being extracted from rice, herbs, and honey, and which was 'very pleasant and comfortable, the morning being cold and raw'. The serving and removing of the dinner was conducted with such silence and solemnity that Macartney likened it to 'the celebration of a religious mystery'. To Macartney's surprise, despite the rejection of his requests, the embassy continued to receive generous hospitality as it made its way south. The Chinese had observed that the English were accustomed to mixing milk with their tea. To ensure that a supply of fresh milk was available officials provided 'a couple of cows in a boat fitted up on purpose'.

At the end of his Journal, Macartney appended some observations on the 'Manners and Character' of the Chinese, which indicated that he found Chinese standards of hygiene unacceptable. Even persons of the highest classes rarely changed their underwear and seldom used pocket handkerchiefs. Even a Manchu of distinction would publicly call upon his servant to search for a louse which was troubling him. Macartney also commented generally on Chinese eating habits. He described the use of chopsticks, which he found 'not very cleanly' and added: 'They are all foul feeders and eaters of garlic and strong-scented vegetables, and drink mutually out of the same cup which, though sometimes rinsed, is never washed or wiped clean.' Furthermore they 'had no water-closets nor proper places of retirement; the necessaries are quite public and open' and the constant removal of ordure caused a stench almost everywhere one went.[14]

The first published account of Macartney's embassy was written by Aeneas Anderson, Macartney's valet. Anderson admitted that before he and other members of the embassy arrived in China, they had been affected by accounts of the indifference of the Chinese concerning their food. For example, they had heard that the Chinese did not discard animals which had died of disease, a report which made them very cautious of eating hashes and stews. He added that their suspicion had been confirmed when they saw pigs, which had died of disease aboard the *Lion*, and which were then thrown overboard, being picked up by the Chinese, and subsequently eaten, 'accompanied with frequent marks of derision at the English for their foolish extravagance'. At first he had supposed that such behaviour was restricted to the lower classes and arose from poverty, but he later found that even mandarins practised this 'custom in domestic economy, at which the eager appetite of the starving European would revolt'. The similarity between this allegation and that made 50 years earlier by Anson is so striking as to arouse suspicion of plagiarism.

Anderson found fault with other aspects of Chinese food. On 6 August 1793, as the embassy began its journey upriver to Tianjin, Macartney recorded that the provisions for the day had been distributed in 'great abundance'. Referring to the same day, Anderson conceded that the beef supplied was of very good quality, but he was critical about the bread, which he described as 'nothing more than flour and water', which they had been forced to toast 'before we could reconcile it to our appetites'. The roast meat had 'a very singular appearance' because it had a gloss like varnish 'nor was its flavour so agreeable to our palates, as the dishes produced by the clean and simple cookery of our European kitchens'. The wine, too, had 'an unpleasant flavour' and tasted more like vinegar than wine.

On the day that Macartney had mentioned that the provisions supplied had been tainted, Anderson recorded that the decision had been taken that henceforth the embassy would cook its own food, because

> the Chinese are so very dirty in their mode of cookery, that it was impossible for the inhabitants of a country where cleanliness is so prevailing a circumstance of the kitchen, unless compelled by severe hunger, to submit to it.

He, too, criticized Chinese table manners, describing the use of chopsticks and bowls containing rice and fried vegetables, 'which food they glut down in a most voracious manner'. Although it was 'not a very delicate picture to present to the attention of my readers', Anderson found it necessary to describe how two of the Chinese sailors aboard stripped and picked vermin from each others clothes 'and proceeded to eat them with as much eagerness and apparent satisfaction, as if they were a gratifying and delicate food'.

Nevertheless Anderson's reactions to Chinese food were not entirely condemnatory. He observed that the method of cutting up meat in butchers' shops in Beijing resembled that used in England. When the embassy was awaiting the audience with the emperor at Jehe, for some reason the amount of food supplied to the party was less than half the usual amount, As a protest this food was left untouched, which resulted in a profusion of hot dishes being produced. And if Anderson was suspicious of Chinese savoury foodstuffs, he was warm in praise of the confectionery: 'their cakes of every kind are admirably made and more agreeable to the palate than any I remember to have tasted in England, or any other country'.[15]

Other members of the embassy offered their own opinions on Chinese food. Sir George Staunton, the secretary to the embassy, exclaimed that the ordinary Chinese had no scruples about eating the meat of animals which had died by accident or from disease. 'This people know no distinction of clean and unclean meat.' He conceded that the Chinese, being for the most part vegetarian, must in the first instance feel 'horror and disgust' at the 'proposal of destroying any sensitive being, for the purpose of gorging upon its vitals'. But once they were reconciled to the deed, the choice of animal was 'little more than a matter of taste or fancy', and so they were willing to eat dogs or even vermin.[16] On the other hand Dr James Dinwiddie, the 'mechanic', or experimental scientist attached to the embassy, was more adventurous in his approach to Chinese food. Having observed a Chinese official, a 'good hearty fellow' eating a meal, he took the opportunity to taste every dish 'and found them extremely good and well flavoured'. When aboard one of the junks which took the embassy upriver to Beijing, on one occasion he had perforce to eat as the Chinese did

> We dined at noon, on a leg of mutton cooked with rice, sitting cross-legged upon the floor, without either chair, table, cloth, knife, fork, or spoon, and we had not sufficiently practised the chopsticks to be able to make any use of them.[17]

John Barrow, a man from a humble background, who had risen under the patronage of Sir George Staunton to become the comptroller of the embassy, also gave a more positive view of Chinese food. Referring to the incident described by Anderson concerning the Chinese scavenging pigs which had been thrown overboard from the *Lion*, he asserted that the animals had not died of disease, but had been 'bruised to death'. The Chinese had picked them up eagerly and then washed them and preserved them in salt. Whereas Anderson had commented disparagingly on the cooked food provided for the embassy when it was *en route* to Beijing, according to Barrow, what was provided was 'a most sumptuous breakfast of roast pork and venison, rice and made dishes. . .' He was even more enthusiastic about 'the most excellent dinner' served to make amends for their uncomfortable lodgings. It consisted of

> a vast variety of made dishes very neatly dressed, and served in porcelain bowls. The best soup I ever tasted in any part of

the world was made here from an extract of beef, seasoned with a preparation of soy and other ingredients. Their vermicelli is excellent, and all their pastry is unusually light and white as snow. We understand it to be made from the buck wheat. The luxury of ice, in the neighbourhood of the capital, is within the reach of the poorest peasant . . .

Although Barrow was complimentary about the food provided for the embassy, he was under no illusions about the poverty of Chinese peasants. They could only obtain salt fish on rare occasions by bartering their vegetables, and a 'morsel of pork to relish their rice is almost the only kind of meat the poor can afford to taste'. Moreover, they had little milk, nor butter, nor cheese, nor bread, all of which, with potatoes, formed the chief sustenance of the peasantry of Europe.[18]

TRADING AT GUANGZHOU

After 1760 the only port open to trade between Westerners and Chinese was Guangzhou. During the trading season, a community of a few hundred Westerners did business there with the Chinese merchant monopoly known as the Hong merchants. Relations between the foreigners and the Hong merchants were apparently very good, although a British surgeon, C. Toogood Downing claimed that the reality was that foreigners regarded the natives with dislike and contempt, and the Chinese called the strangers barbarians and seemed to loathe them as real demons and inferior spirits.

Downing's references to Chinese food reflected this ambivalent relationship. He described a market where dogs and cats were offered for sale as food, and claimed it was

very revolting to the feelings of the European upon his first visit to China, to observe the natives preparing to make their meals upon those domestic animals which he has always been accustomed to look up with a degree of fondness and affection.

He accepted that the 'craving appetite and calls of hunger will generally overthrow the strongest ties of affection and gratitude' and he recalled that during the siege of Jerusalem a mother had eaten the flesh of her own murdered daughter. But, he observed, whereas Chinese of the upper ranks are 'as fastidious and expensive in their food as any people in the world', the 'lower orders are altogether as filthy', which in time led to a 'total loss of discrimination as to the quality of the food eaten'.

Downing reviewed articles of Chinese food, beginning with luxuries such as bird's nest soup. There was, he said, a difference of opinion among Europeans on the palatableness of 'this singular compound', with 'some asserting that it is absolutely nauseous and disgusting, while others who have tasted it maintain that is very properly ranked among the greatest delicacies which can be brought to table'. Turning to the food of the poor, he remarked that the 'lower orders of the Chinese would appear to be almost omnivorous'. In addition to eating dogs and cats, the very poorest people also ate rats and mice, the skinned rats being displayed for sale 'hung up by dozens with a small piece of wood passed across from one hind leg to another'.

Downing made several references to Western food habits in China. British sailors, after subsisting for four of five months on salt meat, looked forwarded with pleasure to fresh meat being brought on board and regaling themselves on 'the beef and plum-pudding of Old England'. Their main encounter with Chinese drink was in the form of spirits sold in Hog Lane, or smuggled aboard ship. However, the Hong merchants were in the habit of entertaining the officers of the ships for which they had given security, and this gave rise to a curious form of dining. The guests were received in the banqueting-room and seated in pairs at small tables. The meal began with toasts, and then 'an attempt is made by each of the foreigners to attack the smoking viands upon the tables'. Because of their difficulty in handling chopsticks 'it is very seldom that the new comers are able to catch with them any of the delicate morsels, which float about in the savoury soups and gravies'. When the guests had satisfied their curiosity by examining the succession of dishes placed before them, and had drunk copiously of the warm wine supplied, the

Chinese dinner was completed. Prejudice had prevented many of the guests from even tasting the 'curious dainties' which had been set before them, and even those who had had the courage to attempt them had eaten very cautiously, 'lest they should detect themselves in the act of devouring an earthworm, or picking the delicate bones of a cat'. However, their host, understanding their predicament, had provided in another room 'a capital dinner after the European fashion', where 'good cheer' might be partaken 'without fear or hesitation'.

The same suspicion was evident when Chinese encountered Western food. When a new Hoppo (the official in charge of foreign trade) was appointed, he was invited to a 'first-rate breakfast after the English fashion' by the foreign community. The breakfast was served on a snow-white cloth and consisted of 'Blancmanges, jellies, and fruits . . . in addition to the more substantial viands'. The Hoppo, who had the meal to himself, eyed each dish carefully and then waved everything away 'without finding a single article suitable to his delicate stomach'. On another occasion, although the Hoppo again refrained from eating, his inferiors did enjoy the hospitality of the 'foreign devils'. Downing commented that an unprejudiced spectator 'would see in the manners of these natives, an exact resemblance to those of the Europeans who dine at the tables of the Chinese. Prejudice prevents them from eating freely, but they yet cannot resist tasting the curious dishes set before them.'

Downing devoted one chapter of his book to tea, his purpose being to correct the confusion and to respond to the accusations which had arisen over the methods of tea production. He attempted to clarify the difference between green and black teas, the two classes of tea to be found in every grocer's shop in England, but he could not resolve the dispute over whether these were obtained from two different plants, or whether the difference arose in processing. He confidently asserted that copper vessels were not used in the manufacture of green teas and concluded that the legitimate manufacture of tea employed no deleterious process. How then, he asked, could one account for the injurious effects which were universally acknowledged to arise from drinking Hyson or Twankay? He rejected the suggestion that this arose from the addition of some unwholesome ingredient to the tea. It was more likely because these green teas, which were never drunk by the Chinese, were dried by a slow process, which did not rid the plants of anything baneful. Black tea, which was subjected to greater heat, might have a less delicate flavour, but perhaps this was a loss worth sustaining. Downing also referred to an instance when the American demand for the green tea known as Young Hyson was so strong that supplies ran out and the Chinese supplied a 'vile substitute', which was quickly detected by the inspectors. He added that many other examples might be adduced to show how far the Chinese tea-merchants attempted to deceive foreigners. This led Downing to look forward to the day when the tea plant might be cultivated in other countries in sufficient quantities to supply the European market independently of China.[19]

One final view of the Chinese and Chinese food in pre-treaty days may be included, that of W. C. Hunter, an American merchant who had lived in Guangzhou for twenty years. Hunter had learned Chinese and was sympathetic towards some members of Chinese society, notably the Hong merchants, whom he described as honourable and reliable. On occasions he and his fellow merchants were entertained by one of the merchants to a 'chopstick' dinner, signifying 'that no foreign element would be found in it'. The lavish meals included bird's-nest soup, plovers' eggs, bêche-de-mer, sharks' fins and roasted snails. With these delicacies, and many other dishes, they drank wine made from rice, from green peas and from a fruit called *Wang-pe*. He found these feasts very enjoyable, even when the novelty had worn off, and he firmly dismissed the suggestion that guests were served with roast or boiled puppy as a *bonne bouche*. Nevertheless he found it necessary to quote some facetious verses which suggested that dog meat *was* served on these occasions. Hunter also defended the 'heathen Chinee' from charges of adulterating tea with willow or elm leaves, or increasing its weight with iron filings, ingenious processes which he said were not practised before the first Opium War. Hunter was one of the foreign merchants detained in 1839 by Imperial Commissioner Lin Zexu pending their surrender of the stocks of opium. The foreigners had become so reliant on their Chinese servants that they did not know how to cook the simplest ingredients. Bread was toasted to death, eggs boiled to the consistency of grape-shot, and rice, when prepared, 'resembled a tough mass of glue'. Such was the result of an early attempt by Westerners to cook Chinese food![20]

THREE

Nineteenth-century Reactions to Chinese Food

Under the Treaty of Nanjing which concluded the first Opium War (1839–42) five Chinese ports: Guangzhou, Xiamen, Fuzhou, Ningbo and Shanghai, were opened for trade and residence to British merchants, a right which was soon extended to other Western nations. In these treaty ports Western communities were established. In terms of nationality the largest groups were British, American, French and German and in terms of occupation they were for the most part officials, merchants and missionaries. Their residence in China was of varying duration. Catholic missionaries were said to come for life and other missionaries and officials, who were expected to learn Chinese, anticipated a residence of many years interrupted by rare periods of home leave. Merchants, and others with commercial interests, who arrived in China early in the nineteenth century, might well have anticipated spending a long period on the China coast, and becoming one of the 'twenty-years-in-the-country-and-speak-the-language' men.[1] These intentions were often to be frustrated, as many of the early Western residents in China died young. Later in the century life expectancy improved, but the population of the treaty ports became more transitory, with many of the inhabitants spending limited periods of time in China, and others merely visiting the country.

WESTERN DESCRIPTIONS OF CHINESE FOOD

In the years following the first treaty settlement attitudes towards Chinese food remained supercilious and dismissive. Sir John Davis, who wrote the standard text on the Chinese and later became Governor of Hong Kong, included in the 1848 edition of his book a description of a Chinese dinner served to Captain Laplace, a French naval officer. According to Laplace the first course included 'salted earth-worms, prepared and dried, but so cut up that I fortunately did not know what they were until I had swallowed them'. The dishes which followed, all of which 'swam in soup' included 'sharks' fins, eggs prepared by heat, of which both the smell and taste seemed to us equally repulsive, immense grubs, a peculiar kind of sea-fish, crabs, and pounded shrimps'. The banquet continued with birds' nest soup, pastries, rice and concluded with fruit. At the end of the meal Laplace's host 'displayed his satisfaction by loud laughs, to which was perpetually joined the sonorous accompaniment of his somewhat overloaded stomach'. Laplace could not bring himself to copy this usage, which he said in France would have been deemed as more than extraordinary, although the Spanish continued 'this remnant of the grossness of the olden time'.

Davis had spent many years in China and had a good knowledge of Chinese. His book contained the first extended description of Chinese food and cooking by a Westerner. He noted that Chinese cookery had a closer resemblance to French cookery than to English, because the Chinese, like the French, used ragouts – highly seasoned dishes – rather than plain articles of diet. The tastes of wealthy Chinese ran in the direction of sensual pleasures including gastronomy, but some of the delicacies esteemed by the Chinese, he cited the hawk-moth, had few attractions for Europeans. The prevalence of Buddhism was the reason for the low consumption of meat. Some Western vegetables were now being grown in China, including peas introduced by the Dutch, which were generally eaten in the pod in stews. Chinese cabbage was used in Western embassies as a substitute for lettuce. Davis reiterated that the common people were omnivorous and ate dogs, cats and rats. The 'great save-all' however was the pig, the flesh of which was by far the commonest meat. He quoted Tacitus as an authority for the claim that frequent consumption of pork produced or predisposed to leprosy, a claim which he considered corroborated by the evidence that leprosy and cutaneous infections were common in China. He noted the immense quantity of salt used to preserve food, in particular fish, which was then dried in the sun. The '*haut goût*' (Davis was too refined to write 'stink') of dried fish appeared to be a recommendation to the taste buds of the Chinese.[2]

Davis's comments on Chinese food were moderate and balanced when compared with the tirades which sprang from the pens of some Western residents, whose contemptuous references to Chinese food matched a commonplace dismissal of virtually all aspects of Chinese culture. A visitor to Guangzhou in 1863, who disguised his identity behind the initials P.G.L., was particularly revolted by the food market, where he saw what he supposed to be sucking pigs, but which on closer examination proved to be dogs with their tails artistically twisted round. He recalled that he had recently buried a favourite horse. In the night 'they', meaning the Chinese, had dug up its remains and stripped every particle of flesh from its bones. P.G.L. added 'I need not say that for the next few days I was very careful of beef-steaks.'[3] Other Westerners argued that the Chinese propensity for cruelty was reflected in the way that they treated animals intended for food. Dr D. F. Rennie recounted two examples of cruelty which he said had been related to him by a Shanghai merchant. The first described how a turtle could be cooked alive in a tureen, which had an aperture for its head. A container of highly spiced wine was put within its reach. As the temperature of the water increased, the turtle grew ever more thirsty, and drank the wine so that, by the time it was dead it was 'impregnated with the vino-aromatic seasoning'. Another story described how ducks' feet were cooked by placing the live birds on a hot iron plate over a fire.[4]

A better-informed description of some aspects of Chinese eating habits, and in particular of Chinese restaurants, was written by John Henry Gray, the Archdeacon of Hong Kong. Chinese restaurants, he noted, differed from their Western counterparts in a number of particulars. Most restaurant buildings were of several storeys, with the kitchen occupying the ground floor, the public hall for humbler customers on the first floor, and the more select apartments on the upper floors. A bill of fare was placed in each room, and the order was taken by a waiter. At a large dinner party as many as a hundred dishes might be served. The feast began with toasts drunk in wine, guests smoked between courses and it was not unusual for a gentleman to show politeness by using his chopsticks to place a portion of food from his own plate into the mouth of a neighbour. There was no tablecloth, but a piece of coarse brown paper was provided for each guest with which to wipe his lips, a necessary process because of the amount of oil used in Chinese cookery. At the end of the meal guests were supplied with towels, which Gray purposely refrained from calling clean, and a basin of hot water. Gray recalled that this same custom was described in the Bible, in Kings II. Behind the restaurants there were numerous soup-stalls where one could enjoy a good and cheap meal. At hotels the dinners provided differed from those served in restaurants, in that they usually consisted of roast pork, roast duck, boiled fowl and rice, or fish and rice. Tea-saloons were very numerous. They had large kitchens where cooks 'remarkable for their cleanliness' were engaged in making all sorts of pastry. According to Gray it was impossible for any foreigner who was a lover of order not to find that these institutions were far superior to the ale-houses and gin-palaces that disgraced the cities of more civilized lands.

Gray wrote a book describing his walks around Guangzhou. His second walk passed one of the twenty-odd small restaurants which served dogs' and cats' flesh. As one entered the dining-room through the kitchen one could see the flesh of dogs and cats being fried with water-chestnuts and garlic in oil. A bill of fare for one such restaurant read as follows:

Cat's flesh, one basin	10 cents
Black cat's flesh, one small basin	5 "
Wine, one bottle	3 "
Wine, one small bottle	1½ "
Congee, one basin	2 cash
Ketchup, one basin	3 "
Black dog's grease	1 tael 4 cents
Black cat's eyes, one pair	4 cents

Gray added that dogs' flesh was supposed to strengthen the body and serve as an antidote to summer sickness. The flesh of black dogs and cats was preferred because it was thought to be

Street scene, 1880s.

more nutritious. The people who frequented these restaurants were respectable shopkeepers and artisans. In southern China the Hakka Chinese commonly ate dog meat, but in Beijing there were two or three shops which offered dogs' flesh as food. The Guangzhouese (Cantonese) considered eating dog meat to be contrary to the will of the gods and it was particularly repugnant to Buddhists. Gray added that the flesh of rats was also an article of food in some parts of the country including Guangzhou, where in winter dried and salted rats were sold in poultry shops. They were eaten by both men and women, but women ate rats because it was believed that they offered a cure for baldness.[5]

Another authoritative description of Chinese food may be found in the revised edition of S. Wells Williams, *The Middle Kingdom*, which was published in 1883. Williams, an American missionary, began by noting the contribution which Chinese food had made to the 'odd character' which the Chinese bore abroad, even though 'uncouth or unsavory viands' formed only an infinitesimal portion of their food, and feasts not one thousandth of their meals. In general the Chinese diet was 'sufficient in variety, wholesome, and well-cooked', but it used too much oil and too much onion and garlic to suit European tastes.

Williams then reviewed items of Chinese food and cooking methods. He explained how rice could be steamed 'without forming a pasty mass, as is too often the result when boiled by cooks in Christian countries'. He described the vast range of vegetables available, including at least twenty varieties of 'cucurbitaceous plants', though these vegetables were inferior to their equivalents in the West where science had improved their size and flavour. He noted the plentifulness of fruit, commenting that the most delicious of the citrus fruits was the 'mandarin orange', but he was less impressed by Chinese pickles, which were eaten in enormous quantities but which foreigners found detestable. He remarked that a Chinese table, with no bread, butter or milk upon it, seemed ill-furnished to a foreigner, but if such a criticism was made to a Chinese the answer would be 'You eat cheese, and sometimes when it can almost walk.'

Williams had read Gray's description of the consumption of dogs and cats. Few articles of food, he said, had been so associated with the tastes of the people as kittens, puppies and rats had been with the Chinese. American school geographies often contained pictures of baskets holding 'these unfortunate victims of a perverse taste (as we think)' or strings of rats and mice, thereby conveying the idea that these things were the usual food of the people. Visitors to China had heard that the Chinese devoured everything and so on arrival they immediately enquired if these animals were eaten. When they heard that this indeed was the case, they perpetuated the idea that these formed common articles of food. However, one could live in Guangzhou or Fuzhou for years without ever seeing rats offered for sale as food, other than as a medicine or an aphrodisiac. Rats and mice, and many other undesirable things, might be eaten 'by those whom want compels to take what they can get'. Dog meat appeared on the menus of perhaps half a dozen restaurants in Guangzhou, but it was an expensive delicacy.

Williams then turned to other items of food eaten by the Chinese. He noted that 'they are perfectly omnivorous with respect to aquatic productions', and that every possible way of catching or rearing fish was practised in one part of the country or another. Some insects, including silk-worms, were eaten, these being 'fried to a crisp when cooked'. These and water-snakes were decidedly the most repulsive things the Chinese ate. In his opinion the art of cooking in China had not reached any high degree of perfection. Like French cooking it was eco-nomical, consisting mainly of stews and fried dishes rather than baked or roasted dishes. The articles of kitchen furniture were few and simple. The cutting of food into small pieces secured thorough cooking with less fuel. Meat soups were seldom seen and there was nothing to compare with the immense variety of desserts known in the West.[6]

One of the most extensive and condescending attacks on the Chinese and their eating habits was made by the American mis-sionary A. H. Smith, whose book *Chinese Characteristics*, first published in 1890, went through five editions within a decade. According to Smith, the Chinese 'are not as a race gifted with the extreme fastidiousness in regard to food which is frequently developed in Western lands. All is fish that comes to their net, and there is very little which does not come there first or last.' Animals were eaten in their entirety whatever the cause of their death. These animals included dogs and cats, and Smith quoted examples known to him personally of villagers having eaten dogs which had been poisoned with strychnine.[7]

Nevertheless a few Westerners boldly suggested that the West might learn from the Chinese in the matter of food. In 1872 W. H. Medhurst, the British Consul in Shanghai, pub-lished *The Foreigner in Far Cathay* in which he sought to correct erroneous impressions of aspects of Chinese life. It was a fallacy, he said, to suppose that the food of the Chinese consisted of 'dogs, cats, rats, and other garbage', a fallacy which was so prevalent that he had been asked by persons oth-erwise well-informed whether foreign residents in China were not unfortunate enough to find themselves restricted to the same diet. He would not assert that dogs and cats were never eaten, and he himself had watched a mob of boat-people fight over the carcasses of some horses which had been shot because they had contracted glanders. But, in his opinion, the Chinese as a race were not 'foul feeders'. The masses rarely ate meat, and if they did it was usually pork. The higher classes consumed delicacies almost unknown to European palates – Medhurst included jelly-fish and ducks' tongues among his examples. He added,

> Some of these can be recommended as well worthy of introduction to our own tables, where possibly they might be rendered even more toothsome by the science and experience which European artists could bring to bear upon their cooking qualities. There is a soup common to first-class dinners in China, composed of shark's-fin, bird's-nest, and sea-slug, with pigeons' or plovers' eggs floating entire on its surface, which I consider quite equal, if not superior, to any of our richest soups, excepting perhaps turtle.[8]

TEA

Throughout the nineteenth century tea continued to be the Chinese product most commonly ingested by Westerners. In the previous century the effect of tea-drinking on health had been a matter of dispute. The well-known British traveller Jonas Hanway had declared that tea was bad for the teeth, caused nervous disorders, was an emetic, was corrosive and should not be drunk by those over the age of 40, and that the vast sums of money spent on tea would be better used to promote industry. In the years before the Opium War rumours had circulated about the adulteration of tea, or its mixture with harmful substances. John Francis Davis had noted how the sudden increase in the demand for tea at Guangzhou was calculated to injure its overall quality. He quoted an East India Company tea inspector's report of 1833 which detailed attempts to pass off spurious or adulterated teas among the various kinds of black tea. But this, wrote Davis, was nothing in comparison to the effrontery which the Chinese displayed in the manufacture of green teas from damaged black leaves. He himself had

Method of making 'caper' tea, mid-1850s.

visited a laboratory where black tea was mixed with turmeric, Prussian blue and gypsum. The Chinese themselves did not consume these kinds of green teas; they were solely for exportation, and it was apparent that they were producing these teas surreptitiously.[9]

In 1848 Robert Fortune was sent to China by the East India Company to obtain the finest varieties of tea plant and to convey them to the government tea plantations in the Himalayas. Fortune visited the district in Anhui province where green tea was first processed. There he observed the preparation of green tea for export by colouring it with gypsum and Prussian blue, not to transform black tea into green tea, but to manufacture a product which was deemed more appealing to Westerners. He commented,

> I could not help thinking that if any green-tea drinkers had been present during the operation their taste would have been corrected, and, I may be allowed to add, improved. It seems perfectly ridiculous that a civilized people should prefer these dyed teas to those of a natural green. No wonder that the Chinese consider the natives of the west to be a race of 'barbarians.'

He estimated that the amount of colouring matter added to make the tea look 'uniform and pretty' amounted to half a pound in every 100 pounds of coloured green tea. 'And yet,' he remarked, 'tell the drinkers of this coloured tea that the Chinese eat cats, dogs, and rats, and they will hold up their hands in amazement, and pity the poor celestials.'[10]

As a result of Fortune's journey 'Upwards of twenty thousand tea plants, eight first-rate manufacturers, and a large supply of implements were procured from the finest tea-districts of China, and conveyed in safety to the Himalayas,' so preparing the way for the eventual replacement of China tea in the Western market with tea grown in India and Sri Lanka. China tea was brought to Europe aboard the tea clippers of the 1850s, the most famous of which was the *Cutty Sark*. The clippers sailed from Guangzhou to London or New York in as little as 90 days. To compensate for the increased costs, the public was per-suaded that 'new season' tea was superior in taste, and that old tea deteriorated in flavour. The clipper races and the glamoriza-tion of the first teas faded after the Suez Canal was opened in 1869. For a long time, perhaps until the end of the First World War, teas from India and Sri Lanka were regarded as inferior to those of China, but before the end of the nineteenth century China's exports of black tea were clearly in decline. The main factors bringing this about were the lower price and more con-sistent quality of tea grown on plantations in South Asia and picked by a docile workforce. Popular taste came to prefer the stronger flavour of Indian tea, a change which may have been accelerated by the claim, made in some Western newspapers, that China tea was unsanitary.[11]

SOCIAL INTERCOURSE WITH THE CHINESE

Although many Westerners described Chinese food, social intercourse between Chinese and Westerners was very limited. Only on formal occasions were Western officials entertained by Chinese officials. An instance of such an encounter occurred in 1854 when J.A.T. Meadows, the British consul at Ningbo, accompanied by Robert Hart, later to achieve fame as the

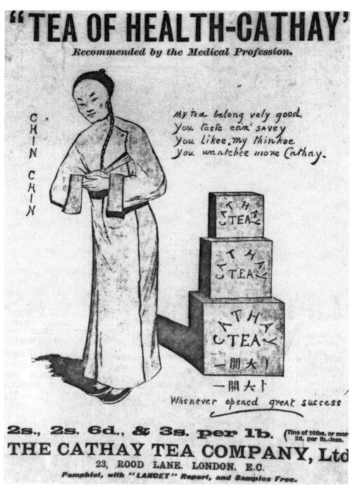

British newspaper advertisement for tea, *c.* 1911.

Inspector-General of the Imperial Maritime Customs, paid a courtesy call on the Circuit Intendant, who Hart described as a 'fat old fellow', with 'dirty hands and long nails'. They were offered tea and then cakes, preserves and other delicacies, the Intendant handling the cakes with his fingers, which made Hart feel 'a little queer'. There followed small cups of 'Whiskey'. Following the accepted practice they 'presented cups' and '*chin-chin-chinned*'. Afterwards they called on the district magistrate, who provided a substantial breakfast with meat. As Hart, who had newly arrived, could not manage his chopsticks, he used his fingers and a fork to eat. Later Hart was involved in the negotiations with the Zongli Yamen, the prototype Foreign Office, and in that context had further experience of Chinese entertaining, which he did not enjoy. Only in the case of Hengqi, one of the members of the Zongli Yamen and formerly the Guangzhou Hoppo, could he say 'his tiffin-table is one that a foreigner can sit at without any feeling of disgust'.[12]

This Western distrust of Chinese food was aggravated by the Hong Kong bread-poisoning affair. In 1856 an incident involving a small ship, the 'Arrow' led to a second war between Britain and China. British ships bombarded Guangzhou and the Chinese responded by burning the foreign factories and by offering rewards for the heads of foreigners. In January 1857 an attempt was made to poison the entire Western population of Hong Kong by putting arsenic in the bread. Some 400 Europeans were taken ill, though none died as the dose of arsenic was too large to be kept down. The dispute over the handling of the 'Arrow' incident led to Palmerston calling a general election in Britain. In the election campaign he described the Chinese 'a set of kidnapping, murdering, poisoning barbarians'.

That view was not shared by the Earl of Elgin, the British plenipotentiary sent to China to resolve the dispute. Elgin presented himself as an enlightened and cultivated person, an aspiration shared by his private secretary Laurence Oliphant,

A restaurant in China, 1870s.

and this was reflected in their attitude towards Chinese hospitality. Soon after their arrival in China, Elgin and Oliphant visited a Chinese restaurant in Macau, a very early record of Westerners choosing to eat in such a place. Despite the 'novelty of the implements' Oliphant managed to make a very satisfactory repast from year-old eggs, sharks' fins and radish soup, shrimps made into a paste with sea-chestnuts and other ingredients. Thereafter he showed some enthusiasm for Chinese food. After the capture of Guangzhou he traversed the narrow streets where 'cooked viands hissed and sputtered on the heated iron, titillating with their savoury odour the nostril of the hungry passenger'. Later he dined with the Shanghai Intendant and praised the way in which the mutton and turkey was served, 'carved at a side-table in a civilized manner, and handed round cut up into mouthfuls, so that the refined chopstick replaced throughout the rude knife and fork of the West'. But he found the custom of 'collecting a heap of delicacies from every dish in your neighbour's plate,' 'decidedly objectionable'. Oliphant was always willing to try new things. On a trip on horseback from Tianjin, he met children locust-hunting. 'I had the curiosity to eat one', he wrote, 'and thought it not unlike a periwinkle.'[13]

For a Westerner to take a meal with an ordinary Chinese was still an unusual event. In 1863 John Gavin, a Scottish civil engineer posted to Hankou was invited to a Chinese wedding. He sent home a description of the dinner

As in everything else, Chinamen begin at the wrong end so we got dessert first, all sorts of fruit, sugar candy and stinking stuff which we had to take with chopsticks, then came the substantial dishes which we also had to eat with chopsticks.

He noted that if one wanted to be particularly polite to one's neighbour, one drew one's chopsticks through one's mouth to clean them before using them to serve him.[14] At about the same time Edward Bowra joined the staff of the Imperial Maritime Customs in Tianjin. He had mixed impressions of his first Chinese dinner. He ate what he believed to be sea slugs 'little, white, delicate, shrimplike articles and not by any means unpalatable', bird's nest soup, which was 'very like vermicelli or coarse strings of isinglass', and bamboo heads, which he thought most succulent. He compared the Chinese wine offered to 'a one-and-sixpenny bottle of South African port with a quart of water and a pint of treacle added.'[15]

WESTERN RESIDENTS IN THE TREATY PORTS

Westerners living in the treaty ports retained a strong and emotional preference for their native food. Harry Parkes, the future British minister in China, had arrived in China at the age of thirteen and had eaten many Chinese dinners, but had tired of these 'plethoric feasts'. When he landed in England in 1850

> I hurried to the best chop-house I could see, and ordered an English beef-steak with potatoes and ale as concomitants . . . I gave a cheer as I swallowed English beef, English ale, and English potatoes – though to tell you the truth, though a secret, the former was ill-cooked and the latter was underdone, owing undoubtedly to my hurry to obtain possession of the viands. But though I praised them and called them excellent, the insidious things waited until I got into the railway carriage, and then disagreed with me.[16]

Other Western members of treaty port communities shared Parkes' preference for familiar food and eating habits. When in December 1854 Robert Hart was entertained to dinner by J.A.T. Meadows, the British consul at Ningbo, he wore formal dress, the meal started with soup, followed by fish, and then an 'immense joint of Beef', which Hart was asked to carve and which he 'hacked most horribly'. The meat was accompanied by yam, which one of the missionary members of the party attempted to cut up, but it flew off his plate onto the floor.[17]

Foreign residents in the treaty ports had to decide what they would eat and how they would have it prepared. Chinese markets could supply a wide variety of foodstuffs, although some of these were disallowed as inedible by Western standards or unacceptable on grounds of hygiene. The latter issue came to the fore in the 1860s, when the publication in the United States of books on disinfectants made people more conscious of the relationship between dirt and disease.[18] Concerns over food hygiene in China gave rise to a wide variety of informed and fanciful claims. One particular objection to eating Chinese vegetables was the use made of 'night-soil' as a fertilizer. Another was the condition of Chinese slaughterhouses. C.F.R. Allen, the British consul at Ningbo in the 1880s, discovered that meat for foreigners' consumption was slaughtered alongside diseased buffaloes and donkeys. He and his family switched to eating Australian corned beef and North China mutton brought by the daily steamer from Shanghai.[19] Many Westerners bemoaned the lack of fresh milk, but when a supply was available, it was common for the supplier to be accused of adulterating it. Oliver G. Ready claimed that a friend of his had actually found a small live fish in his morning cupful of milk.[20] Undoubtedly standards of food hygiene in China were lower than those now expected in the West, and Westerners in China frequently suffered from ill health and premature death, which on occasions were attributable to contaminated food. However, excessive drinking and an ill-balanced diet probably caused much of the ill health experienced.

Western residents of the treaty ports normally employed several servants, including a cook who was expected to provide a variety of dishes acceptable to the palate of his employer. Most of these cooks were Chinese, but wealthy Western merchants employed French cooks. The resultant cuisine was predominantly European, although some concessions were made to the range of foodstuffs available. Very little was taken from Chinese cooking methods, but curries were served. There is little evidence that an Anglo-Indian cuisine, such as was commonly served in British households in India, was replicated by an Anglo-Chinese cuisine in China.

In the first half of the nineteenth century, Western or at least British eating preferences were for rich and substantial meals. According to Dr James Henderson, who worked in Shanghai and was familiar with the eating habits of the commercial classes there, most of his patients begin dinner with a rich soup, and a glass of sherry; then they partake of one or two dishes with champagne; then some beef, mutton, or fowls and bacon, with more champagne or beer; then rice and curry and ham; afterwards game, then pudding, pastry, jelly, custard, or blancmange, and more champagne; then cheese and salad, and bread and butter and a glass of port wine;

This 'AWFUL repast' concluded with dried fruit, more wine, strong coffee and cigars. Henderson suggested that a more suitable diet would be a plain joint of mutton, beef, or fowl, with rice. As he regarded Shanghai water as too dangerous to drink, and was convinced that tea was poisonous, he recommended the drinking of a moderate quantity of sherry or wine, perhaps half a bottle a day.[21]

Supplies of food sent from home provided a reminder of home comforts and a reaffirmation of emotional ties. John Gavin, a Scottish engineer who moved to Hankou in 1863, received parcels of food from his sister and mother. His sister sent a bun and some shortbread, which, he wrote were very nice and had kept perfectly. However he told his mother, 'Dinna send me a Gordon cheese, they don't go down in this climate,' and added that he would rather have a supply of jams and jellies, which cost him at least six shillings a pot in Hankou.[22]

This reluctance to consume Chinese food was very apparent in the arrangements made for provisioning British troops stationed in China. In the 1860 campaign Edward Barrington de Fonblanque exclaimed,

Why do we lead such artificial lives, and within a few miles of Pekin acquire all the luxuries of London? – English beer, and French and Spanish wines; sauces and pâtés from Fortnum & Mason, and soda-water from Schweppes?

The markets of Tien-tsin are wonderfully supplied. There you have fish, meat, game, vegetables, and fruits in the greatest profusion and at the lowest prices. There is a Celestial Quarter, whose confectionary [sic] and sweetmeats are unrivalled in their way; and our cooks might take some useful lessons from their Chinese fellow-craftsmen.

Fonblanque contrasted British habits with those of the French soldiers, who 'saved their money for better times', ate 'native chow-chow' and drank samshu (rice spirit) as a liquor, while Englishmen insisted on having capers with their boiled mutton.[23]

By the 1870s treaty port communities had organized the supply of Western food and drink. Single men, particularly those who served in the Imperial Maritime Service, lived in messes, where the importance of preserving national identity was stressed. On the island of Gulangyu (Kulangsu) off Xiamen, European stores could be bought, ice and aerated waters were produced locally, and a source of fresh milk was planned.[24] Tinned food was now widely available and this became a major source of nutrition for Westerners residing in China.[25] Paul King, who served in the Imperial Maritime Customs in Shantou (Swatow), described how bachelors ate in the 1870s. Breakfast, of tea or coffee and an egg, was taken alone. Tiffin at noon was a more substantial meal, often consisting of 'spatch-cock chicken', as fresh meat, other than poultry, could only be obtained from visiting steamers. At dinner, which was taken at eight, white linen mess jackets and duck trousers were worn. Sherry, claret and bottled beer were drunk at table and whisky and soda afterwards. Dinner was necessarily largely 'metallic'.

Tinned soup, tinned fish, tinned meat, tinned vegetables and Christmas tinned plum pudding . . . Tinned sausages were the great stand-by in those days, served with green peas (also from a tin). No wonder the white man's digestion not seldom failed him after years of exclusive feeding on chicken and tins.

Such was the prejudice against Chinese food, that little local produce other than chicken was consumed, although in the summer a Chinese cook served rock cod at beach picnics. King later suffered a severe attack of sprue, that is, an inability to digest food, perhaps due to the eating habits he had adopted.[26] In the treaty ports of the interior Western residents could not rely on local stores and had to provide for themselves. In 1882

W. D. Spence paid a short visit to Chongqing on the upper Yangzi, taking with him jam, marmalade, butter, coffee beans, baking and curry powder, two casks of Apollinaris water and nine dozen bottles of wine and spirits. A decade later Westerners posted to Chongqing were still bringing with them six months' supplies of food packed in tin-lined cases.[27]

The preference for Western food was most marked at Christmas, when the consumption of traditional Christmas fare affirmed the allegiance of exiles to their culture. Robert Hart celebrated Christmas 1854 with a missionary family. The main course consisted of boiled mutton, roast pheasant and a roast goose. This was followed by 'Plum-pudding, Mince Pies, Tarts and *Blanc Mange*. All patronized Plum-pudding of course.'[28] Oliver Ready, a merchant living in Hankou, spent Christmas 1889 shooting game. He described his solitary Christmas meal:

> Pigeon soup
> Woodcock
> Boiled pheasant
> Cold roast beef
> Plum cake ('a Christmas present from a Norwegian
>   lady') ablaze with Whisky
> Cheese
> Pumelo
> Whisky and water
> Tea[29]

TRAVEL IN THE INTERIOR

Some Westerners travelled far from sources of Western food and had to subsist on Chinese food. Between 1844 and 1846 the Abbé Évariste Huc, with his superior Father Gabet, travelled to Tibet and then, after having been expelled from that region, crossed China to Guangzhou. Huc, a Gascon with an ebullient temperament, claimed to have a superior knowledge of the Chinese, and he derided earlier accounts of Chinese food. Some descriptions of Chinese meals, he asserted, had been plagiarized from earlier accounts or had been elaborated with fanciful suggestions: that the Chinese prepared dishes with castor oil, or that their favourite dainties were 'shark's fins, fish-gizzards, goose-feet, peacock's combs', suppositions which Huc knew to be absurd. A real Chinese dinner was a very odd thing in the eyes of a stranger, but the Chinese were equally astonished by the Western manner of dining. Huc alleged that all Chinese were gifted with 'a remarkable aptitude for cookery', and could produce culinary marvels with extremely simple means. Cooks in the service of mandarins had in their possession a vast store of recipes, and when called upon to demonstrate their skill, they could perform surprising feats.

At times Huc and Gabet stopped at government resthouses, or, as Huc described them, 'communal palaces'. At a resthouse in Sichuan they were offered delicious iced lemonade, juicy fruits and melons, rather than the customary tea. They learned that this had been provided at the express order of the viceroy because 'such are the customs of the people who come from the western seas'. However, when crossing Hubei they stayed at a succession of miserable inns where they had difficulty in procuring enough food to prevent them from dying from hunger. Better fortune awaited them at Nanchang, the capital of Jiangxi province. With extraordinary effrontery the two missionaries installed themselves in the temple of the god of literature. There they elected to take their dinner, supplied by the *'maître d'hotel'*, in full view of the populace, who, Huc supposed, anticipated great amusement from seeing how 'Western Devils' consumed their food. Their saying grace, and making the sign of the cross, seemed to promise something interesting to the spectators. But then Huc and Gabet were at pains to eat and drink in the most rigorously orthodox Chinese fashion. They picked at some melon-seeds exactly as if they 'had been born on the borders of the Yellow River, instead of the Garonne', and they used their chopsticks with 'perfect ease and gravity, as if we had done nothing else all our lives'.[30]

The plant collector Robert Fortune had also learned to conform with Chinese customs. On his travels, he wrote:

I had discarded all European habits and luxuries. Chopsticks were substituted for knives and forks, tea and light wines for stronger drinks, and a long bamboo Chinese pipe for Manilla cheroots. By these means I had arrived at a high state of civilization and politeness.

Fortune liked Chinese food. At one inn where he stayed dinner was served on a table in the hall:

> The fare was plain and homely. There was a large basin full of boiled rice, with other smaller ones containing fish, eggs, and pork. The vegetables consisted of cabbages and bamboo. The latter I thought extremely good, and always ordered it during the remainder of our journey.

On another occasion he stopped at a Buddhist temple. The food offered was vegetarian, which he found very palatable, adding that some of the vegetables were prepared in such a manner as made it difficult to believe that they really were vegetables.[31]

In 1868 T. T. Cooper, an English merchant who described himself as a pioneer of commerce, made an adventurous journey from Chongqing to Burma. He stayed at inns and subsisted on the basic fare of rice and salt cabbage. Once he was entertained by a group of Chongqing merchants to a dinner consisting of 'fish soup, boiled and fried fish, stewed ducks, mutton and fowl'. At the end of the meal two young merchants told him that he was 'more like a Chinaman' than the foreigners in Hankou. They sat smoking and drinking samshu for a long time. Cooper, responding to what he took to be the genuine hospitality of his hosts, commented:

> I felt that I was seeing Chinese life from a stand-point hitherto unknown to most Europeans, especially Englishmen; and I felt much gratified with this my first admission into the private life of the people whose manners and customs I had adopted.

Nevertheless there were limits to Cooper's toleration of Chinese food. In the far west of Sichuan a French missionary, who knew from experience the hardships of the route that

A Chinese kitchen, showing food being prepared, c. 1894.

Cooper had followed, entertained him to an 'unexpected feast of roast kid, potatoes, bread and butter'. Before he left for Tibet he had a blacksmith make him a gridiron, 'a culinary means of deliverance from the everlasting round of greasy Chinese stews'. With this, and an iron cauldron, he produced a meal of grilled pheasant, pork chops and boiled potatoes, washed down with rice wine, and so 'forgot, for a time, that I was alone in the West of China, far away from friends, surrounded by a people buried in the darkest superstition, and liable at any time to fall a victim to their passions or prejudices'.[32]

Another adventurous traveller, Archibald Colquhoun, accomplished part of his journey by boat. His Chinese chef invariably cooked pork for his meals

> But as stewed pork, roast pork, pork sausages (terrible things they are!) and pig's-foot *gelée* are apt to pall upon the uncultivated Western palate, we were forced to enter a protest against the too frequent repetition of these Chinese dainties ... We had a hard struggle with the cook, but he relaxed so far as to vary the pork *menu* with dried duck and salt eggs.

Colquhoun maintained that Chinese food was 'by no means the horrible mess' which Europeans generally believed it to be. Even the food of his boatmen 'often looked by no means bad'. He was sure that eleven hours' work would make him relish it, although a trial of it had not prepossessed him in its favour. However his description of the eating habits of the muleteers and coolies who accompanied his expedition, which he likened to pigs around a trough, illustrated the superciliousness which was his usual attitude to things Chinese. His relief when he reached Bhamo and was entertained by American missionaries was palpable: 'No words, that I can employ, could ever depict the feelings with which we seated ourselves before a snow-white tablecloth, covered with little delicacies, which the good Americans insisted on producing for us.'[33]

At the end of the century, Isabella Bird, at the age of 64, went up the Yangzi to Wanxian by boat and was then carried in a sedan chair across north-east Sichuan. An experienced traveller, she preferred to take her food with her and only buy a few fresh items locally. She remarked, 'The reader may be amused to learn the singular monotony of my diet. I had a cup of tea made from 'tabloids,' and a plate of boiled flour, every morning before starting, tea on arriving, and for 146 days, at seven, curried fowl or eggs with rice.'

At one point on her journey she was instrumental in reviving a Chinese woman who had attempted suicide by eating opium. The woman's relations had expressed their gratitude by offering her a meal

> which I reluctantly ate out of coarse, unglazed basins: a strip or two of fat pork, some bean curd floating in grey sauce, some black beans, tasting like rotten cheese, some small onions, pickled dark brown, some rice, mixed with chopped cabbage, and some chopped capsicum.

This incident led her to summarize her views about Chinese food, a topic with which she felt familiar as she had been spending two hours a day observing its preparation. The only Chinese delicacy she could eat with equanimity was old eggs, which she had tasted at a Chinese dinner in Seoul. On her travels she enjoyed steamed dumplings, which made good toast. Bean curd, however, resembled 'in insipidity unflavoured *blanc mange* made with Carrageen moss'. She approved of the meat and vegetable patties, and the cakes of wheaten flour or millet, topped with treacle or candy, sold by itinerant pie-men. She believed that the idea of Chinese food held in the West was considerably astray. It was supposed that the delicacies consumed by the rich as a form of conspicuous consumption were typical of Chinese food. In fact the Chinese diet included four times the variety of vegetables used in the West. Wholesome and excellent meals were often produced in dark and unsavoury surroundings, and anyone who travelled much in the interior learned to find Chinese food palatable. Her chief objections to it were the amount of vegetable oil used and the prevalent flavour of garlic. Without doubt Chinese food was preferable to the 'fishy and vegetable abominations known as "Japanese food"' which she had tried some eighteen years previously.[34]

MISSIONARIES AND CHINESE FOOD

The attitude of Western missionaries to Chinese food depended in part on the religious denomination to which they belonged. Catholic missionaries identified themselves with their congregations and, because of their low salaries, learned to live on Chinese food. Protestant missionaries based in the treaty ports responded to Chinese food in much the same way as other members of the expatriate community, that is to say by partaking of it very sparingly. The Church Missionary Society (CMS), the society supported by the Church of England, epitomized an attitude towards Chinese food in its practice of using loaves of stale, foreign-made bread and watered-down claret at communion services. When a CMS missionary suggested substituting rice-cake and tea, this was vetoed because of its wider implications.[35]

John L. Nevius, an American Presbyterian missionary, remarked that although China furnished nearly every article of food that might be found in the United States:

The native mode of preparing and cooking it is, however, very different from ours, and, in many respects, not suited to our tastes and habits. Most missionary families have an American cooking-stove, and servants are taught to prepare food according to our way, so that our tables and meals correspond very nearly to what we have been accustomed to at home.[36]

Nevius found it necessary to justify the employment of Chinese cooks by missionaries. If they did not do so, he said, they would neglect the 'special work to which Christ had called them'. Chinese cooks, available at five dollars a year plus board, learned Western cooking techniques including how to make bread and butter, skills taught them by missionary wives and by women missionaries. In 1866 Martha Crawford, wife of a Southern Baptist missionary, published a book entitled *Zao yangfang shu* (Preparing Foreign Food) which was intended to help foreign wives explain to their cooks how to prepare suitable meals. It contained 270 recipes, including such Tuscaloosa specialties as frizzled beef and fritters and sour milk biscuits.[37] The *English-Chinese Cookery Book* by J. Dyer Ball, published in Hong Kong in 1890, continued this practice. His recipes included Yorkshire Pudding with Roast Beef and Toad in the Hole. He also explained how to cook bean sprouts: 'cut off the roots and put into a saucepan, and boil with water, and a little salt for half-an-hour till soft'.

Missionaries stationed in treaty ports made forays into rural areas, and this could necessitate their eating Chinese food. The Revd R. H. Cobbold, who had spent eight years in Ningbo, declared that experienced travellers left their own baskets of provisions behind them, for one seldom reached a village where one could not find some refreshment, whether it be bean soup, 'three cornered *no-me* rice-puddings, boiled in a wrapper of plantain leaf, and eaten with coarse sugar', or something in the way of sausages, 'pork and onion chopped fine, with bread-crumbs and white of eggs to give consistency, made up into balls of the size of a large walnut'. This food might not always be palatable, because tastes differ, but the traveller might rest assured that the 'sensual Chinaman' would not greatly offend against the 'laws of *gourmanderie*'.[38]

Hudson Taylor, the future leader of the China Inland Mission, was convinced that only by identifying closely with the Chinese would missionaries reach them spiritually. When he arrived in China in 1854 he stayed with other Protestant missionaries but found it extremely difficult to live within his salary. He wrote home that if he had quarters of his own he could live on rice, not bread as that was too expensive, and drink tea without milk or sugar. Two years later he was travelling in the hinterland of Shantou and making his supper from congee, that is rice gruel. On another occasion, he stayed at an inn near Ningbo. The food offered was cold burnt rice and snakes fried in lamp-oil. As he was unwilling to reveal that he was a foreigner he attempted to make a meal of this, but with little success.[39] In 1865 he founded the China Inland Mission (CIM), which was to observe the principles of evangelism that he had established for himself.

> Let us in everything not sinful become Chinese that we may by all means 'save some'. Let us adopt their dress, acquire their language, seek to conform to their habits and approximate to their diet as far as health and constitution will allow.[40]

When, in 1866, the first CIM missionaries left Shanghai for the interior, the men put on long Chinese robes and had their hair shaved in front and false pigtails woven into their back hair. The women tied their hair in buns and wore loose native gowns. By so doing they took a stance on an issue which was to divide the missionary community for decades: whether or not to wear native dress. The attendant question – whether or not to adhere to a diet of Chinese food – was never debated in the same open terms. However, it was an issue which was to split the missionary community, with the CIM taking the lead in identifying with the Chinese. At the first CIM mission at Hangzhou, CIM missionaries ate their meals in a bare hall at a plank table set with bowls and chopsticks. Before long one of the group, Lewis Nicol, revolted against the ruling about wearing native dress. Sent to an out-station he there re-assumed Western clothes and began to use knives and forks.

Timothy Richard of the Baptist Missionary Society also ate Chinese food, emphasizing the economy he thereby achieved. He breakfasted on millet gruel and for lunch he bought four rice dumplings from street hawkers, which cost him less than a penny.

> My evening meal was luxurious. Instead of taking it at home I usually went to a restaurant. There I would order one evening chi-p'ien (a course of the white meat of a chicken boiled into soup and nicely flavoured), and the next evening ii-p'ien (a dish of good fish with well-flavoured soup). After this meat or fish course I would order four little steamed loaves of bread, the size and shape of a small glass tumbler. With these I drank as much native tea as I liked, and the whole meal cost the extravagant sum of not more than one hundred and twenty cash, or sixpence.[41]

In December 1877 Richard was working in Shanxi at the height of a famine which cost some nine and a half million lives. He wrote home, 'That people pull down their houses, sell their wives and daughters, eat roots and carrion, clay and refuse, is news nobody wonders at.' If that were not enough to move one's pity, he added, then the sight of unburied corpses being devoured by hungry dogs, and children being boiled and eaten up should do so. Richard distributed the meagre funds he had at his disposal, and called on the recipients to pray to God to have pity on them. He supported the government's programme of relief, but he also encouraged the formation of famine relief committees among Western residents in China and abroad. In London a committee of the China Famine Relief fund published an illustrated pamphlet entitled *The Famine in China*. One of its illustrations, which showed peasants stripping off the bark from trees for food, was accompanied by an appeal 'Ye who spend large sums every day on your food, will you not give these sufferers a cup of soup?' Not content with organizing immediate relief, Richard urged reform on the Chinese government, arguing that only by adopting Western science and technology could China avert further disasters.[42]

Charlotte Diggs Moon, known as Lottie Moon, of the Southern Baptist Mission, worked alone in Pingdu, Shandong from 1885. She claimed it was her practice to eat, sleep and dress as she saw the natives doing, but she wrote 'I do not enjoy Chinese food, and drinking tea does not suit me, but social intercourse is one way of winning the people.'[43] She was in Shandong in the years prior to the 1911 revolution, when the cost of living soared and the region was beset by plague and famine. The following year, suffering from depression, she donated all her savings to a famine relief fund and resolved to stop eating entirely. Irwin T. Hyatt suggested that 'by dying precisely as gruesomely as did the friends she was unable to save, she could make death itself a means of achieving closeness to them'. Her name has been remembered as an example of selfless giving, and in various publications, including the *Lottie Moon Cook Book*. This contains no Chinese recipes, but is a reprint of *Mrs Hill's New Cook Book*, published in 1872, a collection of 300 recipes from Virginia that Lottie Moon used when offering her Southern hospitality in China. The book is still sold to support the Southern Baptist Mission.[44]

THE BOXER UPRISING

The lifestyle assumed by Westerners living in North China was upset by the Boxer Uprising of 1899–1900. The uprising cost the lives of many missionaries, particularly of the China Inland Mission, and led to the celebrated 55-day siege of the Western legations in Beijing. One of the best-known missionary accounts of these events, *A Thousand Miles of Miracle in China*, detailed the providential escape of the Revd Archibald Glover and his family from the Boxers. At one point they were stripped of their clothing and were starving. In desperation the children collected weeds and they made a herbal meal. These uncooked weeds, Glover said, were truly 'the bread of affliction', but because they were sanctified by prayer, they became 'the bread of blessing'. Later on their journey they were passed from prison to prison. Their staple food was 'wet' or 'dry' rice, that is to say rice gruel, or plain cooked rice. Sometimes it was varied with raw eggs, or a preparation of bean-curd, 'which looked and tasted not unlike junket'. Their usual drink was an infusion of beech or elm leaves, which was dignified by the name of tea. Near the end of their flight they reached a London Missionary Society mission station and there, at last, they were given 'what appeared in our eyes a veritable feast': fish, fowl and potatoes, with preserved meat and fruit. But best of all there was milk, 'a Nestlé solution too delicious for words'.[45]

When the Westerners were besieged in the Beijing Legation area, the contents of two Western shops, Imbecks and Kierulffs, provided a stockpile of food and of alcoholic drinks, especially champagne. Those besieged also had access to a grain shop on Legation Street containing nearly 200 tons of wheat, as well as quantities of rice and maize, although much of the rice was yellow unpolished rice, which to eat was like chewing sand. As the spring race-meeting had been held in early May, the stables were still full with some 150 ponies and some mules. This food had to suffice 1,200 Westerners and some 3,000 Chinese Christians for an indefinite period. Provisions were organized by Auguste Chamot, the Swiss proprietor of the Hôtel Pékin and his American wife, and later a food committee was established to supervise the distribution of food. Chamot found some mill-stones and transformed part of his hotel into a mill, supplying the besieged with bread. Various communities formed messes for their eating arrangements. One of the largest groups was composed of American missionaries. For practical, rather than ideological purposes, the Congregationalists ate their meals first, followed by the Presbyterians and then the Methodists. A committee of three women, one from each mission, worked out the daily menu and gave their orders to the Chinese cooks.[46] During the siege many of the ponies and mules were eaten, the first pony to perish being the one belonging to Edward Conger, the United States Minister, on the grounds that 'he hated for-eigners as bitterly as do the Chinese'. An improvised kitchen was constructed in front of the theatre in the Legation grounds. There Chinese cooks wearing chintz aprons boiled horsemeat in large kettles.[47] Later, in the French Legation, an attempt was made to vary the menu from the eternal horse goulash by preparing 'horse steak à la mode and horse schnitzel'.

During the siege Westerners continued to prepare and consume their food in a manner close to their ordinary habits. Lady Macdonald, the British Minister's wife, fed 40 Europeans three times a day. At table only one dish was served and nobody, except the Italian chargé d'affaires, thought of dressing for dinner. Tinned beef, the *pièce de résistance*, was served of necessity with rice. For luxuries the besieged had 'a good stock of jams, tinned fruits, tinned vegetables, sardines, tinned mackerel, Liebig's extract, a big box of Stilton cheese, coffee, tinned butter, and white flour.'[48]

A notable incident, an instance of food diplomacy, was the dispatch by the Empress Dowager – regarded by the besieged as the cause of their misfortunes – of three cartloads of provisions, including water melons, aubergines, flour, and 'an uneatable Chinese vegetable', to the legations. Various explanations circulated on why this food had been sent – perhaps it was because the British minister had informed the Court that 'the ladies felt the need of ice, eggs, and fresh fruit', perhaps it was a conciliatory gesture on the part of the Empress Dowager, who now realized the folly of having encouraged the Boxers. The gifts were received with mixed feelings by the besieged, who either condemned them as paltry presents from people who were trying to kill them, or suspected that the food was poisoned.

During the siege efforts were made to distribute food equitably among Westerners, but the treatment of the Chinese Christians was not so fair. These refugees lived in shacks in the grounds of the residence of Prince Su. They were allocated some food, but their supplies were quite inadequate and they were reduced to stripping the trees of leaves and bark. Carrion crows and dogs were shot for them by the sentries and the converts ate them raw. When two ponies were found to be infected with a parasitic worm, the meat was sent to the Chinese Christians.

FOUR

1900–49: Western Impressions of Chinese Food in China

By the beginning of the twentieth century, for a Westerner to visit or reside in China had become so commonplace that descriptions of Chinese food had lost much of their capacity to intrigue or to shock. However, as the century wore on fresh opinions began to be expressed about the merits or otherwise of Chinese food and whether Westerners should eat it.

THE TREATY PORTS

Westerners living in the treaty ports were almost unanimous in their dismissal of Chinese culture and, by extension, of Chinese food, and this view was communicated to the increasing numbers of casual visitors to the country. The tone was set by the diplomatic community in Beijing, whose duties included occasionally eating Chinese meals. Both Daniele Varè, the Italian chargé d'affaires and Dr George Morrison, the Beijing correspondent of *The Times* left patronizing descriptions of one such occasion. On 10 October 1913 they attended the ceremony at which Yuan Shikai was inaugurated as the first President of the Republic of China and copied down the English wording of the menu.

The Bill of Supper
The food is made of swollow – The food is made of fine fish – The food is made of shrimp – The boiling chickens – The spinach and fine meet – The cake is made of yellow hen's eggs – The boiling fish – The boiling duck – The vegetables – The canned fruit – The fruit – The coffee.[1]

Most of the Western residents in the treaty ports were not obliged to attend such functions and they distanced themselves as far as possible from all things Chinese, including Chinese food. The menu for the Shanghai Paper Hunt Club annual dinner for 1936 began with hors d'oeuvres and Dutch pea soup. This was followed by fried sole with lemon, broiled quail on toast and *contrefilet* of beef served with Yorkshire pudding, roast potatoes and spinach. The meal concluded with apple pie, cheese, fruit and coffee.[2] Western habits at dinner parties were described waspishly by Somerset Maugham. 'Each course,' he noted, 'was served with the appropriate wine, sherry with the soup and hock with the fish; and there were two entrées, a white entrée and a brown entrée, which the careful housekeeper of the nineties felt were essential to a properly arranged dinner.' As for the conversation, it was less varied than the courses. The guests talked of sport, but China bored them all, in fact they were 'bored to death with each other'.[3] This segregation was extended to accommodation on ships operating in Chinese waters. There was usually a saloon class for foreign travellers, with foreign food and furniture, and a Chinese first class, with Chinese food served at round tables.[4] On special occasions the treaty port community relied heavily on the ingenuity of their Chinese cooks in preparing and presenting the appropriate food. One St Andrew's Day a Scots family living in Changsha explained to their cook how haggis was made. He bought eight goats' stomachs, hearts and livers and the family then made them into haggises.[5]

Westerners visitors were warned about eating in China. In Carl Crow's 1931 *Handbook for China*, travellers were advised that the main Chinese cities now had European or American style hotels, which offered Western food and that an increasing number of Chinese inns were becoming Europeanized. These offered a 'more or less edible travesty' of the five-course *table d'hôte* which all Chinese cooks believed to be necessary to the sustenance of the foreign life. In addition they carried stocks of tinned provisions which the traveller could use for the preparation of his meals. 'Chinese food is quite wholesome and many old residents eat it regularly, but it contains too many strange dishes to be palatable to the inexperienced,' Crow warned.

Travellers were urged to avoid food which had not been thoroughly cooked, especially green salads. Crow said that although this was good advice, it was often ignored by older residents with no apparent ill effects. He added menacingly that an old resident might do many things without harming himself, but if a newcomer were to do the same, it would send him to the doctor, thence to the hospital and possibly to the undertaker.[6]

Few treaty-port residents journeyed far into the interior of China, but in the summer months wealthier residents removed to hill stations, the most popular being Guling in Jiangxi, known as 'China's Switzerland'. There the Guling Store sold 'Guling Brand' preserved provisions.[7] At the Journey's End Hotel the proprietor offered 'Grilled rainbow trout. Crab home-grown salads. Fresh prawn curries'. For some treaty port residents, for example the sugar agents of Butterfield and Swire, travelling was part of their job. One agent, Gordon Campbell, recalled that in the 1920s sugar agents preferred to take European food with them, mostly in the form of tinned food and bottled water. Campbell also took his own bread, which in time grew harder and greener. He did not eat much Chinese food, as he was not fond of it and he was very doubtful what he was eating – he had once eaten a beef steak in a Chinese inn, which at the time he thought quite edible, but he discovered later that it had come from a cow that had died the previous day. Another agent recalled having been a guest at a seventeen-course meal, all the courses being of water-originating food. The feast, which lasted for three hours, was an experience which he was glad to have had, but was not anxious to repeat.[8]

How to establish social relations with Chinese by sharing their food was a problem touched on by the American writer Alice Tisdale Hobart in her novel *Oil for the Lamps of China*. In the 1920s her husband had worked as a manager for the Standard Oil Company, and Stephen Chase, the hero of her novel, holds a similar position in Manchuria. Oil company agents were expected to travel extensively and to deal constantly with Chinese customers. On his journeys, Chase subsists on a diet of eggs and coffee. His encounters with Chinese food form part of the negotiations with Chinese merchants over contracts, negotiations in which Chase is constantly trying to avoid being out-manoeuvred. On one occasion, at the start of discussions about arrangements for an oil agency, he is invited to a feast, a circumstance which puts him immediately on his guard. His host insists on placing choice pieces of meat on his saucer, but while the other guests eat with sucking sounds of satisfaction, Chase's sense of alienation increases. For a brief moment he is able to enjoy the well-cooked foods and to share the pleasures of the other diners, but this moment does not last. He becomes baffled by the 'strange sameness' of the faces of the other Chinese as the meal stretches on until mid-afternoon. Then a drinking game begins, with the intention of getting Chase drunk. In exasperation he breaks away, exclaiming to himself that he has wasted the day. After several more days of discussions a bargain is struck, and Chase in turn offers a feast to his customers in the name of the company. The table is illuminated by a great oil lamp, a present from the Company, but even its light does not reveal to Chase how he has been outwitted in the negotiations. This incident was typical of the dilemma which Chase faces and which dogged oil agents of the time: he strives constantly to learn the Chinese way of doing business, but the company's philosophy is to teach the Chinese 'modern business methods'. The nearest Chase comes to bridging the gap between himself and the Chinese is when he forges a friendship with a man named Ho, who becomes his Chinese adviser and travelling companion. But even though he counts Ho a friend, the two men do not eat together, for Chase sticks to his eggs and coffee and Ho prefers his own food. These and other experiences finally convince Chase that the white man and the Chinese are 'two races alien at heart', yet drawn together in the struggle for progress.[9]

Not all treaty port residents rejected Chinese food. According to Fay Angus, who grew up in Shanghai in the 1930s, it was acceptable for Western children in the care of their amahs to eat street food. She liked best the long strips of twisted dough deep-fried in peanut oil. Her mother wondered why she had no appetite for the formal European dinners served so elegantly at their house in the evening.[10] Another dissident voice was that of Averil Mackenzie-Grieve, wife of a 'distinguished sinologue', who lived in Gulangyu in the 1920s. She compared the allegiance of the British of the treaty ports to their own food to that of the Chinese in Malaya to Chinese food. The latter, when they had made good, no longer wore the long robe or the silk cap and they drank three-star brandy instead of rice wine, but they still gave feasts 'with bird's nests, sharks' fins, old black eggs and the same slugs which the Malays call *trepang*'. The same was true of the British.

> All over the exotic, the disdainful, often ruthless and baffling East, little groups were sitting as we sat: stiff-shirted, low-necked, exclusive, eating roast chickens and bread sauce, Cadbury's chocolate soufflé, Huntley & Palmer's biscuits, tinned Stilton cheese; drinking Scotch whisky and Portuguese wines . . .[11]

ADMIRERS OF CHINESE FOOD

The colonial attitudes of the Westerners in the treaty ports were challenged by the Nationalist revolution of 1925–7, and some modifications occurred in social relationships in its aftermath. Meyrick Hewlett, who in 1928 became the British Consul-General at Nanjing, formed a 'close and intimate relationship' with C. T. Wang, the new Minister for Foreign Affairs. He could never forget 'the whole-hearted enjoyment of a dinner at his house'. In return Hewlett entertained diligently and expensively: 'Two or three dinners of eighteen people were given by me monthly.' Then he and C. T. Wang inaugurated an International Club, which was intended to promote better international relations., Hewlett declared, 'There was not a happier meeting-ground for all nationalities anywhere in China.'[12] Some Western firms found it politic to alter their practices towards Chinese employees. When M. W. Scott arrived in Hong Kong in 1934 to work for Butterfield and Swire, he was greeted by one of the firm's British-educated Chinese assistants and immediately taken out for a 'chop stick meal'. Some missionaries also changed their lifestyles in the direction of more equal relationships with Chinese colleagues, a relationship which included sharing food. In 1927, at meetings of the Senate of the West China Union University, tea was served by one Chinese and one foreigner. Chinese tea and pastry were provided and one foreign cake. At the All-China Conference on religious education held in 1931, Western and Chinese delegates ate together for the first time.[13]

In the interwar period some Western admirers of Chinese culture developed an aesthetic appreciation of Chinese food. Richard Wilhelm, a German teacher, who spent 25 years in China, mainly in Beijing and Qingdao, wrote *The Soul of China*. What, he asked had the East to teach us? Part of his answer was how and what to eat. According to Wilhelm the public traffic of a European restaurant, with possibly two different groups sitting at the same table, would be regarded as coarse and disagreeable in China. Chinese people met to eat and also to enjoy themselves. A Chinese meal could be 'a small masterpiece of social communion'. The European habit of just swallowing dishes was alien to the Chinese, who were not ashamed to honour a good dish. Wilhelm claimed that the Chinese had been masters of cooking since time immemorial, and quoted the case of Yi Yin, who persuaded King Tang, the founder of the Shang dynasty, to employ him because of his culinary skills and in due course became the king's right-hand man. Wilhelm also described some of the specialist restaurants to be found in Beijing. At one, the owner killed a pig a day and the menu was entirely composed of recipes using pork. At another 100 different versions of Beijing duck were offered. At a third, presumably a Mongolian restaurant, the dishes were all of mutton and in the winter one could order a 'fire pot'. At a fourth the proprietor had in a dream seen the souls of the animals he had eaten. They accused him of murder and only spared his life when he promised never to kill an animal again. In return the animals gave him secret recipes for vegetarian food. The story of his conversion was recounted on the walls of the restaurant, which served roasted pig, sharks' fins, swallows' nests, fish cutlets and a hundred other things, all prepared on a strictly vegetarian basis. These restaurants were frequented by connoisseurs. Other restaurants had adopted features of European cuisine, such as sauces made with milk and various kinds of bread.[14]

Shortly before Japan occupied Qingdao, Wilhelm met the Estonian philosopher Count Hermann Keyserling. Keyserling, who had left Europe in disgust, was immensely impressed by Chinese culture, not least by Chinese food. He was taken to one of the 'out-of-the-way gourmet restaurants which are as typical of Beijing as they are of Paris'. There the 'atmosphere of refined culture' and the 'pure culinary idealism' of the *maître d'hôtel* turned him into a gourmet. 'Why,' he asked, 'should the palate be regarded as less than the eye and the ear? A great cook is creative in the highest sense.' At one restaurant he was served duck six times in succession, but 'its preparation was so delicately varied that it did not give the effect of repetition'. For technical mastery he admired most a dish of pickled jellyfish. Although he was ashamed to admit it, at first he had shuddered at a dish of maggots, but it turned out to be 'exceedingly delicious'.[15]

In the 1930s Beijing attracted a small coterie of Westerners who had come to China to experience, before it should disappear, what they regarded as oriental wisdom and the art of living. Among them were the poets William Empson and Harold Acton and the writer Osbert Sitwell. Sitwell showed his commitment to things Chinese while still in Nanjing. Having ordered a cup of tea he was brought 'something that reminded me of a wet Saturday afternoon in a Hindhead boarding-house'. He was told that the hotel only served Ceylonese and Indian tea, so in protest he sent out for a cup of 'coolie, green tea'. Beijing, he found, was 'the paradise of the Chinese gourmet', boasting as many as 6,000 restaurants which offered the cuisines of every province. Whereas drama, sculpture and music were in decline, cookery, which also ranked as an art, survived in its pristine splendour. A European chef would give precise answers to queries about quantities of ingredients or the length of time of cooking, but a Chinese chef would respond, 'As much as you judge to be right for it.' This commitment to art extended to the siting of restaurants and to the presentation of meals. It was most apparent in an enumeration of some favourite dishes:

a soup said to be made from stock over sixty years old; Fried Prawns; Turnip Cakes à la Shantung; White Fungus cooked in Wine; Tortoises' Eggs; Bamboo Shoots with Shredded

Ham and Sea-slugs, à la Szechuan; Boiled Bear's Paws; Scalded Mutton; Fried Fish-lips; Roast Turtle; Minced Pork and Cabbage with Mushrooms and Bamboo Shoots, served in rind of Bean Curd; a kind of black Caviare, boiled in vinegar and red pepper . . .

These dishes might sound outlandish, but their ingredients were no more remarkable than those for *Vol-au-vent Toulousien*. Somewhat surprisingly Sitwell concluded 'Chinese food *is* excellent: though to some – and to myself among them – the best European food seems better.'

Before he left Beijing Sitwell wandered through the streets observing the street vendors who sold 'bowls of hot soup, of varying quality, peanuts, sweets of a hundred different kinds, dried melon and sunflower seeds, cigarettes, sarsaparilla, and regional dishes such as "fried bean curd"', as well as roasted chestnuts and dumplings and many other things. Even the bowls they used were beautiful. The sight of the stalls and the sound of the vendors' street cries irritated some Europeans and Americans. Others found these sights romantic, almost lovely. To Sitwell they also implied 'destitution in both buyer and seller', and the cries sounded like 'the very voice of poverty'.[16]

George Kates moved from Hollywood to Beijing in 1933 and became an expert on many things Chinese. For this reason he was often invited to diplomatic dinners and ate the cheeses and drank the wines of the country of his host. But his real passion was to identify himself with the culture of upper-class life of old China which was fast disappearing around him. Emulating Confucius's 'princely man', he lived simply in a house furnished with carefully chosen antiques, and ate sparingly. He contrasted this lifestyle with that of the 'little man', the ordinary Chinese, whose experience of hard times had made 'eating, if possible pleasurable eating', an imperative. All profitable relationships in Chinese society were cemented by banqueting. No Chinese, he asserted, needed convincing of the actual pleasures of the table. Whereas the princely man watched his table manners, the little man had no inhibitions at the meal table, apart from observing the etiquette of seating. This led Kates to offer a general assessment of the contrast between food in China and the West:

Westerners have been known to return from a Chinese feast apparently replete; then, after a few hours, the chopped and highly flavored food already half digested when served, prepared moreover to be eaten chiefly for taste, with the mild wine, leave them wondering themselves at how little they feel satisfied. In matters both of food and drink, we in the West have quite other methods of replenishing our energies than have the more sensitive, the less heroic and more delicate, Chinese.[17]

Other writers offered a more down-to-earth appreciation of Chinese food. Nora Waln, a young American woman, was the guest of the wealthy Lin family who lived on the Grand Canal. She had been invited to stay there because her eighteenth-century forebear, J. S. Waln of Philadelphia, had done business with a Lin ancestor who was a Guangzhou merchant. The China she saw as she approached the house was a land of plenty: the itinerant cooks on the wharves cried their wares,

> The cauldrons gave off a delicious steam which whetted my hunger. Thick meat and vegetable soup, piping hot! Crusty golden dough-nut twists! Sweet steamed yams! Flaky white rice! Roasted chestnuts! Pork dumplings. Buns of light steamed bread! Grain porridge! Candied red apples! Nougat-stuffed dates! Fried noodles! Bean-curd of rich brownness!'

However ladies did not eat from street vendors and so her party dined modestly at a restaurant, where they ordered the usual 'five dishes' of chicken, shrimps, pork, pigeon eggs and a fish soup, costing one dollar per person. But as they ate an unpleasant incident occurred, a reminder that they were living in lawless times. A soldier, presumably from a warlord army, came in, demanded food and then paid in useless currency. After he had left the innkeeper threw the note, and the chopsticks which the soldier had used, into the fire.

For Nora Waln, to enter the Lin household, where six generations lived under one roof, was like Alice stepping through a looking-glass into another world. On the night of her arrival her maid helped her undress and bathe. She was provided with a pair of ivory chopsticks with silver handles and ate from a robin's egg blue bowl. The meal began with three dishes, each cooked 'in such a different and delicious sauce that I was eager to possess the recipes to send home to my sisters'. There followed a fish soup, which was served in sea-green china and the meal was completed with steamed rice served in a transparent white bowl. She finished her meal with hard white winter pears and a cup of jasmine tea, and after wiping her face and hands with a hot towel, fell asleep on the brick bed.[18]

Emily Hahn, the prolific American writer, arrived in Shanghai in 1935 and fell in love with the city. 'Let aesthetes sigh for Peking,' she wrote, 'Shanghai is for now, for the living me.' Her enjoyment of life extended to many aspects of Chinese life, and most particularly Chinese food. In Shanghai, she discovered, one could have one's elevenses at any hour of the morning: 'boiled or fried noodles with ham or tiny shrimps or shreds of chicken'. For afternoon snacks there were 'endless sorts of sweet or salty cakes stuffed with ground beans or minced pork or chopped greens'. Her Chinese partner liked 'coolie food' best, plain dishes of bean sprouts and salt fish and ordinary cabbage, but he was also knowledgeable about Chinese food and Hahn would listen to long discussions about how to prepare particular dishes. She made brief forays into the countryside, visited monasteries, and ate meals of Buddhist vegetables.[19]

All the writers mentioned so far make only passing references to cooking Chinese food. In 1935 Corrinne Lamb published *The Chinese Festive Board*, one of the first Chinese cookbooks directed at a Western readership.[20] In her introduction she explained that over the last twenty years she had partaken frequently of Chinese hospitality, not only in the treaty ports, but also in the interior, and not only at the tables of the wealthy, but also at those of peasants, innkeepers and even cameleers. She had learned that Chinese cooks possessed the rare ability to work the same marvels with the lowly cabbage as with birds' nests which cost $16 an ounce. She now hoped to make some of the dishes she had tried available to strangers to China and to foreign guests within her borders.

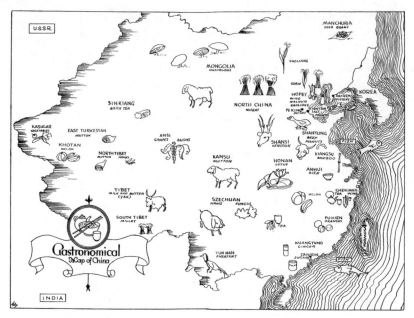

Gastronomical map of China, 1935.

She began with comments on the Chinese diet and eating habits. She pointed out that rice formed the staple for only about two-fifths of the Chinese people, the majority depending on wheat, barley and millet. As for rats 'such things are never heard of, though it is true that snakes are eaten in South China'. Whereas the destitute in China sought food at any time, peasants and artisans ate regular meals. *Petit déjeuner* consisted of tea and 'a ring of light batter fried in deep fat'.

> I warn you, you would not like it. It is a sort of prehistoric doughnut. Cold, limp, insipid, and shining in its coat of cooled grease, it is not the sort of thing which would appeal to one at seven o'clock in the morning . . .

The two main meals were taken at about 10 a.m. and between 4.30 and 6.00 p.m. Each consisted of a staple, in the form of rice or flour, and selection of one to four dishes, the contents of which depended on what was available in the market. These meals were supplemented by 'the widespread habit of nibbling at food between the regular meals', a habit which was 'consistent with the irregularity characterizing most other Chinese activities'.

She continued with chapters on table etiquette, Chinese dinner parties and the wine bowl, in nearly every instance emphasizing the advantages of the Chinese way of eating. The niceties of Western table manners, she suggested, did not permit the full enjoyment of food. In China the diner was at liberty to indulge himself as he thought best. The use of chopsticks saved washing up and a steaming Turkish towel was preferable to a dainty Irish linen serviette. She then described the etiquette of a Chinese dinner party. If it was a formal occasion, an invitation written on a red card would be sent. The most distinguished guest would be seated in the place of honour facing the doorway. Each guest would choose a dish from the menu and the host would add his selections. During the meal drinking games were played, and perhaps some 'dainty little acquaintance in a nearby sing-song house', smelling of cheap Japanese scent, would sing.

Her recipes, she claimed, came from Beiping restaurants.[21] These had been difficult to compile because of the speed at which a Chinese chef operated, his disdain for measured quantities and his reluctance to expose the secrets of his craft. She had tried to cook these recipes on a foreign stove, using foreign utensils, but had been forced to switch to a mud stove, tin cans, copper ladles, gourds and calabashes. From this she had concluded

> that rice can only be cooked in a brass kettle, fish can only be fried in an iron *ch'ien tzu* with a broken handle, mutton can only be stewed properly in a vessel made from an empty petrol can, and tea can only be prepared in a pot with the spout broken off. Dishes should only be washed with a whisk-broom, kitchen utensils should not be washed at all but wiped out, and lusty singing, merry conversation, folk songs and dances should always be engaged in when preparing anything really difficult.

Her book contained 50 recipes and some advice to the American housewife on their preparation, often suggesting that the resulting dish would be tastier than American plain cooking. Instead of using canned bean sprouts, which had lost their crispness, the housewife was advised to produce her own by sprouting a quantity of navy beans. Instructions were given for preparing 'smothered chicken' which was described as very superior to the ordinary boiled chicken. The recipe for 'chicken and peppers' was the Chinese version of chicken *à la King*, but instead of being served with a cream sauce it was made with a 'highly poignant' (*sic*) sauce, which was as unusual as it was appetizing. The book then offered useful advice on ordering a meal in a Chinese restaurant. Some 260 dishes were identified and about 100 of these were marked with an asterisk, indicating that they were dishes which always called for appreciation. Those eating in restaurants were told that it was customary to add 10 per cent to the bill as a gratuity to the waiters, and 'a further twenty cents to the puller of each private rickshaw or fifty cents to the chauffeur of the car in which the guests arrive'.

In *The Good Earth*, first published in 1931, which sold over a million copies in the 1930s, Pearl Buck developed a new theme by expressing a sympathetic attitude towards the food of the ordinary Chinese peasant. The novel's main protagonist, Wang Lung, is driven by a desire to own land. Buck interwove an account of his struggle to achieve this with references to the food that he ate and the moral values which that consumption implied. Early in the novel, Wang Lung marries a simple peasant woman who becomes his working partner. Her culinary skills – she has been brought up as a kitchen slave – transforms the fare on which Wang Lung and his father had been subsisting. At their wedding meal the guests are served with fish and pork. Wang Lung, as custom dictated, deprecates the food as poorly prepared.

> But in his heart he was proud of the dishes, for with what meats she had the woman had combined sugar and vinegar and a little wine and soy sauce, and she had skilfully brought forth all the force of the meat itself, so that Wang Lung himself had never tasted such dishes upon the tables of his friends.

However this good fortune is not to last. Famine strikes, the family starves, and cannibalism is reported in the village. Wang Lung, following the dictates of filial piety, gives what little food they have to his father, but he refuses to sell his land. He and his family flee south and subsist from begging and charity. There he learns something of the social implications of diet:

> In Wang Lung's country a man, if he had a roll of good wheat bread and a sprig of garlic in it, had a good meal and needed no more. But here the people dabbled with pork balls and bamboo sprouts and chestnuts stewed with chicken and goose giblets and this and that of vegetables, and when an honest man came by smelling of yesterday's garlic, they lifted their noses and cried out, 'Now here is a reeking, pig-tailed northerner!'

In time Wang Lung grows rich, his wife dies, he stops working on his land and he begins to eat dainty food: 'those things which rich men use to force their lagging appetites'. But as he approaches death, he sits clutching a handful of the good earth and reverts to the eating habits of his youth, preferring to have one of his sons 'stir up meal in hot water and sup it as his father had done'.[22]

POLITICAL SYMPATHIES, WAR AND CHINESE FOOD

Pearl Buck's father, John Lossing Buck, was a Presbyterian missionary who had made an important survey of the income of Chinese farm households. His daughter's sympathy for Chinese peasants may be attributed to her Christian upbringing and her knowledge of the rural economy. Other Westerners' views of the Chinese were determined by their political principles. None had greater sympathy for the poor and oppressed than did the radical American journalist Agnes Smedley. In an essay entitled 'Peasants and Lords in China', she described a visit to a village near Wuxi in Jiangsu, where in 1928 a peasant uprising supported by the Communists had been suppressed harshly. Of necessity she had to take hospitality from the local landlord, who served them tea 'with devastating pomp and solemnity'. Later, when they were eating dinner, they heard the rattle of chains and the shuffling of feet in the corner of the great hall. The noise was made by two peasants lying on a heap of straw, chained hand and foot. They had been tortured to force them to betray the local peasant leader. 'And all the time we were feasting!' Smedley exclaimed angrily.[23]

An appreciation of peasant food became a test for the political sympathies for all those who had dealings with the Communists during the early years of the Party's development. Otto Braun, the German Comintern military adviser, the only Westerner to complete the Long March, failed that test, thereby confirming Mao Zedong's suspicion of him and of the value of Comintern advice. Braun persisted in preferring bread to rice and he made and dried his own sausages. On the other hand the American reporter Edgar Snow, who visited the Communist headquarters at Yan'an in 1937, not only lived on the fare available, but put weight on as well. As a concession to a Westerner he was given bread made with graham flour, which when toasted he found not bad. On one occasion he managed to obtain the ingredients to make a simple chocolate sponge cake, substituting pig's fat for butter, but his improvised oven did not work properly and the result was a two-inch lay of charcoal at the bottom of the tin and the rest of the mixture still in 'a state of slimy fluidity'. Nevertheless he and his friends ate it.

> Besides that I lived on millet – boiled millet, fried millet, baked millet, and vice versa. Cabbage was plentiful, and peppers, onions and beans. I missed coffee, butter, sugar, milk, eggs, and a lot of things, but I went right on eating millet.[24]

Political sympathies were relevant elsewhere. Joshua Horn went to China in 1937 as the ship's surgeon on a cargo boat which had a Chinese crew. He had an altercation with the ship's third officer, whom he described as 'a racist, a fascist, a braggart and a snob'. His daily inspection of the ship took him into the Chinese crew's quarters, where he noted that although their accommodation was poor, their food was much more appetizing than that served to the officers. The Chinese cook, sensing that his interest in the food extended beyond the purely medical, offered him a tasty concoction and showed him how to use chopsticks. Horn sat with the Chinese sailors showing his approval of their cooking by sign language. Later in the voyage he landed at Shanghai and was invited to his first Chinese banquet, of 'crisp sucking pig, mandarin fish, plovers' eggs, roast duck, truffles and soups of surpassing delicacy'. Whenever it seemed that gluttony had been subdued, another succession of dishes appeared. But after the meal, as he was returning home, he saw a young Chinese being marched away to be shot on suspicion of being a Communist. The juxtaposition of these two events caused Horn to reflect on 'the pain, the misery, and the degradation which was China. I thought of the contrast between the meal I had just eaten and the gnawing hunger of millions of Chinese,' and he predicted that the Chinese would soon rise in revolution to destroy the evil, the oppression and brutality.[25]

The outbreak of the Sino-Japanese War in 1937 brought a stream of Westerners to China who were sympathetic to the Chinese cause, and this predisposed them to adopt a favourable attitude towards Chinese food. Among them was Bernard Llewellyn, a volunteer driver for the Friends' Ambulance Unit's China convoy, which was operating in south-western China. He noted the squalor in which many Chinese lived, their cruelty to animals, and the tragic consequences of war and famine. Nevertheless he contrasted his view of China with that of many Westerners, in particular Americans, who hated China because they had never discovered it. Were they even to leave the coastal cities, they took their 'own food tinned food and fruit juices and ice-boxes with them'. Llewellyn however declared that on his travels in China he had found a contentment which he had not enjoyed elsewhere. He stayed at Chinese inns where

the food was brought on, piping hot, and tasting more delicious than any roadside meal you could find in any country of the world. Fried chicken, bean curd, liver and onions, scrambled eggs, bean sprouts, noodles in delicious soup and, if the restaurant was near a big river, a whole fish cooked in a sauce of surpassing excellence.

A Chinese cook preparing dumplings, 1940s.

The kitchen end of a village rice-shop, 1940s.

When drinking tea at these inns he found time for reflection:

> it was not just tea poured out of a convenient pot or urn such
> as you might get in an English café; nor was it hot water
> poured over a tea-bag to produce a liquid which was once
> handed me quite unapologetically as tea in an American
> restaurant. It was tea you selected yourself from a score of
> jars – green tea or red tea or scented tea or chrysanthemum
> tea. It was born of a few dry and wrinkled leaves in the
> bottom of the glass: when boiling water was splashed over
> them they came to life and opened and flowered like bulbs in
> a garden.[26]

Other visitors, although sympathetic to the Chinese cause,
were less sure about Chinese food. In 1938 W. H. Auden and
Christopher Isherwood spent six months gathering material for
a book about China at war. Their impressions, which at times
were facetious, were accompanied by comments on the food
they had eaten. Entertained by the Governor of Guangdong
province, the table-setting reminded them of a competition in
watercolour painting, with the chopsticks resembling paint-
brushes, the various sauces the paints, the tea-bowls the
paint-water and there was even a tiny paint-rag on which the
chopsticks could be wiped. But then, remembering that the
country was at war, they added that when a new dish was served
the host made a gesture towards it with his chopsticks, 'like a
cavalry-commander pointing with his sabre to an enemy position, and the attack begins'. They travelled on a train which
offered a special European menu. After one trial they rejected
this as too nasty, but the boredom of Chinese dishes later drove
them back to it. They met the Australian journalist W. H.
Donald, Jiang Jieshi's political adviser, who enquired about
their plans. When they replied that they intended to go to the
north, Donald warned them that it was a hard road and added
'in a lower, dramatic tone', 'You may have to eat Chinese food.'
Auden suggested that he himself must eat Chinese food, but
Donald's reply was 'Never touch the stuff! It ruins my stomach.'
Before their journey was half over their views on Chinese food
were coinciding with those of Donald. In Zhengzhou every

third person they saw seemed to suffer from some serious illness, 'And the foodstuffs they were buying and selling looked hateful beyond belief – the filthiest parts of the oldest and most diseased animals; stodgy excrement-puddings; vile, stagnant soups and poisonous roots.'

They made a detour to the hill station at Guling which, compared to the reality of China below, was 'all far, far too beautiful to be real'. But at a restaurant in Tunxi reality reasserted itself. Isherwood noticed that bamboo was being cooked in all its forms, including the strips used for making chairs. That, he thought, was so typical of China:

> Nothing is specifically either eatable or uneatable. You could begin munching a hat, or bite a mouthful out of a wall; equally you could build a hut with the food provided at lunch. Everything is everything.[27]

Another wartime visitor was the Methodist minister Harold B. Rattenbury who, having worked for twenty years in China, returned in 1939 to be 'an ambassador of sympathy and understanding between British and Chinese of goodwill and common purpose'. The record of his visit was filled with references to improvements occurring in China and the hospitality of the Chinese he met. He travelled for three days with a Dr Miao, a prominent Nationalist who in the past had demanded that Britain return to China the hill station at Guling, but who was now anxious to present a friendly face to a British visitor. On the first day they ate a lunch of chicken and rice at a new restaurant with an English-speaking chef from Kunming. The night was spent at a new China Travel Service restaurant, which was utterly different from the inns on the old salt track from Sichuan, 'covered with the dust of centuries and filled with the vermin which had sucked the blood of countless coolies'. At restaurants, Rattenbury recalled, Dr Miao 'knew how to pick his dishes, and perhaps knew the weakness of foreigners. In consequence, I never enjoyed Chinese fare as I did those three glorious days.'[28]

In *Face to Face with China*, published in 1945, Rattenbury set out to show that 'Chinese and British, the East and the West, were meant to be friends and builders together of a new and more humane world'. In a chapter entitled 'Home' he described Chinese food and domestic eating habits in such a way as to make the differences between East and West more endearing than challenging. He remarked that much had been written about delicacies such as bird's nest soup, but he would concentrate on the ordinary meal. In Central and South China the staple was rice, but this was rice steamed dry 'unbelievably different from the soggy form in which rice is eaten as pudding in Britain'. Accompanying the rice was a selection of dishes of vegetables, fish, meat and eggs, this constituting a 'first-class meal for an ordinary family'. How the Chinese housewife, using only a large frying-pan, managed to produce so many varied and succulent dishes was a mystery that would baffle many a Western woman. Furthermore Chinese cooking and eating habits led to a great saving in washing-up. The kitchen was also important because it was where the kitchen god resided, whose task at New Year was to take the record of good and evil doings of the house to higher authorities. As a missionary Rattenbury could only reject this as superstition, but he conceded that 'Simple folk regard these things differently from the sophisticated, and there have always been men and women of both types in China as in the West.'[29]

The most distinguished Western visitors met the leaders of Nationalist China. In November 1941 Eve Curie, the daughter of Marie Curie and an ardent French patriot, made a 40,000 mile tour of the war zones of Africa and Asia. Her travels took her to Chongqing and Chengdu, where she had interviews with various diplomats and military leaders. Her sympathies for the Chinese cause were put to the test when she was called upon to eat contrasting examples of Chinese food. In Chengdu the Governor entertained her to an elaborate meal of fourteen courses which she found supremely good. It included 100-day old eggs, which she said tasted like very strong Roquefort cheese. 'I ate them with reverence for their rarity and respectable age, but with no enthusiasm whatsoever.' A few days later, when her truck taking her back to Chongqing had broken down, she walked up to a mud house on the top of a hill, where she found a half-crippled woman with a frightening face.

From her she bought peanuts and two hard-boiled eggs for lunch. 'We thanked God,' she wrote, 'that peanuts and eggs had shells to protect them from sick Chinese hands.'[30]

Robert Payne was *The Times* correspondent in China at the time of the siege of Changsha in 1942, and subsequently taught English literature to university students in Chongqing, the Nationalists' wartime capital. His account of his years in China is suffused with empathy for the delicacy of Chinese taste and sympathy for Chinese suffering at the hands of the Japanese. On one occasion he was offered *tieguan'in* tea from Fujian province. It was, he said, impossible to define its taste, 'but the heavenly satisfaction which comes over you when you have drunk it is something which I have never known before in the same degree'. Later, when at the University of Kunming, he exclaimed that he had more admiration for the Chinese professors there than almost any group of men: they lived like Diogenes, with very few possessions and only a few books; they were continually on the verge of starvation, but were completely unconscious of the heroism of their lives.[31]

Disillusionment with the Nationalists was expressed by the American writer Graham Peck. He was in Luoyang, the old capital of China, in the summer of 1941, when the Nationalist forces were collapsing before a Japanese offensive. On the wall of the restaurant that he patronized there was a poster listing orders from the Generalissimo, Jiang Jieshi, on the conduct of officers and officials. One order read 'No public banquets unless absolutely necessary.' In the restaurant a group of officers was having a lavish meal. A family of refugees stood by silently, gazing 'with narrowed, starving eyes' at the food they were eating. Eventually one of the officers picked up a morsel of meat in his chopsticks and threw it towards the children. The meat landed in an ornamental pond, and, when the children rushed to fish it out, one of them fell into the water. This so amused the officers that they threw more food into the pond. But when an officer dropped a piece of meat beside his leg and a child lunged for it, splattering water over the man's shiny boots, he roared and kicked the child. The officers, tiring of the joke, had the waiters throw the beggar family into the street.[32]

Other writers were sharply critical of the Nationalist regime.

The American journalists, Theodore H. White and Annalee Jacoby contrasted the Nationalist government's indifference to the lot of poor peasants, to the Communist policy of taking their needs seriously. In *Thunder Out of China*, published in 1946, the issue of food was central to that indictment. They noted how Chongqing had changed as a consequence of its role as the Nationalists' wartime capital. Refugees had come from every part of China, bringing with them their own cuisines and restaurants. By the middle years of the war, when a luxury group had grown up in the city, 'its tables were almost as good as those of imperial Peking – for those who had the price'. However, in February 1943 rumours of a famine in Henan rolled into Chongqing 'like tumbleweed blown by the wind'. White and Jacoby headed for Luoyang and entered the famine area. Each large town had at least one restaurant open for those whose purses were full. On one occasion they ate a meal in such a place, but for them the spicy food was tasteless, for hungry people watched them eat, inhaling the smell of the food with shuddering greed, their eyes tracing each steaming morsel from bowls to lips and back. For a fortnight they recorded what they saw, peasants dying of hunger at the roadside, an inefficient relief effort, government officials who did not live lavishly by Western standards, but whose tables steamed with hot wheat buns and fresh meat. The night before they left they were guests at a banquet served by government officials at Zhengzhou. White kept the menu:

> They served us sliced lotus, peppered chicken, beef, and water chestnut. We had spring rolls, hot wheat buns, rice, bean curd, and fish. We had two soups and three cakes with sugar frosting. It was one of the finest and most sickening banquets I ever ate.

This had taken place in the midst of a famine which had caused the death of two to three million people. But back in Chongqing White and Jacoby found that 'the equanimity of the capital was unruffled'. Their reports of dead bodies lying about, and of dogs digging up corpses, were dismissed as figments of their imagination.[33]

Apart from Edgar Snow, mentioned earlier, only a handful of Westerners reached Yan'an, the Communist wartime capital. They included the American photographer Ilona Ralf Sues who had worked for the Nationalist government in the 1930s. After the Japanese invasion her sympathies turned away from the Nationalists and towards the 'down-trodden, under-privileged Chinese masses'. She travelled to the Communist-held areas, where she observed that commanders and fighters ate the same food and endured the same hardships. She shared a picnic meal with Zhu De, the military leader of the Long March, and Peng Dehuai, commander of the First Front Army. Sues contributed some tins of vegetables and fruit, Peng brought peanuts and candy, but the *pièce de résistance* was three pheasants shot with scarce ammunition by the best marksmen in the squad and cooked by Zhu De himself. From there she continued to Yan'an, stopping at inns where the only food available was 'grayish water-noodle soup, stale steamed bread, and an occasional egg. Oh yes, and some dark-brown pickled turnip, which at least had a taste.' The scene was one of dire poverty, with swarms of half-naked beggars in every village. But at Yan'an there were no beggars. Sues and her companions could eat either in the Eighth Route Army mess 'on a strict millet-and-salt-turnip or millet-and-pickled-cabbage diet, with an occasional egg', or at home, where they often got noodles instead of millet, fresh vegetables and even some pork. She appreciated this hospitality, but her heart was won by the commitment of the Communist leaders to ensure that none should die of famine, that there should be a bowl of millet for everyone.[34]

Agnes Smedley also entered the Communist-held areas and spent some months with men of the Eighth Route Army and shared their hardships and meagre diet.

I wonder at the Chinese people. Our only food is millet or rice, and one vegetable. To-day we had rice and turnips. Sometimes it is squash or potatoes. And on this we live. There is no fat, no sugar, and for days no meat at all. I have a little money left . . . So I am able to buy an occasional chicken. My whole group of six eat it. This gives us a little protein and a tiny bit of fat.

In 1940 she was with a detachment of the Communist New Fourth Army in Hubei province, which had the support of local guerrilla groups. Although food was very scarce, some 50 of the local guerrilla leaders entertained Smedley and an Irish Catholic priest. She recorded, 'we all gathered around two long boards on which a feast of rice, turnips, and peanuts was spread. It seemed like a glorious dinner, and after we had eaten and made speeches in praise of freedom, we sang the songs of our countries.'[35]

William Band, a university lecturer in Beijing, and his wife, joined up with the Communists in the Hebei Border Region. They attended a science conference at which he read a paper on the property of liquid helium at minus 271 degrees centigrade. As it happened it was extremely hot and the middle of the fly season. The Bands' description of the food arrangements suggest that their political sympathies were sorely tried.

> The chief food was plain rice gruel, served piping hot; bean curd soup was almost the only other hot item. These were paraded through the village street, supposedly covered from the flies. In the dining-room we kept everything covered the whole meal through. Anyone anxious for something to eat would sing out:
>
> 'All get ready!' A wave of the hand over the table and 'Bzzzzzz . . .' go the flies. Someone lifts a cover, we all take a hasty chopstickful, and down drops the lid before the flies can get inside.[36]

A later visitor to Yan'an was the American journalist Harrison Forman. He portrayed the Communist-held areas as a society where peasants, through hard work and ingenuity, and through the development of labour exchange brigades and co-operatives, had achieved a frugal but secure existence. Even the Communist leaders participated in food production, with Mao Zedong raising American onions on his little vegetable patch and Zhu De, commander of the Eighth Route Army, planting lettuce and cabbage. Forman met Mao and his wife Jiang Qing in one of the cave residences. Both were plainly dressed and the refreshments offered were 'weak tea, cakes and candy made locally, and cigarettes'. Mao chain-smoked 'his abominable Yan'an cigarettes' and youngsters ran in and out of the cave, seizing pieces of candy.[37]

While wartime visitors to China were perceiving Chinese food through the refracting mirror of their political preoccupations, Westerners from the treaty port communities were confined to detention camps, and forced to accept what food was available. Fay Angus, who had grown up in luxury in treaty-port Shanghai, was interned in the Girls' Language School in Yangzhou. She recalled:

> Our food was basic and standard for two-and-a-half years. The morning meal consisted of cracked wheat or *congee* (rice gruel), complete with weevils or maggot-like worms, and the evening meal brought us SOS (Same Old Slop). SOS was an apology of a stew. We were lucky to find two small pieces of pork floating in our bowl of watery soup, and maybe a piece or two of turnip or carrot.

In 1944 the Japanese camp commandant allowed the inmates to go meatless for two weeks and then on Christmas Day they received one cup full of savoury cubed pork per person. 'We discovered our taste buds, though dormant, were not dead,' Angus wrote, 'they were readily activated and satisfied at least for that one meal in our two-and-a-half-year imprisonment.'[38]

CIVIL WAR AND COMMUNIST VICTORY

For some months after the defeat of Japan in 1945, an uneasy truce subsisted between the Nationalists and Communists. Then a civil war broke out which resulted in victory for the Communists. In this period the contrast between the lifestyles of the two sides, not least in the manner of their consumption of food, continued to be an important element in the Western assessment of their claims to be legitimate representatives of the Chinese people. Among those who represented the merits of the Communist side was the writer Robert Payne, who had previously criticized aspects of the Nationalist regime at

Chongqing. In 1946 he flew into Yan'an and interviewed several Communist leaders, including one guerrilla leader, who told him that the food was good, but not plentiful. He added,

> The leaders of the Government got the best food, he received the 'medium mess' and the common soldiers and administrators were in the third category. I said it was not very communistic. He answered: 'We have to do that. All the food is adequate – have you seen a single person looking pale or starved? – but we agreed long ago that the leaders should have the best. After all, it happens everywhere else, and the difference between the three categories is hardly noticeable.'[39]

In 1946 the American reporter Jack Belden, a man 'who knew the seamy side of China, where the lice lurked' made an adventurous journey through the Red areas of North China. During a previous visit to China he had gone 'from one Guomindang general to another, eating special delicacies from their well-laid tables, while peasants were scraping the fields outside the yamens for roots and wild grass to stuff into their griping stomachs'. Now he was determined to identify with the peasants. Almost immediately the strength of his sympathy for the Communist cause was tested. He was taken to be an UNRRA representative, and a possible source of food and grain, and so was treated as an honoured guest. His guard, who claimed to know his habits, told the villagers that he only ate sweet things. But that made little difference

> for the food that was brought was a piece of salted pork fat and a bowl of greasy greens. I found it very unappetizing, but seeing that they were poor and had put themselves out for my benefit, I ate as much as I could swallow without being sick.

On his travels Belden encountered many more examples of poverty. At one teahouse where he stopped, he munched raw carrots and drank hot water – there was nothing so luxurious as tea. He spent some days with an armed working team and ate nothing but millet and a few carrots. One traumatic night he joined a raiding party which seized and executed a landlord. Before they set off they ate a supper of wheat cakes sprinkled with black cotton-seed oil, and bowls of millet. The wheat cakes looked appetizing and reminded him of giant *crêpes suzettes*, and 'that made me think of my French wife and I was sick for home'. When he emerged from what the Communists called the Liberated Areas he found the gulf between Jiang Jieshi's supporters and the peasants wider than ever. In Shanghai officials and businessmen were 'eating five bowls of rice at one sitting and complimenting one another on the tastiness of the Mandarin fish, the Gold Coin Chicken, the fatted Beiping duck and the specially warmed yellow wine' while out in the country the peasants were eating millet husks. Therein lay the essential dynamic of the revolution which was about to occur.[40]

Another American, William Hinton, spent the spring and summer of 1948 in the village of Long Bow in Shanxi province. Eighteen years later he published an edited version of his notes in the revolutionary classic *Fanshen*. Like Belden, Hinton's sympathies were firmly on the revolutionary side and with the peasants who formed the mass of its support. Also, like Belden, Hinton had to demonstrate his sympathy for the peasant cause by living alongside them and eating with them. The first test of his commitment came when he found that his clothes were infested with lice. Peasants, he observed, pursued lice with their fingers and squeezed them until they burst. As he could not face doing that, he found a pair of chopsticks, picked the lice out 'like delicacies off a banquet table', and crushed them with a stone. The more severe test was the food. At first Hinton ate at the District Office, but as the security situation improved it was decided that he should eat out like the rest of the team members did. Every day he and his interpreter gave their meal tickets to a poor peasant's wife in return for a noon-time meal. Some of the homes they visited were spotlessly clean, but others were filthy. One belonged to a former collaborator whose house had been confiscated. The six members of his family, including his daughter who was dying of tuberculosis, now lived in a two-roomed shed. The living room was 'a shambles, smoke-blackened and cluttered with scraps, wheat roots, broken tools, crocks. and rags' and there was an overpowering odour of decay. There they were given 'lukewarm corn dumplings in bowls caked with the dried leavings of many a previous meal.' Hinton knew that the bowls, the chopsticks, the very air that they were breathing was infected with tuberculosis. He also knew that every land reform worker had to go through this test. His interpreter was eating her dumpling 'as if it were a sugar bun'. She was doing her job, so the least he could do was to eat the corn dumpling he had been given. He concluded that eating in peasants' homes had put them in touch with people in a way that a thousand meetings never could.[41]

FIVE

Westerners and Food in Communist China

After the Communist seizure of power in 1949 only a handful of Westerners remained in the country, and access for foreign visitors was severely restricted. Until President Nixon's visit to China in 1972, only under special circumstances were Americans given official permission to visit China. However, a few Europeans and other Westerners were granted entry and recorded their impressions of the new society and of the food available there.

Inevitably these Westerners were favourable to the regime. Joshua Horn, the English doctor whose trip to China in 1937 has already been noted, returned to the country in 1954 and worked as a surgeon, dealing with cases involving the reattachment of severed limbs. He declared that his main motive for returning was to follow the revolutionary road taken by the Chinese people. Sometimes he went to the countryside to visit his patients, who were often peasants, and shared their millet porridge, wheaten pancakes and eggs. More of his time was spent in hospital. He was deeply impressed by the 'deep-going democracy' practised there, which contrasted strongly with the bureaucracy of hospitals in the West. One feature of this was that all staff, whether doctors, nurses, Party functionaries, or boiler-men, ate together in one huge dining-room. They collected their own food and paid for it with the food tickets bought once a month. He calculated that, on average, his lunch cost sixpence.[1]

In late 1954 James Cameron was sent to China by the London *News Chronicle* and claimed that during his visit 'I saw a great deal more than has been seen for some years.' Chapters in his book were devoted to topics such as women, temples, intellectuals and the land, but some of the most animated passages concerned food and his quest to experience the real China. He travelled 7,000 miles without ever once meeting with a dish 'that in any way resembled anything I had ever seen produced in Europe as "Chinese food"'. Whatever else had changed in China, it was still possible to eat sublimely there. He described a meal he had eaten at a Beijing Muslim restaurant, the outside of which he said 'resembled a carman's pull-up in the English Midlands that had fallen upon evil days: almost wholly without charm of any kind'. However the excellences of the meal challenged description. The restaurant was a 'fire-pot' house. The fire-pot was placed on the table and a waiter brought the ingredients for making the sauce: 'His tray was a wonderful sight, like a painter's palate – scarlet pepper sauce, brown shrimp oil, green minced leeks, bean-curd cheese, hemp-seed paste.' One took wafer-thin slices of mutton, held them momentarily in the bubbling pot, plunged them into the sauce and then ate them. He had never tasted mutton cooked so deliciously, nor did he know of a more convivial way of dining, seated round a circular table, with the burnished bronze fire-pot hissing in the middle. Moreover 'this incomparably delightful meal' cost about tenpence or twelve cents in Western money. He also ate at a restaurant which claimed to serve Beijing duck at its best. He used his description of this meal as an opportunity to discourse on Chinese food and etiquette. Of the duck he exclaimed, 'Disliking gastronomic ecstasies as I do, I can say no more than that mankind has perhaps developed no better way, so far, of consuming his servant, the duck.' Throughout the meal he noted that the only concession to the new social system prevailing in the country was the necessity of proposing a toast every five minutes or so. For salutations of especial importance: to Guests, Democracy, Peace, Chairman Mao, 'the call was "bottoms up!"'

Between his enjoyment of these meals Cameron made 'an earnest and considered effort to grasp the details of the contemporary situation in China'. Something of this situation was revealed to him when travelling by train from Beijing to Shanghai. At Zhenjiang station hawkers wheeled trolleys along the platform, selling 'sweets, steam-bread, ducks pressed out flat like flounders . . . and chickens roasted complete'. But a loudspeaker intoned 'Listen, comrades – there is a meal being served aboard the train. This is different from the old days, comrades, when only the exploiters could be served in this way; we work for the people now, and you may eat on the train for three thousand yuan. We suggest you do not buy food outside the train; it will have been exposed to the germs and the flies.' So Cameron went to the dining-car, where

> they gave me a meal abominable beyond reasonable compar-ison; all around me people were eating a bowl of rice, seaweed and pork-ribs that looked unendurably appetizing, but nobody would let me eat that. Mine was the special one; it cost a thousand yuan more – in their courtesy they had groped blindly towards some vague conception of the European cuisine: a burned piece of cow's flesh on a piece of toasted bread.[2]

Robert Guillain, a correspondent for *Le Monde*, visited China a few months after James Cameron. Guillain, who had been to China twice before, in 1937 and 1946, compared the China of old with what he described as the New China. His memories of old China were of war, graft, humiliation, hunger and death. At the height of a military debacle he had attended his first Chinese banquet at the invitation of the mayor of Shanghai. The fare served was sumptuous. Among the 40 dishes was 'a bowl filled with small pieces of meat arranged in the shape of chrysanthemum petals', which proved to be ducks' tongues. After the banquet the mayor announced that the Japanese were about to launch their final attack on the city and that the Chinese would choose death rather than flight. He agreed to meet foreign journalists the following morning at the scene of the final battle. When they arrived at the rendezvous the mayor had already fled.

After his 1955 visit, Guillain declared 'These Chinese are no longer the same.' Whereas in the past hygiene had been appalling, on this occasion he travelled 1,000 miles before seeing his first Chinese fly, at a cold-snack stall on Changsha station. To avoid touching the food with her hands, the girl serving at the stall was manipulating a pair of forceps, like a big pair of sugar tongs, a tool which Guillain discovered had been distributed to state restaurants throughout China. Once again he was invited to a banquet, not as the guest of a corrupt and defeated regime but as the guest of Zhou Enlai, the Prime Minister of the Chinese People's Republic. The event took place in the extended former French Hôtel de Pékin. Three thousand people attended, including innumerable foreign personages, many dressed in their national costumes. According to Guillain it was 'an Asiatic family party given by Grandma China'. The drink flowed, and in addition to rice wine there were several types of champagne and port made in China. Zhou Enlai circulated among the guests, stopping occasionally to drink a toast. Orchestras then appeared, and to Guillain's astonishment 'Asiatics and Whites from the popular democracies danced together.' Nor was hospitality of this kind an unique occasion. Foreign delegations, whether visiting Beijing or the Hotel of the Love of the People in Guangzhou, were provided with impeccable accommodation and food which bore no resemblance to the meagre daily fare of the ordinary Chinese. This, for Guillain, was one aspect of a new China where foreign delegates were deliberately misled by scenes of happiness and success, while the people endured a 'terrifying uniformity and regulation'.[3]

In 1960 Zhou Enlai hosted yet another banquet for foreign visitors in the Xinqiao Hotel in Beijing. On this occasion the principal guest was Field-Marshal Montgomery, and also invited was Felix Greene, a British-born writer long resident in the United States, who had first visited China three years previously. The banquet included dishes such as 'jasmine chicken soup', 'three-coloured sharks' fins', 'duck with tea flavour.' After Zhou Enlai had welcomed his guest, Montgomery gave a speech in which he declared 'I find the Chinese people happy and cheerful, whereas in the Western world it is considered that the Chinese people are very depressed and unhappy . . .' His comments were to be denounced in the Washington *Star* by General Albert C. Wedemeyer, former chief-of-staff to Jiang Jieshi. 'Obviously he is unaware,' Wedemeyer wrote, 'of the ample evidence concerning the massive famine in China.' Greene took Wedemeyer's remark as an example of

Washington's ignorance of what was happening in China. The banquet which Montgomery and Greene had attended coincided with the crisis caused by the policies of the Great Leap Forward. In 1960 famine caused a drop of ten million in China's population.[4]

Conditions in China in the aftermath of the Great Leap Forward were described by Sven Lindqvist, a Swedish student who studied at Beijing University. On one occasion there was an epidemic of dysentery among the foreign students in his dormitory. Lindqvist commented, 'our excrement was like the waters of the Yellow River'. The students were highly dissatisfied with the hygiene arrangements in the dining-room, but dared not voice their views openly. One morning they found that the noticeboards had been decorated with the international plague sign of the skull and crossbones. Suspicion lighted on a South American student, who was subjected to severe harassment by the authorities and was eventually forced to leave the country. Lindqvist remarked, 'In a socialist society nothing is apolitical. Even food is political food, and criticism of the food is political criticism.' His description of Chinese food was an indictment of the political conditions prevailing in China. In the dining-hall the students could choose between 'Chinese and so-called western food, but both were so tasteless and lacking in nourishment that loss of hair and other deficiency diseases were common'. The winter months of 1960–1 were marked by appalling shortages.

> The main winter food consists of poor-quality gritty rice and old dried cabbage. The bread is eked out with synthetic flour and gives you a headache. Milk and eggs are out of the question, but sometimes you get a sauce with meat flavouring. After the meal the students go and wash out their bowls under the hot-water taps. That winter they drank the dishwater, to get the last grain of nourishment out of their food.

Lindqvist admitted that these grim living conditions were 'a natural corollary of China's present stage of economic development', and that it was essential to experience them if one was to understand Chinese society and the reactions of the Chinese.

During his two years in China he had observed some improvement in the food supply. But his strongest impression was of the situation in the spring of 1961, when students were so hungry that they were climbing trees to break off the buds and eat them, when all they talked about, and all they thought about was food. The average age of these students was about 21, but many of them were already grey-haired.[5]

Nevertheless, throughout the 1960s and the Cultural Revolution, official Western delegations continued to be treated to gastronomic experiences. In 1966 a Franco-Italian group spent four weeks in China on what its disillusioned French guide described as 'a Red Tour for millionaires'. Their first dinner was at the Lacquered Duck restaurant in Beijing. Before the meal started the guests were plied with beer, red wine and *maotai*. Then began the ritual of a Chinese meal 'sharks' fins, salads, bamboo shoots, rotten eggs, roots, leaves, stalks, chicken and pork'. The high spot was the lacquered duck, and as an added treat they were given the duck's liver 'a delicacy which would send our French gourmets into ecstasies'. The meal cost each delegate the equivalent of ten francs, which was 'exceptionally cheap for our Western purses'. It was obvious that the meal was the sort of luxury which the ordinary man or women could seldom afford, and the French guide expressed her concern about the dishes they had barely touched. She was told that as soon as they had left the restaurant staff would fling themselves on their leavings like a flock of vultures. 'That,' she concluded, 'allayed my thrifty bourgeois scruples.'[6]

Ross Terrill, an Australian journalist revisiting China in 1971, used his knowledge of Chinese to escape from the routine of official banquets and to experience the proletarian relationships instilled by the Cultural Revolution. He described a meal he had taken at a neighbourhood eating house on the Nanjing road in Shanghai.

Décor is at the level of a public toilet. Chairs are the old wooden kitchen variety, and the wooden floorboards are hospitable to many a splash or piece of food (but no cats or dogs or flies) . . . But the food is excellent. It costs under Y3 (the yuan is forty cents) for two. To remember what dishes to bring to what table, waiters fix a numbered clothespin on a bowl in the center of the table: '7' is 'noodles with fish,' '16' is 'chicken soup.' . . . Stacks of small red stickers hang on the walls. A notice says: if you have an illness, put a sticker in your bowl when finished, and special care will then be taken when washing the bowl.

Before leaving China, Terrill went to Guangzhou and walked around the 'pulsating alleys' of the city, which he noted were crowded and far from affluent. 'Yet no one is in rags; no one sits around in that state of hopeless-looking poverty all too familiar in Asia. Clothing is simple, clean, neat; food is wholesome.' He then described a meal in one of Guangzhou's fine restaurants, followed by a farewell banquet when his hosts went out of their way to satisfy his every known whim.[7]

In *Political Pilgrims*, published in 1981, Paul Hollander discussed the use of hospitality to influence the views of 'political pilgrims', that is Western intellectuals, when visiting the Soviet Union, China and Cuba. He pointed out the importance of food in this context. Whereas good meals in themselves did not change people's views on political systems, they often contributed to a sense of well-being, which predisposed the visitor to a 'positive, affirming attitude' toward the social environment in which he found himself.[8] China had a long tradition of using hospitality, and in particular lavish banquets, to cause Western visitors to experience a sense of gratitude and indebtedness, as the record of Lord Macartney's Embassy in the late eighteenth century testifies. After the 1949 revolution this technique was extended to Western intellectuals and sympathizers who were admitted to China, to obtain their favourable opinion of the regime, preferably expressed in print.

The visits, in 1971 and 1972, of Henry Kissinger, the President's Assistant for National Security Affairs, and then of President Nixon himself, illustrate how effectively the Chinese use food as a diplomatic weapon. On his secret visit Kissinger was in the care of Marshal Ye Jianying. On arrival the Marshal invited him to one of the many meals of staggering variety and quantity that caused me to speculate to our hosts that somewhere thousands of years ago a Chinese had been accused of starving an important guest and they were determined not to allow this to occur again.

At a crucial stage in the discussions Zhou Enlai made a forceful presentation of the Chinese point of view. When Kissinger attempted an equally firm response, which threatened a confrontation, Zhou stopped him, pointing out 'that the duck would get cold if we did not eat first'. At lunch over Beijing duck, the mood changed and the negotiations for Nixon to visit China progressed.

Writing later, Kissinger remarked that after ten trips to China, these banquets now seemed very stylized, but

[i]n February 1972 they were still marvelously novel and imbued with the deft little touches with which the Chinese demonstrate that they consider their visitor special. They had acquired a list of Nixon's favourite tunes, and their splendid army band played a selection of them at each dinner. There were formal banquets on four of the seven nights we were in Beijing: a welcoming banquet by Zhou Enlai; a return one hosted by Nixon; and feasts in our honor by the municipalities of Hangzhou and Shanghai.

At these banquets, 'not only did the courses of the meal seem to go on forever, but each Chinese at the table, in keeping with Chinese custom, concentrated on making sure that every American plate was filled with heaps of food.' Accompanying the food were toasts in *maotai*, a brew which Kissinger opined was not used as airplane fuel as it was too combustible. When Nixon returned to the United States, to demonstrate the liquor's potency to his daughter he set fire to a bowl of it and nearly set fire to the White House. The state banquets were televized live on the morning shows in America, and according to Kissinger they performed a 'deadly serious purpose', showing the peoples of the two countries that a new relationship was being forged.[9]

After Nixon's visit, a stream of Westerners, many of them Americans, availed themselves of the opportunity to visit China. John Kenneth Galbraith went to obtain 'a privileged view of the Chinese economic system', but spent much of his time eating. Perhaps to cover the limitations of his knowledge of China, in his account he often adopted a facetious tone. At the welcoming dinner in Guangzhou, 'Being hungry when the food arrived, I consumed plentifully. Full, I felt better. Alas, there was a mistake; that food was not the dinner, but only the first of seven equally stunning courses.' Later, at a luncheon in a restaurant in the Summer Palace outside Beijing, he adopted a 'new meal strategy', eating more moderately of the early dishes, but then discovered that there were twice as many courses as before. At the first hotel he and his companions stayed at, they asked for chopsticks, but were then served 'beef bouillon and lamb chops'. He described the dinner served at an old Beijing restaurant as 'perhaps the most exquisite I have ever consumed. It consisted of absolutely nothing but duck – duck hearts, duck liver, duck tail, duck wings, brown crisp duck skin, duck fuselage, duck soup from the bones.' At the end of a visit to the Beijing Number 2 Cotton Textile Mill, his group ate in the canteen. Fifteen different dishes were placed on the table, and then some more appeared. 'Each was irresistible and so intended.' They were entertained to dinner in the Great Hall of the People by Guo Moruo of the Academy of Sciences, a dinner which 'put to shame any minor nutrients Nixon may have had'. Not surprisingly, towards the end of his visit, when faced with a ceremonial dinner given by the Scientific and Technical Association of Shanghai, a dinner of fifteen or twenty dishes, including one which was decorated with a nightingale carved from a pumpkin, he felt unwell and ate little and drank nothing.[10]

There was, however, one discordant voice, that of the Belgian sinologist Pierre Ryckmans, who wrote under the pseudonym Simon Leys. Ryckmans had become disillusioned with the regime in China during the Cultural Revolution, and in his book *Chinese Shadows* which first appeared in 1974, he was sharply critical of the attitudes of the 'pro-Maoist Western intelligentsia'. He accused them of blindness to the truth of what was happening in China, and of a deplorable failure to find out more about how ordinary Chinese people lived, having never taken a bus, or eaten a bowl of noodles at a corner stand. 'Why risk going to a "native" eating place, when every day they can enjoy a wonderful banquet paid for by the state?' he asked. He mocked the ritual of the state banquets for foreign visitors hosted by Zhou Enlai in the Great Hall of the People. The seating arrangements were the result of 'some complex algebra that would have fascinated the Duc de Saint-Simon' – so complicated that guests sat in the same company at all subsequent banquets, which ensured that conversational topics were soon exhausted. Throughout the meal a band played tunes such as 'The Chuang Minority Loves Chairman Mao with a Burning Love'. As for the cooking, it 'may appear fabulous to American journalists raised on hamburger and chop suey', but on a Chinese scale it ranged from 'good' to 'average'. He claimed that in Beijing the only thing to do which had been left more or less untainted by ideology was to gorge oneself at a restaurant – the low quality of the fare did not warrant a more refined word. Cheap restaurants had the Spartan look of an army canteen. The 'posh places', where bureaucrats entertained foreign guests, were decorated 'like a small-town dentist's waiting room'. If one were invited by a bureaucrat with clout the meal might be delicious, otherwise it would be rather poor.

A favourite destination for Westerners visiting rural China was Dazhai in Shanxi, home of the famous production brigade which had inspired the slogan 'Let us learn from Dazhai!' Ryckmans described the village as 'a sort of Lourdes or Fatima' for the faithful, who went to see the hillside terraces painfully dug by peasants with their bare hands. A feature of the visit was the banquet given by the village headman, whose face was nearly as well known as that of Chairman Mao. He wore on his head the carefully knotted towel that peasants working in the sun used to wipe away their sweat. Chinese officials arrived in 'old clothes, artistically patched and rumpled'. The banquets were no less delicious and abundant than those provided in the Beijing, Guangzhou or Shanghai palaces for foreigners, but here they are touched with a well-studied primitivism, a shrewd naïvety. In the usual vast array of dishes, some dissonant notes are skilfully struck – a dozen hard-boiled eggs on a tin plate here, a bowl of gruel there – and added to the usual choice of wines, beers, soft drinks, and alcohol is a fearful local spirit. The gourmet brave enough to taste it is suddenly drenched in sweat, giving him the virile and exalting sense that he is somehow communing with the hard task of building socialism.[11]

Leys mocked the 'China experts' such as the Australian journalist Ross Terrill, whose book *800,000,000: The Real China* was quoted above. Terrill's favourable description had been written in one of the 'bleakest and darkest periods' of China's recent history. That he should enjoy 'the peace and brightly coloured hills and valleys of China . . . the excellence of Chinese cuisine' was, to Leys, quite disgusting.[12]

Some Westerners did have closer encounters with the Chinese people. In 1976 Orville Schell, a writer fluent in Chinese, was a member of an American party which was given

'Educated youth' in the Chung Non Central Co-op Canteen, Shanghai, 1976.

exceptional access when it toured China. Schell was desperately anxious to encounter the 'real Chinese' and to an extent his wish was granted, as he was allowed to spend time working in the Shanghai Electrical Machinery Factory. There he experienced in an extreme form the uniformity and utilitarianism which Westerners, used to choice of accommodation and diet, found difficult to accept. The workers were housed in dormitories and bought meal tickets for their meals in the cafeteria. Breakfast was a bowl of rice gruel or a few buns, but lunch was more substantial. The cafeteria had three luncheon shifts, for which the workers queued holding their tin cups, dishes and chopsticks in small net bags, 'such as French housewives carry at the market'. After having collected their food they sat at concrete tables. On his first day at work, Schell ate garlic shoots, cabbage soup and rice. One of his fellow workers ate a small whole salt fish, and another broad beans and a five-ounce bowl of brown noodles. The food was eaten rapidly, and bones and gristle was spat out on the table. There was little conversation and at the end of the meal the workers rinsed their dishes in long concrete sinks. Garbage was sent to a neighbouring commune as pig food. Later, reflecting on his spell at the factory, Schell admitted that he sometimes could not make his mind up about the country: was China perhaps some utterly new experience 'in which all the caveats against too much regulation, regimentation and organization ought not to be reconsidered?' He did not answer his own question.[13]

WESTERN STUDENTS AND TEACHERS IN CHINA

A different perspective on Chinese food was provided by those Westerners who went to China as students and teachers. Frances Wood, who went to China in 1975 as an exchange student, gave a wry account of student life in the years after the Cultural Revolution. At first she was housed in Spartan accommodation in the Foreign Languages Institute in Beijing, but later studied at Beijing University. Foreign students ate their regular meals of Western food in the canteen, and they supplemented their supplies at the Friendship store, where they could buy Edam cheese with a pink wax rind, small packets of butter, and caviar from the Amur River which was so cheap that they ate it in huge quantities for Sunday breakfast. They varied their diet by eating at Chinese restaurants, for example at the Long March restaurant just opposite the university. Among the dishes she enjoyed were: Ants Climbing Trees, vermicelli made from bean starch with peppery minced pork (the ants), and Pockmarked Mother-in-law's Beancurd (which she did not explain further). In the restaurants they patronized there was a tendency to segregate foreigners in a side room, whereas the foreign students wanted to eat with 'the masses' even if that meant listening to a chorus of spitting and seeing a heap of chewed bones on the table-top. She sometimes visited a restaurant at Wudaokou which served *baozi*, or steamed buns, stuffed with meat, cabbage and onions, and eaten with soy sauce and a little vinegar. On winter days they were very warming, but awkward to eat with chopsticks when wearing an outer coat and padded cotton mittens. Foreign students were expected to participate in manual labour and on one occasion she worked on a commune about a half-hour bus ride from Beijing. After doing jobs such as bundling cabbage, she had lunch with a peasant family, squatting in the courtyard, 'eating bowls of home-made noodles in soup with matchstick slivers of cucumber and a dab of sour-plum sauce'. On another occasion she breakfasted at a 'carter's roadside caff', which served 'soup thick with onions and beancurd', and '*youtiaor*, long deep-fried salty doughnut-like things', to dip into the soup.[14]

An American anthropologist, Steven W. Mosher, seeking 'to penetrate the private world of the villager', spent a year from 1979 to 1980 on a commune in South China. He was then expelled by the Chinese government for his comments on what he regarded as the true situation in rural China. At first Mosher took his meals with a peasant family in the commune where he was living – meals which often consisted only of steamed rice and a plate of diced salted turnips. Some evenings there was an extra dish of turnip greens, string beans or spinach from the family's private plot, and once or twice a week a small fish or a few slices of pork fat would appear on the table. After a month of living on this diet, recurrent minor illnesses and steady weight loss convinced him that he should make other arrangements. Defensively Mosher pointed out that several Chinese cadres who had lived in villages during the land reform period from 1963 onwards, when the policy of the 'Four Togethers' required them to live, study, work and eat with the peasantry, had also suffered from chronic stomach trouble.

Mosher was enraged by the corruption of cadres. He quoted a saying, 'High-ranking cadres have front-door deliveries, middle-ranking cadres go in the back door, while ordinary people beg.' One example of this unfairness was the eating arrangements which prevailed in the teahouse – not an old-fashioned village café, but the four-storey building erected by the commune. The bottom two storeys were for peasants, who sat on backless stools at unfinished wooden tables. This lower teahouse was self-service and the menu only offered spare ribs, from which most of the meat had been trimmed, or fried pork fat, along with one or two kinds of greens. On one occasion Mosher tried to eat there, but a matronly attendant had shouted 'you don't want to eat down here. It's unsanitary and the food is no good.' So he was forced to go upstairs, though not before he had noted the indifference of the peasants to her announcement 'that would have had most Americans bolting from the teahouse'. In the upper teahouse he found banquet-sized tables, waitress service, and a menu which included chicken, fish and lean pork, and sometimes duck and eel as well. This, he remarked, was to ordinary peasant fare 'what a meal at Twenty-One is to a TV dinner'. Twice Mosher tried to challenge this arrangement by inviting peasants to eat with him in the upper teahouse, but his guests were treated rudely and accepted their lot of eating in the lower canteen. These incidents convinced Mosher that the claim that the 'New China' had benefited the Chinese peasant was a myth.[15]

In 1987–88 Rosemary Mahoney participated in a teacher exchange between Radcliffe College and the University of Hangzhou. Her description of student life emphasized the inefficiency of the administration and the dire conditions under which students lived and worked. The People's Republic, in the years immediately after the Cultural Revolution, had little time for the simple enjoyment of life, and this was particularly apparent in the matter of food. As a 'foreign expert' Mahoney was housed in the foreigners' building and ate apart from her Chinese colleagues. Most of her colleagues were extremely wary of befriending a foreigner, the main exception being a young Chinese teacher of English literature she referred to as Ming Yu. In an early encounter Ming Yu brought Mahoney a bag of 'soft brown disks the size of coat buttons and dusted with a yellow, pollenlike powder'. She was at first told that these were mushrooms and later that they were dried meat. Afterwards, when Ming Yu had gone, she tried one of the disks and found that it was pickled lemon peel. Misunderstandings and awkwardnesses of this sort pervaded her impressions of China. On another occasion Ming Yu took her to the live market, where the abundance of produce was evidence of Hangzhou's increasing prosperity. They watched 'a fat man with thick lips and a sagging face' sell a black puppy with white-mitten paws to a customer. Mahoney commented that this was the first dog that she had seen in China. Ming Yu explained primly,

> Dogs are not allowed in the city. There's no room for them. They bite people and transmit disease. They used to be a hazard, so they are forbidden now. Besides, no one thinks of them as pets. People eat them.

Mahoney protested that in her view to eat a dog, man's best friend, was a loathsome practice. Ming Yu replied that dog meat was a warming food and was considered a good thing to eat in winter. She had seen photographs of Americans walking with a dog attached to a rope, and of dogs sitting on laps and beds, but the Chinese would not consider allowing that.

Mahoney was invited by her students to eat dinner in their dining hall, a barn-like room with a raftered ceiling. Endless rows of tiled tables stretched over the wet cement floor. The students were expected to queue for their food but, Mahoney observed, like all Chinese in crowds, they pushed and elbowed each other relentlessly. Her friends collected five dishes and five bowls of rice.

The food looked terrible. The dumplings had dried out and turned a chestnut brown, the cabbage was boiled down to a kind of film, floating on top of the soup, and there was a dish of meat that looked like minced pencil erasers. Only the rice and the bowl of fried peanuts looked edible to me.

Her friends ate with spoons, rather than chopsticks, so that they could eat faster. As they ate they discussed their food preferences. Mahoney insisted that she liked a lot of Chinese food, in particular sweet-and-sour soup, the little dragon dumplings and the way the Chinese cooked cuttlefish and noodles with pig's liver and fragrant mushrooms. One of her friends described how her mother cooked duck and how home cooking was different from the loathsome food served in the canteen. That moment of agreement ended abruptly when Mahoney asked them if they had eaten dog. They replied that of course they had. Mahoney commented that she found it strange not to see dogs on the streets and asked whether they had all been slaughtered. She was told no, they were mostly 'sent out into the country', sharing the same fate as dissidents. But she suspected that the truth was that dogs were cruelly slaughtered.[16]

Justin Hill, a 21-year-old working with Voluntary Service Overseas, spent two years between 1993 and 1994 teaching English at the Advanced Training College in Yuncheng, an industrial town in the extreme south of Shanxi province. Hill, who aspired to 'get under the shell of Chinese life', in part achieved this through eating Chinese food. At first he was only invited to meals and banquets in restaurants, as was usual when entertaining foreigners, but after two months, to his surprise, he and a fellow teacher were invited by a member of staff, Mr Cao, to visit his parents-in-law in the countryside. When they arrived at the house, they were offered sweets, peanuts and local pastries stuffed with date paste and encrusted with sugar, and they watched as Cao's mother-in-law made *jiaozi*, steamed buns stuffed with minced pork and chives. Much later they sat down to eat.

Only we three ate, Cao, Mario and I, while the rest of the family cooked and replaced our cooling bowls of *jiaozi* with fresh hot ones. Bowl after bowl. I was stuffed to the eyeballs, and on refusing, was implored by the mother not to be polite but to honour her by eating another bowl. Throughout all this she apologized for her poverty, the common food, and the rustic conditions, telling me that China was still a developing country.

As they rode back on their bicycles, Hill reflected that this was the first time they had been invited into a Chinese home and had eaten with Chinese people. He felt that at last he had crossed the threshold and was just beginning to get to know China.

Hill described himself as 'plump in the way most Westerners are'. His size was of great interest to Chinese people, who often told him that he was fat. On one occasion a Chinese friend encouraged him to drink a health tea, the label of which described it as 'Fat-lowering, weight-losing, halitosis-allaying, clears away heat to stop itching, relaxes the bowels . . .' However, if a foreign teacher were to lose weight, this would imply that the college was not feeding him properly and the result would be a loss of face. This was not likely to happen, Hill declared, for he ate better than he had ever done in his life, subsisting on a diet of stir-fried, boiled and steamed fresh vegetables, and not a processed foodstuff in sight.[17]

GETTING TO KNOW CHINA THROUGH ITS FOOD

Mass tourism to the People's Republic of China began shortly after the fall of the Gang of Four in October 1976. Between 1978 and 1982 the number of persons visiting China rose from 1.8 million to 7.9 million. The vast majority of these visitors were residents of Hong Kong and Macau, but a significant minority was composed of Westerners from the United States, Australia and Western Europe. Many of these visitors joined organized tours and followed well-trodden routes. Others were independent travellers, or at least travellers who hoped to step aside from the prescribed route of guided tours.

One of the publications to address this new market was *The China Guidebook* edited by Fredric M. Kaplan and Arne de

endars and plastic chopsticks), this only shows that westerners don't appreciate the same things when going out to eat.
While most westerners need to feel they've got value for
money by the quality of the ambience and service, for most
Chinese the quality of the food is paramount. Good restaurants gain a reputation solely for the quality of their food, no
matter what the décor and no matter how far out of the way.[23]

Nowadays travellers are advised that no visit to China is
complete without the consumption of an authentic Chinese
meal rather than the bland substitute served in the restaurants
recommended by tourists agencies. A recent Thomas Cook
guide book, having urged the visitor to set aside concerns about
hygiene and stomach upsets, continued

> if you do not take your courage in hand, click your chopsticks
> together a few times to satisfy sceptical Chinese diners that
> you can operate them, and plunge head first, so to speak, into
> real Chinese food, you cannot say that you have understood
> and savoured the taste of China.[24]

Part II: East to West

Keijzer which first appeared in 1979. One section gave independent travellers advice on Chinese food.

> Dining in China can be a problem for those used to eating what they want, when they want. The simplest option is to take most of your meals in the hotels, although it is important to observe scheduled dining hours. Hotel food is usually good and reasonably priced. Most often, it is best to order the fixed house dinner . . .

If one wanted an average restaurant meal, the visitor should arrive early – 4.30–5.00 p.m. for dinner – and 'not be overly concerned about hygiene or crowds'. If the restaurant was full it was not considered rude to stand behind the seats of customers who were finishing their meals. One could order from the menu by looking at the prices or by pointing at what looked good on other people's tables. Visitors were warned that as the Chinese did not use soap for washing dishes, cleanliness was often a concern in public restaurants, so many local people carried their own chopsticks and were careful about selecting where they ate. Buying food from street stalls was hazardous, particularly from stalls near hospitals, where hepatitis might be endemic. Readers were warned that the Chinese ate items which were totally repugnant to Western culture, and then told that 'Even to sedate Western palates, [sea] slugs or [bears'] paws can be quite palatable.' The guide advised that after three weeks of traditional banquets the visitor might wish to vary hotel tourist fare by eating in small local restaurants. There were however drawbacks to doing so: the tablecloth and chopsticks might be greasy and dirty and the cement floors littered with bones and gristle. But, by eating in such an establishment, 'You'll catch a real glimpse of how the Chinese live and what they eat.'[18]

At about the same time that the early editions of the *China Guidebook* were appearing, the United States' and British embassies in Beijing were co-operating in producing a little guidebook for Western visitors to the capital. It listed over 70 hotels and restaurants with brief comments on their characteristics. Six of the restaurants mentioned were Beijing duck restaurants, one of which had a takeaway service. In the section on Northern Chinese restaurants, one offered imperial special-ities including minced pork with sesame seed cakes; another served salted roast duck, a Shanxi speciality, which was said to be 'rather expensive, but worth it'. The Duo Wei Zhai restau-rant was

> On the northern bank of the canal north of the Sanlitun diplomatic area. A new, four story restaurant which does not have any particular regional specialty. Very nice surround-ings. Food good, but rather expensive. Delicacies such as dog and cat available if ordered in advance.[19]

By the 1990s, some guidebooks were giving frank appraisals of the sort of food upon which more independent and less afflu-ent travellers might expect to subsist. Readers of the *Lonely Planet* guide for 1991 were warned that China was a poor coun-try and that most people could not afford to eat like cadres. The outstanding food was restricted to classy city restaurants. In the backwaters the visitor would be living on steamed or fried rice, a few varieties of fried meat and vegetables, dumplings, bean curd, noodles and soup. Food was generally better in the south than in the north, and during the winter 'northern Chinese food can be perfectly dreadful'. Chinese restaurants did not follow the Western fashion of providing dimly lit, intimate sur-roundings: the average government-run canteen seated hundreds of people at a time and resembled an aircraft hangar. There were many privately run restaurants, which were more pleasant to eat in, but foreigners usually paid more than local residents. The guide offered a final word of advice to the inde-pendent traveller: 'in remote places or on long bus trips it helps to have a small bag of emergency rations such as instant noo-dles, dried fruit, soup extract, nuts, chocolate etc.'[20]

The opening of China stirred Colin Thubron, a prolific travel writer and Mandarin speaker, to make an ambitious jour-ney through the country. Throughout his travels he stayed in the cheapest places into which Westerners were allowed, and whenever possible ate Chinese food with Chinese people. However he found his plans impeded by 'an ancient apartheid' which still divided Westerners from Chinese travellers. Sometimes at hotels he was chivvied out of the dining-hall into a private room.

> Here, alone with the ghosts of banqueteers and a huge, off-white circle of tablecloth, I would sit like a penguin on the rim of an ice-floe, poking my chopsticks into four or five little dishes of dried meat, beancurd, cabbage or sea-cucumber, and plotting escape.

Occasionally he did get off the tourist trail. Staying near Wuhu for tenpence a night in a hostel room overlooking the latrines, he ate a meal of rice and beans with a peasant family. In Suzhou a college schoolteacher and his family entertained him to a meal of home-made dumplings. In a bamboo shelter near a monastery on Mount Emei he found a man cooking by the flare of a lamp. He was so tired that although he could not distinguish what he was eating he 'bolted it down as a bulwark against the cold'.

Thubron's contradictory feelings towards food in China reached a crescendo in Guangzhou, where, it seemed to him, 'nothing edible was sacred'. This, he declared, reflected 'an old Chinese mercilessness towards their surroundings'. In the Wild Game Restaurant he interrogated the waitress for anything he could bear to eat. She recited the menu:

> Steamed Cat, Braised Guinea Pig (whole) with Mashed Shrimps, Grainy Dog Meat with Chilli and Scallion in Soya Sauce, Shredded Cat Thick Soup, Fried Grainy Mud-puppy . . .

Even though the mud-puppy turned out to be a fish, Thubron had suddenly turned vegetarian. Forced to choose meat he ordered python broth, followed by braised python with mushrooms and braised wildcat. The domestic tabby cat, which squirmed under his table, suddenly seemed to him to be edible – indeed everything around him seemed in peril – the warm flannel brought for his hands, the mosquitoes, the curtains, and what if he should fall from the fourth-floor stair-well? He fed the cat scraps of python and wildcat meat and left the rest, pleading that he was full. Later he went to the food market, and found kittens, dogs, monkeys and a row of owls for sale. Defiantly he bought a barn-owl, and released it surreptitiously from his train window the following night.

From Guangzhou Thubron turned north and escaped from cities. Camping in remote spots, he sometimes subsisted on preserved dates. By the time he reached Yunnan he was suffering from an 'insidious attrition' which affected almost all Westerners who travelled for long alone in China, a malaise which was the result of various factors. Since leaving Guangzhou he had scarcely eaten a nutritious meal. Breakfast in the south was 'a bowl of rice porridge laced with gherkins, an impenetrable steamed bun, a few peanuts and a glass of hot sweet milk'. Even though he had lost a stone in weight, the bun and gruel remained inedible. He was also oppressed by the 'buffeting in trains', the 'mass and proximity of bodies, their bawling and spitting,' the 'pervasive smell – cooking-oil, urine, stale fish'. He concluded that, like everyone else, he was a victim of vitamin deficiency. In Thubron's mind this condition was related to the suffering which the Chinese people had endured during the Cultural Revolution, which had left a legacy of 'split families, brutalised psyches, a whole skein of invisible divides'.[21]

By the end of the twentieth century travel guides were making a more positive assessment of eating in China. The *National Geographic Traveller* advised the American tourist willing to spend $50–75 on a meal to try the Roast Duck Restaurant at 32 Qianmen Dajie in Beijing.

> Even in the gritty and cheap zone as you walk in, the duck is miraculously good. For the price of a McDonalds back home, you can pick up a half duck that will make your stomach swell.[22]

The *Lonely Planet* Guide also suggested that visitors to China should revise their expectations when eating out.

> Although Chinese restaurants have a reputation in the west for being noisy, tasteless and basic (formica tables, tacky cal-

endars and plastic chopsticks), this only shows that westerners don't appreciate the same things when going out to eat.
While most westerners need to feel they've got value for
money by the quality of the ambience and service, for most
Chinese the quality of the food is paramount. Good restaurants gain a reputation solely for the quality of their food, no
matter what the décor and no matter how far out of the way.[23]

Nowadays travellers are advised that no visit to China is
complete without the consumption of an authentic Chinese
meal rather than the bland substitute served in the restaurants
recommended by tourists agencies. A recent Thomas Cook
guide book, having urged the visitor to set aside concerns about
hygiene and stomach upsets, continued

> if you do not take your courage in hand, click your chopsticks
> together a few times to satisfy sceptical Chinese diners that
> you can operate them, and plunge head first, so to speak, into
> real Chinese food, you cannot say that you have understood
> and savoured the taste of China.[24]

SIX

The Globalization of Chinese Food
– the Early Stages

NINETEENTH-CENTURY BEGINNINGS: THE UNITED STATES AND CANADA

The first stages of the global spread of Chinese food date back to the nineteenth and early twentieth centuries. A major factor in that spread was Chinese migration to Western countries, in particular to the United States, Canada and Australia, and the establishment of Chinese communities in these countries.

The discovery of gold in the Sacramento Valley in 1848 encouraged migration from South China to the United States and by 1851 it was estimated that about 25,000 Chinese had arrived in California. Most were engaged in placer mining or in domestic or manual labour. Because of the shortage of women domestics, some worked as cooks. At first the Chinese migrants were given a friendly reception. Chinatown in San Francisco became something of a tourist attraction and Chinese restaurants were established, among them the Macao and Woosung Restaurant on the corner of Kearny and Commercial Streets.[1] Of these restaurants William Shaw, a gold miner, commented

> the best eating houses in San Francisco are those kept by Celestials and conducted Chinese fashion. The dishes are mostly curries, hashes and fricasee served up in small dishes and as they are exceedingly palatable, I was not curious enough to enquire of the ingredients.[2]

Less sophisticated restaurants served the mass market. Tsing Tsing Lee built the Balcony of Golden Joy and Delight which

135

seated 400 customers at a time. Meal tickets cost $20 for 21 tickets. Chinese eating houses displayed triangular yellow silk flags and offered 'all you can eat' meals at a fixed price and this attracted western miners' custom when their funds were low.[3] To supply these restaurants, and the Chinese population at large, food was imported from China. By the 1860s the Chinese were paying $500,000 duty on imported goods such as sauces and dried oysters.

However from 1852 disorder in the mining districts, coupled with anti-foreign feeling, engendered racial tensions and prejudicial comments. The Chinese community in California was abused in the pages of the *Alta California*, one complaint against the 'no ways partickler Celestial' being his addiction to rats and lizards. Whereas even the bear turned away from tainted food, 'John' despised nothing of the creeping or crawling kind. Even though flour, beef and bacon, and other fare suitable to white folk abounded, the Chinese rejected these, and their eating habits were enough to turn the stomach of the 'stoutest Anglo-Saxon'. These vitriolic, racist comments elicited a reply from a Chinese immigrant. After having thanked the American people for their kindness, he asked:

> When or where did you ever see any of my countrymen eat rat, lizard, or earth-worm? Have you ever visited any of our provision stores? Did you ever see anything of the kind? Did you ever take the trouble of investigating, as you ought to have done before condemning in such unfeeling language our manners and customs?[4]

However this defence was not heeded, and the Chinese migrants were stigmatized as posing an economic threat, as being unable to comprehend the principle of democracy, and as bringing with them filth and disease. The Chinese restaurants lost their Western clientele and were patronized almost exclusively by Chinese. At times hostility towards Chinese as economic competitors was combined with slighting references to their eating habits. In a novel published in San Francisco in 1878, one character said of the Chinese:

They follow our hard-working people close on their heels, steal their trades, cheapen labor, and then sit down to a dinner of rice and potato sprouts, such as a hearty white would starve on.[5]

Forced to seek alternative employment, Chinese immigrants turned to the laundry business. By 1870 there were 176 Chinese laundries in San Francisco, and these businesses, set up to 'wash barbarians' clothes', were established all over the city, well beyond the confines of Chinatown, and were providing a service primarily to white clients.[6]

In the 1860s Chinese migrants spread out from California. One group of about 1,000 arrived in Virginia City, Nevada, where Mark Twain was working on a newspaper. He visited the Chinese quarter at night, noting how in every hut one could see 'two or three yellow, long-tailed vagabonds' smoking opium. He accepted the hospitality of Mr Ah Sing who kept a grocery store at 13 Wang Street. He tried his Chinese brandy and

He offered us a mess of birds'-nests; also, small, neat sausages, of which we could have swallowed several yards if we had chosen to try, but we suspected that each link contained the corpse of a mouse, and therefore refrained.

Nevertheless Mark Twain and a fellow reporter 'ate chow-chow with chop-sticks in the celestial restaurants,' and he concluded that the Chinese were 'a kindly disposed, well-meaning race', and that it was only the scum of society who abused or oppressed them.[7]

Prejudices against the Chinese were given legal backing with the passage of anti-Chinese legislation and from 1882 by the introduction of restrictions on Chinese immigration. Between 1890 and 1920 the Chinese population in the United States fell from over 100,000 to just over 60,000. Chinatowns, in the popular image, and to a considerable extent in truth, were notable for gambling, drug-dealing, prostitution and filth. Yet in the same period the beginnings of an improvement in white American attitudes towards the Chinese may be observed. In California, Chinese labourers were cited as more reliable than

Provision store in San Francisco, *c.* 1885.

other immigrant groups, and Chinese cooks came to be regarded as a luxury only the well-to-do could afford. Some Chinese discarded their queues and began to assimilate with the majority population. The visit in 1896 of Li Hongzhang, the most influential Chinese official of the time, to New York and Vancouver, raised the status of China in North American eyes. It was on this visit that Li Hongzhang supposedly 'invented' chop suey. According to one version of this story, when Li was staying at the New York Waldorf Astoria he rejected invitations to banquets, preferring to eat Chinese food prepared by his own cooks. The cooks, unable to obtain genuine Chinese ingredients, concocted a dish of bits and pieces, *zasui* in Mandarin or 'chop suey', an approximation of the Guangzhouese pronunciation. The origin of chop suey has also been traced back to California at the time of the gold rush, when white gold miners resorted to Chinese eating places and were given dishes composed of scraps of meat and vegetables.[8] In either version chop suey is defined as a dish which was invented in the United States, either as an adaptation of Chinese food to cover shortages of ingredients or to appeal to Western palates.

Chinese immigration to Canada began around 1858 in response to the gold rush in the Fraser Valley of British Columbia. A second wave of Chinese arrived in the 1880s to provide labour for the construction of the Canadian Pacific Railway. As in the United States, at first relations between whites and Chinese were relatively amicable. In 1859 Walter Moberly, engaged in building a wagon road to the mine workings came across a group of Chinese miners.

> The Chinamen received me kindly and made me some tea and mixed some flour and water and made thick cakes of dough which they cut into strips about an inch in width and boiled. They had no other provisions but were looking forward to the spring run of salmon . . .[9]

However anti-Chinese prejudice soon began to be voiced, one of the commonest complaints being the cheapness of the diet on which Chinese labourers subsisted. In 1859 the *Colonist* carried an article which remarked:

> It may do very well for the people in the cities, the merchants, the ship owners and steam boat men to talk in favor of the Chinese, but when a white man is placed alongside a company of these creatures, imported from abroad, and fed on rice and dog-fish, and made to measure the price of his day's work by the price of theirs, there will be complaining and dissatisfaction.[10]

Chinese miners found themselves excluded from the more promising diggings and the response of some was to move into service industries. In 1862 Barkerville had sixteen Chinese businesses, including eight Chinese restaurants. Such Chinese-run restaurants serviced the majority community and may or may not have served Chinese food to their customers. In British Columbia the shortage of women led to a demand for domestic servants, particularly cooks. Chinese men responded to this demand and in the 1870s it was estimated that there were about 400 Chinese servants and cooks in Victoria.

After the mining and railway booms had subsided, restrictions were placed on Chinese immigration and the remaining Chinese community became largely confined to Chinatowns in Victoria and Vancouver. There the Chinese communities were regarded by the majority community as centres of vice and disease, a reputation which was probably well deserved. Racial hostility forced the Chinese out of skilled occupations and they increasingly resorted to laundry and restaurant work and to market gardening. The restaurants either served the Chinese community exclusively, or served Western food to a Western clientele.

THE 1884 HEALTH EXHIBITION IN LONDON

A small number of Chinese sailors had arrived in the East End of London by the end of the eighteenth century and throughout the nineteenth century small Chinese communities were to be found in London, Liverpool, Glasgow and Cardiff. By the 1880s the Limehouse district of London, which bordered on the West India Docks, had Chinese grocery stores, eating houses and meeting places. In Liverpool, a somewhat larger Chinese community had established itself in Pitt Street and neighbouring streets and there could be found a few provision stores and eating places serving Chinese seamen, dockworkers and students. There is no record of these eating places being patronized by Western customers and it seems unlikely that they were.[11] At this time the main entrepreneurial activity of Chinese in Britain, as in North America, was laundry work. The first Chinese laundry in Britain opened in Newington in 1884 and by 1891 they were said to be springing up like mushrooms on Merseyside.[12]

The introduction of Chinese food in Britain took place under very different circumstances to those which prevailed in North America. In 1884 a Health Exhibition was held in South Kensington, London, with an international range of exhibits.

One of its most popular attractions was a Chinese Restaurant. The arrangements for this, which included the supply of food-stuffs and the employment of cooks, were made in China by Robert Hart of the Chinese Maritime Customs. His response to the request to organize the Chinese stand illustrated Western misperceptions of Chinese eating habits:

> The English idea of the Chinese Tea-House and Chinese Restaurant has nothing corresponding to it in China except the fact that there are buildings in which people can buy and eat food and drink tea: if we could supply you with one of them bodily, you would indeed have a slice out of the real life of China, but English sight-seers would neither eat in it nor sit in it, and the Committee would very soon beg us to move it out of that.

Nevertheless Hart sketched a plan for a restaurant and tea-house, and sent shop façades to London. Chinese cooks were recruited from Beijing and Guangzhou, and Hart wrote to his agent in London asking him to arrange their accommodation, telling him that 'Chinamen can be packed close and they will not require palatial apartments.' As for food, 'rice, vegetables and salt fish and pork will be enough:- they are all more or less coolies so to speak'.[13]

The Chinese Restaurant opened a few weeks after the main exhibition had begun. The menu dated 11 September 1884 was written partly in French implying that Chinese cuisine was as sophisticated as that of France, but the names of some of the dishes suggested that some mockery was intended. It read as follows:

HORS D'OEUVRE
Pullulas à l'Huile. Saucisson de Frankfort
Olives
Bird's Nest Soup
Visigo à la Tortue
Souchée de Turbot au Varech Violet
Biche de Mer à la Matelote Chinoise
Shaohsing Wine

Petit Caisse à la Marquis Tsing
Roulade de Pigeon farcie au Pistache
Copeau de Veau à la Jardinière au Muscus
Sharks' Fins à la Bagration
Boule de Riz
Shaohsing Wine
Noisettes de Lotus à l'Olea Fragrance
Pommes pralinée. Compôte de Leechée
Persdeaux Salade Romain
Vermicelli Chinoise à la Milanaise
Beignet Soufflé à la Vanille
Gelée aux Fruits
Biscuit Glace aux Amande pralinée
Glace à la Crême de Café
DESSERT
Persimmons, Pommes Confit, Pêches,
Amands Vert, Grapes
THÉ IMPÉRIAL

London periodicals amused themselves by ridiculing the Chinese restaurant. The *Pall Mall Budget* went through the menu, first suggesting that the hungry sightseer might with confidence order bird's nest soup, which was served in a tiny slop-basin and was excellent. The magazine predicted the soup would probably be naturalized in England from and after 1884. It considered the *biche-de mer*, and suggested that the 'British public will not find these sea-slug pies so bad as might be imagined, their taste being not unlike that of turtle'. The sharks' fin, however, was for 'the more audacious only'. It recommended the lotus seeds, the food of lotus-eaters, to the Poet Laureate, a jibe directed at Alfred, Lord Tennyson. It praised the very expensive tea served, but described as 'excruciating' the music played by the Chinese orchestra to entertain customers.[14] *Punch*, which throughout the summer had published instalments of 'Our Insane-itary Guide to the Health Exhibition', carried the mockery further, complaining that the 'Celebrated Chinese Dinner', for which one paid seven shillings and sixpence, had only the barest claim to be called Chinese. Apart from 'two or three Chinamen carrying kettles', the waiters were Swiss or German or French. The chef *was* French – though he had lived fifteen years in Beijing, ample time to forget his French cookery. The hors d'oeuvres, it noted, consisted of 'olives from Na-ples' and some sausage from the well-known cities near Beijing of 'Stras-bo-urg or Bo-log-na'. If one did not know that the soups were Chinese, one might suppose that one was a watery *consommé* and the other a rather thick mock-turtle. The fish, Truite à la Ling Wang, had a Flowery Land name, but its flavour recalled the restaurants of the Palais Royal rather than those of Hong Kong. Even less convincing were the entrées and desserts. The Shaoxing wine which was supplied after every course did appear to be thoroughly Chinese. It was served hot in small teacups and tasted like 'a mixture of hock, the traditional flavour of furniture polish, and chocolate cream'. For those who liked those articles of food, it was doubt-less very good indeed.[15]

The Chinese restaurant did elicit two more serious responses. A long article by John Dudgeon in the *Health Exhibition Literature* on 'Diet, dress and dwellings of the Chinese,' set out, perhaps for the first time in detail, the argu-ment that the Chinese diet, which contained only a small proportion of meat, was more beneficial to health than the diet of the West. Dudgeon pointed out that the Chinese, despite their ignorance of science, had admirably suited themselves to their surroundings and enjoyed a maximum of comfort and immunity from disease. He explained that the Chinese had hit upon a combination of food giving a 'due proportion of heat-givers, as in starchy food, to be consumed along with flesh-formers, as in fish and seeds of leguminous plants which have a highly nitrogenous character'. In South China the staple diet was rice and fish and in North China the Chinese ate cere-als and pulse. From these circumstances, he concluded,

> valuable suggestions are to be derived by which we might recast our dietary with profit both to our bodies and to our purses. The Chinese have succeeded intuitively, or as a result of their long experience, in the attainment of the maximum of nourishment with the minimum of cost, which ought to be the object of every people and not alone of a government dietary for soldiers and sailors.

Dudgeon was not advocating a purely vegetarian diet: the Chinese were not vegetarians. What he did propose was a great diminution in the amount of flesh consumed and a large addition of farinaceous and vegetable substances making the diet of people in the West more like that of the Chinese.[16]

The menu of the Chinese restaurant was also discussed by Vincent Holt in *Why Not Eat Insects?*, a small work which challenged current views of what should be regarded as edible. He claimed that the 'quaint delicacies' which had been offered at the Chinese restaurant had been well-appreciated by fashionable people who would otherwise turn their noses up at foods such as insects. He explained that bird's nest soup was made from nests constructed from the viscid fluid from the swallows' mouths, and that 'Biche de Mer à la Matelote Chinoise' was sea slug. He pointed out how much prejudice affected our views on food, that if the sea slug were known only by its less common name of sea cucumber, it would be refused by none. The Chinese dinner at the 'Healtheries' had become one of the most fashionable entertainments of the season. Those who had partaken of it would previously have expressed disgust at the thought of eating some of the items on the menu, but fashion had overcome their prejudices, and the food had been pronounced delicious.[17]

AMERICA: FROM CHINATOWN TO BILL LEE'S BAMBOO CHOPSTICKS

The wider availability of Chinese food in the West can be traced to developments in the United States and Canada in the first half of the twentieth century. In those countries the Chinese population, no longer augmented by immigration, and hemmed in by various restrictions on employment, increasingly concentrated on niche occupations, most commonly working in laundries or in the restaurant business.

In the late nineteenth century the strength of anti-Chinese prejudice had made it unlikely that many Westerners would choose to eat Chinese food. An 1893 guide to New York commented that the area around Mott, Pell and Doyers streets was 'a veritable "Chinatown" with all the filth, immorality, and picturesque foreignness which that name implies'. White labourers who visited San Francisco Chinatown still held to the popular view that Chinese food was composed of all sorts of disgusting things. In 1905 anti-Chinese sentiments had been revived by the Chinese boycott of American goods as a protest against discrimination against Chinese immigration. When in 1906 much of San Francisco, including Chinatown, was destroyed by earthquake and the subsequent fires, some ugly anti-Chinese incidents occurred.

However in the early years of the twentieth century this situation began to change. Redevelopment after the San Francisco earthquake led to the creation of a new 'Oriental City' which was cleaner and more attractive than the old Chinatown and which was designed to attract tourists. Dupont Street was lined with clothing stores, grocery stores and restaurants and these received a degree of white patronage.[18] In 1903 the Los Angeles City Directory listed only five Chinese restaurants, but the 1923 edition listed 28. By now there was also a sizeable Chinatown in New York, and some enterprising Chinese had opened restaurants outside Chinatown.[19]

The reason for the change in the image of American Chinatowns has been a subject for debate. One explanation put forward was that restrictions on Chinese immigration had resulted in a gross disparity in the sex ratio of the Chinese population. In 1890 there were 26 Chinese males for every one Chinese female. This disparity encouraged Chinese males to resort to gambling, to prostitutes and to opium, and this in turn led to the rise of vice syndicates. Only when the sex ratio in the Chinese population had become more normal – by 1930 it had improved to 3:1 – did syndicated vice in Chinatowns subside. This explanation was challenged by Ivan Light, who argued that the normalization of the sex ratio was only one reason for the change. He identified as a major factor the economic rivalry which had emerged between the vice syndicates and legitimate Chinese merchants and restaurateurs. The latter wished to attract white tourists to Chinatown, who would eat Chinese food and buy souvenirs, rather than spend their money in vice resorts, so it was in their interests to suppress vice in their communities. In time they gained the support of Chinese and white agencies committed to cleaning up these districts and ending the sporadic violence associated with them, and it was only then that white patronage of Chinese restaurants began to rise. [20]

A rather different explanation for why the Chinese opened restaurants catering largely for the white population is implicit in Xinyang Wang's exploration of the Chinese experience in New York City. Yang noted that whereas much of the Chinese population of the west coast cities lived in Chinatowns, many New York Chinese chose to live in predominantly white suburbs and to endure rampant racial discrimination. He suggested that the reason for this difference was that two different ethnic economies had developed. In San Francisco's Chinatown there were industries which provided employment, but in New York and Chicago the vast majority of Chinese worked in the laundry business or in restaurants which served the white community. Employees in these concerns had to live close to their place of work, hence the scattering of the Chinese population. In 1922 Chinese laundries were the object of a sustained campaign by white laundrymen who accused the Chinese of cutting their prices unfairly. Through the interwar years Chinese laundries continued to be the object of hostility and then of unmeetable competition with the introduction of washing machines into laundries. As a result one of the few economic opportunities for Chinese declined, adding further to the pressure on them to concentrate on catering. Already, by 1918, of the 57 Chinese restaurants in New York, 33 were situated outside Chinatown. Whereas Chinese restaurants in Chinatowns might serve a predominantly Chinese clientele, those in the suburbs perforce had to cater for a white clientele and this made it essential to develop a style of catering which would attract white customers.[21]

According to Rose Hum Lee, it was during the First World War that Chinese restaurants in downtown locations had their greatest appeal. They offered a choice of American or Chinese food and they combined dining with dancing to the music of a well-known band. As such they were the forerunners of

American nightclubs. However the situation which had developed in Butte, Montana was probably more typical of the way in which mass Western acceptance of Chinese food would develop. At the turn of the century Butte was city with a population of about 50,000, many of whom were transient males. It had about 75 restaurants, mostly Chinese owned and operated, which specialized in preparing miners' lunch pails, serving them breakfast and dinner, and extending credit from one payday to the next.[22]

Nevertheless the negative view of the Chinese and by extension of Chinese food persisted. In 1924 Chinese immigration to the United States was further restricted on the grounds that Chinese were unassimilable. Popular magazines reiterated the widely held view that one reason why the Chinese could not be assimilated was because of their eating habits. Their favourite delicacies were said to be rats and snakes; they ate soup with chopsticks, which were believed to be hollow, like straws; their national dishes were chop suey and chow mein and the only other food they ate was rice.[23] Such prejudicial views were replicated widely, for example in Alfred Hitchcock's film, *Rich and Strange*, 1932, which told the story of a young couple who were shipwrecked on a voyage round the world and picked up by the crew of a Chinese junk. The woman befriended the ship's cat, which then disappeared. She later discovered that it had gone into the cooking pot and that its pelt had been nailed to the deck to dry.[24] White children grew up with these prejudices. In Kansas City, in the 1920s, Edgar Snow was taught a chant by a black washerwoman, who perhaps resented the competition from a Chinese laundry.

> Chinaman, Chinaman,
> Eat dead rats!
> Chew them up
> Like gingersnaps!

After he had become a journalist, Snow was asked by the editor of *Feathered World*, a publication owned by the multi-million-dollar corporation Odhams Press, for a photograph showing a Chinese hen laying an egg on a dung heap. The purpose of the assignment was to damage the export to Britain of albumen from Chinese eggs. Snow's wife declined the assignment on his behalf.[25]

However, during this same period, Chinese restaurants gradually spread across the United States and Canada. The Los Angeles City Directory for 1924 listed 28 Chinese restaurants. By 1941 the same publication listed 73.[26] The telephone directories for the city of Philadelphia for 1920 included eight Chinese restaurants among the 23 ethnic and regional restaurants recorded. By 1950 there were 31 Chinese restaurants out of a total of 50 ethnic restaurants in the city. In 1920 there was one Chinese restaurant in Philadelphia per 79,300 people, but 30 years later there was one restaurant per 22,500 people.[27] The rate of expansion of Chinese restaurants was probably quite uneven. Some Chinese restaurants operating in the 1920s were forced to close during the Depression, but the repeal of prohibition in 1933 contributed to an upturn in the restaurant business. In San Francisco's Chinatown a younger generation of Chinese Americans seized the opportunity to promote tourism by renovating stores and investing in modern bars, restaurants and coffee shops. In 1936 two cocktail bars were opened and shortly afterwards Forbidden City, a night club with a Chinese chorus line, added to the tourist attractions. In 1939 the Golden Gate International Exposition brought thousands of visitors to San Francisco and further boosted Chinatown's tourist trade.[28] A similar transformation was brought about in Los Angeles where a new Chinatown was opened in 1938. Tourists were attracted by the pagoda-styled décor and the tiered gates from the set of the film of *The Good Earth*.[29]

Two related points may be made about the gradual acceptance of Chinese food in the United States. One concerns the increased assimilation of second-generation Chinese Americans. By the 1920s Chinese Americans, even those living in Chinatowns, had not only discarded the queue and other features of Chinese dress, but were also taking advantage of education to achieve social mobility. Middle-class Chinese American couples, particularly in cases of mixed marriages, were challenging discrimination in housing and were combining elements of Chinese and Western lifestyles in their homes.

One couple interviewed by Judy Yung spoke both Chinese and English at home, ate Western food for breakfast and lunch and Chinese food for dinner.[30]

The second point concerns how Chinese (and Japanese), who had been forced by economic necessity into self-employment in restaurants, laundries, small retail stores and market gardening, operations which required very long hours of work at low pay, dealt with this situation. According to Ivan Light, Chinese and Japanese small businesses at first depended on an exclusively ethnic clientele but later they showed a marked tendency to branch out into a wider trade. By 1932 San Francisco Chinese were buying American canned goods and patronizing American chain stores. This cultural assimilation was matched by an increase in non-Oriental patronage of Chinese stores and restaurants. In 1929, when the Chinese and Japanese numbered only 2.3 per cent of the population of California, they sold 4.1 per cent of all food products and served 4.3 per cent of all restaurant meals consumed. From this Light calculated that roughly one-half of food commodities retailed by Orientals and roughly half the restaurant meals prepared by Orientals must have been consumed by non-Orientals.[31]

Some examples of how Chinese restaurants began to acquire a Western clientele may be quoted. In San Francisco, from the late 1920s, Chinese merchants began to open full-service restaurants, that is restaurants which served more than chop suey, outside Chinatown. An early example was the New Shanghai Terrace Bowl which opened in 1927 and which solicited non-Chinese customers by distributing coupons in department stores. It later opened a bar and a stage for performances and offered both Chinese and American food. The Shanghai Low on Grant Avenue in San Francisco's Chinatown, which had a large 'Chop Suey' sign on its façade, claimed:

> We serve finest kind of Chinese dishes. Excellent service at moderate prices, private rooms for parties.
> Dining room overlooking Park and San Francisco Bay.
> Please visit our cafe, it is equal to a trip to China.

本樓分設兩層餐房陳設華美五光奪目幽雅超倫
四壁所懸盡是中國名勝畫景而地又附近花園草
木芬芳餐房之內常能引吸新鮮空氣使在坐者悅

意快然故中西人士無論用宴及請讌無不如意週
到且招待殷動所有器具及用具極其潔淨仰各界
君子幸祈留意光顧焉

上海樓主人謹識

SHANGHAI LOW
532 GRANT AVE., SAN FRANCISCO

We serve finest kind of Chinese dishes. Excellent service at
moderate prices, private rooms for parties.
Dining room overlooking Park and San Francisco Bay.
Please visit our cafe, it is equal to a trip to China.

Advertisement for the Shanghai Low restaurant in San Francisco, *c.* late 1920s.

Several restaurants had menus which offered advice to non-Chinese customers on how to order Chinese food. They were told that all Chinese dishes were served in generous portions, sufficient for two or three persons if supplemented by some other order. They were assured that if they had any difficulty in selecting dishes the management or a waiter would be more than happy to assist them.[32]

Some other, less well-known, examples of this quiet expansion may be mentioned. Bill Lee's Bamboo Chopsticks in Bakersfield CA traces its history back to 1922 when the founder's father began to run a produce cart up and down the valley. His son trained as a butcher, opened a butcher's shop and then in 1938 opened the Bamboo Chopsticks with a staff of two cooks and two waitresses. From the outset the restaurant set out 'to bring to Bakersfield a taste of the far east with a unique American flavor'.[33] A Chinese restaurant in Charlotte, NC, operating in about 1932, which offered the typical choice of chop suey and chow mein, was patronized by girls from a nearby school. In Los Angeles the Apablasa-Marchessault gradually attracted white Americans to try Chinese food. A 1935 account read:

> There are several Chinese cafés where you can get excellent dinners – if you know how to order. If you ask for chop suey, they know you for a tenderfoot and treat you accordingly. Real Chinese food is delicate and rare; supposed to be tasted rather than eaten, for the number of courses is stupendous. If really to the manner born, you reach into one general dish with your chop-sticks; it is a clean and delicate way to dine. Unless you go in for too much bird's nest soup and century-old eggs, the prices are reasonable. Bird's nest soup is delicious, but any one can have my share of the heirloom hen fruit.[34]

By 1940 there is clear evidence of the wider acceptance of Chinese food across the United States. In that year the *St Louis Post-Dispatch* described Chinese food as 'among the best in the world'. In New York, which now had a Chinese population of over 12,000, although many Chinese still worked in laundries, many others worked in Chinese restaurants. According to one estimate, in 1941 there were 700 Chinese restaurants, some situated in Chinatown and others scattered throughout the city. On Sundays and holidays, Chinatown was thronged not only with Chinese coming in from outside, but also by a 'great number of Western visitors', who came to eat Chinese food, to buy oriental souvenirs, or just to look around.[35]

During the Second World War, the recognition that the United States and China were allies brought about a substantial, if not a complete, revision of American attitudes towards China and Chinese food. In San Francisco Chinese Americans held 'rice bowl' parties to raise funds to support China's war against Japan. These parties were attended by white Americans who may have associated the symbol of the rice bowl with thoughts of material and cultural superiority, but who nevertheless regarded the Chinese community and by extension the eating of Chinese food more favourably than hitherto.[36] Service overseas led some Americans to realize that 'foreigners had developed tasty ways to cook nutritious meals with a good variety of vegetables and little meat'. Pearl Buck, author of *The Good Earth*, commended a Chinese cookbook to American housewives because from its recipes they could 'learn to use meat for its taste in a dish of something else, instead of using it chiefly for its substance'.[37] Between 1941 and 1943 San Francisco Chinatown restaurants experienced a 300 per cent increase in business.[38]

The situation of the Chinese in Canada at the beginning of the twentieth century was little different from that of the Chinese in the United States. A small and declining Chinese population was accused of taking jobs from whites. In Vancouver in 1915 a campaign was mounted against Chinese laundries and against Chinese pedlars selling vegetables. It was argued that Chinese domestics and restaurants cooks preferred to buy Chinese-grown vegetables and thereby denied white market gardeners a living.[39] In response Chinese Canadians adopted the survival strategy of focusing on niche businesses. The restriction on new immigration in 1923 led to a further decline in the Chinese population, which at the same time was becoming more thinly dispersed, with Chinese moving to every province. At first the most important businesses in these new

A Chinese-owned restaurant in small-town Alberta in the 1920s.

centres of Chinese population were hand laundries, but with the increasing availability of washing machines, Canadian Chinese, like their American counterparts, had to turn to the restaurant business. Most of these restaurants were small, poorly decorated, and labour-intensive, and they usually served inexpensive Western-style food.[40] A few did prosper: a photograph from the 1920s shows a smart Chinese-owned diner in Alberta which served Western food, and which employed at least three white waitresses. Some Chinese working in the food trade achieved a degree of acceptance within the larger community. Of one Chinese who had settled in a small town on the Prairies it was said,

> When the hotel closed down, he started his own restaurant and a store as well . . . He always put in a bag of candy for the children with an order. He sold groceries, dry goods and kerosene . . . He also bought furs and hides . . . He acted as banker on Saturday nights . . . He kept many people from starving during the Depression.[41]

Vancouver's Chinatown remained the largest concentration of Chinese, and the Chinese presence there provoked conflicting responses from the white community. For some Chinatown offered an economic opportunity, to be exploited as a tourist attraction, but for others it presented a threat. In 1919 British Columbia had passed legislation outlawing white women's employment on oriental premises, a law which at first was not enforced. However in 1929, perhaps as a distant response to worries about political developments in China, the White Canada Association was formed to prevent further oriental penetration in British Columbia. Two years later a white waitress in Vancouver's Chinatown was murdered, allegedly by her Chinese lover. Now the practice of employing white waitresses in Chinese restaurants to attract non-Chinese customers came under attack. It was claimed that this practice encouraged vice and that the majority of Vancouver's known prostitutes had formerly been employed in Chinatown restaurants. Eight Chinese restaurants in Pender Street were served notices requiring them to dismiss the 29 white waitresses in their employ. After a lengthy confrontation, Chinatown proprietors were forced to accept that only Chinese-owned restaurants that served English meals to English customers could employ white waitresses. Even this concession was a hollow one, for during the Depression Chinese-operated Western-style restaurants in Vancouver were refused the right to accept welfare meal coupons.[42]

Although in the interwar years Canadian Chinese were a marginalized group, treated as second-class citizens, nevertheless they were becoming more integrated. This improved their image in the eyes of the majority population and opened the way for an appreciation of things Chinese, including the consumption of Chinese food. The proportion of Canadian-born Chinese Canadians was slowly increasing; as was the number of Chinese naturalized as Canadian citizens. More Chinese Canadians were becoming Christians and their ability in spoken and written English was improving. In the 1920s the universities of McGill and Toronto introduced Chinese studies. This more positive image was enhanced in 1936 when the Chinese community in Vancouver played a significant role in the celebrations marking the city's fiftieth anniversary. Chinese merchants sponsored an elaborate 'Chinese Village' project, which stressed the cultural achievements of China and which proved a milestone in the transformation of the image of Vancouver's Chinatown. China's position as an ally during the Second World War further improved this image. By the end of the war the Pender Street restaurant industry was flourishing alongside its grocery and butchers' shops, fish markets and curio stores. Chinese merchants set out to adapt the streetscape in conformity with the oriental image Europeans expected to find. A notable example was the installation of neon lighting on the façade of the White House Chop Suey restaurant on Columbia Street. Whereas before the war the White House was patronized exclusively by Chinese, by 1947 it was reported that the occidental population had moved in *en masse*.[43]

CHINESE FOOD COMES TO BRITAIN

Before the First World War the Chinese community in Britain was very small and subjected to a degree of discrimination and hostility. The use of Chinese labour in the Transvaal in the aftermath of the Boer War, an issue which was prominent in the 1906 election campaign, had raised fears of cheap Chinese labour flooding into Britain. The most dramatic reaction to this fear was the destruction, in one night of rioting in 1911, of all 30 of Cardiff's Chinese laundries. Anti-Chinese feeling on these grounds persisted into the 1920s, when it began to be countered by trade union support for the labour movement in China. Meanwhile accusations of Chinese involvement in drug-trafficking, seduction of young white girls and other evils had been popularized by Sax Rohmer, whose novel *The Mystery of Fu-Manchu* was published in 1913.

In 1911 there were some 668 China- and Hong Kong-born Chinese living in London, some 502 living in Liverpool and a smaller number living in Cardiff. The majority had formerly been seamen, although many of those who had settled had taken up laundry work. In addition a small trickle of Chinese students had begun to arrive. In London's East End there were some 30 Chinese shops and restaurants along two streets, Pennyfields and Limehouse Causeway. The restaurants were patronized exclusively, or almost exclusively, by Chinese. In Liverpool, which claimed to have the oldest Chinese community in Europe, the relationship between the Chinese and the local population was perhaps closer than that in London or Cardiff. Some intermarriage had occurred and a number of Anglo-Chinese families lived in the city. A Chinese restaurant had opened as early as 1907, and between the wars the number of Chinese restaurants in Liverpool fluctuated between two and six. These restaurants were opened initially to serve the needs of the Chinese community. One of these restaurants, the Foo Nam Low in Pitt Street, which was destroyed by a bomb in the Second World War, did attract some English customers who would 'get a big jug and go for a shillings worth of chopsuey'. One enterprising Chinese, whose wife's mother was Jewish and her father Chinese, made fishcakes and sold them in the local pub. Also on Pitt Street were to be found Chinese grocery stores which attracted some non-Chinese customers, one of whom recalled fondly the black jam cakes sold there. Another remembered a shop which sold 'China beetles': 'I NEVER fancied those but most kids liked them . . . As I remember them, they *were* beetles, dried, and they used to pick the legs and shell off them – UGH! I liked everything else they sold, but NOT those things.'[44]

The first Chinese restaurant in central London is said to have opened in 1908,[45] but the Tanhua Lou in Piccadilly, which was operating in 1923 if not earlier, later claimed to be the first Chinese restaurant not only in London, but also in Europe.[46] In the 1920s ignorance of, and prejudice against, Chinese food was still the dominant mind-set in Britain, but a few Westerners, among them the poet and aesthete Harold Acton, had begun to voice their appreciation of it. Acton had lived for some years in Paris and extolled French cooking. When he returned to London he found his 'quick-lunch lounge meals' so squalid that he engaged a Guangzhou man named Chong Sung, who had worked in a Chinese restaurant in Wembley, as his cook. Chong Sung brought with him Chinese bowls, cups, spoons, 'a lacquered canister of tea, cumquats, a pot of ginger, and myriads of smaller parcels of rice, vermicelli, lychees, mushrooms and other dainties like precious herbal and geological specimens'. He proved to be a perfect minister to Acton's poetic muse, for each meal he cooked excelled the last in delicate flavours. However few of Acton's friends would come to dinner because they associated Chinese food with snakes and scorpions. Some suggested that his diet would ruin his health, but he grew plumper and claimed that the green tea he drank at all hours cleared his brain and induced a greater serenity. His friends, influenced by the Chinese bogey-man of fiction, regarded the cook with suspicion, and Chong Sung's feelings were only mollified when Arthur Waley, the famous translator, wrote an elegant Chinese couplet in praise of his cooking. By eating Chinese food, Acton said 'I was half in China, and as time went on I wished to be wholly in China.' Chong Sung departed, leaving Acton to lament the loss of one whose 'ancient civilization had evolved a sublime gastrology which can satisfy the appetite and appeal to the intellect as well'. Some years later Acton started teaching at Beijing University and lived in a Chinese mansion with three successive courtyards, and so fulfilled his ambition to be wholly in China.[47]

By the 1930s several more Chinese restaurants were operating in Central London. Perhaps the most popular among Westerners was the Ley On in Wardour Street, where in the 1930s one could order a single dish, with rice, for one shilling and threepence.[48] There were two or three Chinese restaurants in the West End, their clientele consisting mainly of Chinese students.[49] Choy's Chinese Restaurant opened in the late 1930s and later moved to its present location on the King's Road. The Shanghai Restaurant in Greek Street was also operating by 1939. Outside London the Blue Barn in Cambridge, a tiny Chinese-American establishment which served only three dishes: chop suey, chow mein and fried rice, was open in 1938.[50] Its chop suey was 'a dish of stewed meat and cabbage, awash in tomato sauce'. As dishes at the Blue Barn were substantial helpings and cost about the same as dinner in a Cambridge college, the restaurant was popular with students.[51]

Publicly expressed attitudes towards Chinese food still reflected those of Western residents in the treaty ports. In 1939

The Shanghai Restaurant, Greek Street, London, 1939.

the BBC broadcast a talk by Jean Sterling entitled 'Some typical dishes from China'. She began:

> The Chinese have two meals a day. These meals are called 'Rice' – Morning Rice and Evening Rice. This custom is observed by both rich and poor. They are called Chow Times. It is curious that the meal 'times' should be called 'Rice', and 'food' called 'Chow'. When asking a Chinaman whether he has eaten, one would say, "Have makee chow?" or a Chinaman would say to a foreigner, when wanting to say he had just finished a meal, "Just now have makee chow." For this reason the large rather handsome yellow dogs one sees, are known as Chow dogs, because at one time they were eaten when puppies, as a delicacy.

The talk continued in this patronizing vein. A Chinese cook was a 'naturally born cook', who could prepare excellent Western dishes without ever tasting them. A Chinese dinner was a 'terribly long affair'; the dishes were delicious and their names sounded exciting, but one had to endure receiving food

Rose Hum Lee, writing in 1960, discussed how American attitudes towards the Chinese and Chinese food had changed since the 1940s. In small cities the cafés and restaurants run by Chinese but serving purely American food had virtually disappeared. The independent Chinese vegetable vendor was a figure from the past, and the small grocery stores run by Chinese were passing out of existence. Chinatowns had now become tourist attractions. On Sundays whites and Chinese converged on the Chinatowns of New York and San Francisco looking for Chinese food, relaxation, meetings, purchases and sociability. Along Grant Avenue in San Francisco the restaurants catered for tourists. But elsewhere in Chinatown there were older restaurants which only served banquets and old-world dishes to a discerning Chinese clientele. This Chinatown was the only source of authentic mooncakes, engagement cookies, and multi-course feasts for various occasions and its food shops sold a wide range of imported Chinese food.

Rose Hum Lee noted that the Chinese no longer had a monopoly of the dishes that they had introduced – some of the best Chinese dishes were procured from Japanese, Jewish and American establishments, which employed chefs trained to prepare Chinese dishes. These establishments spent more money on providing an exotic atmosphere and were more alert in experimenting with ingredients that appealed to the American palate. Whereas Chinese restaurants maintained a 'customer-seller' relationship, these new establishments adopted an 'intimate friendly' approach to their clientele. As a consequence many Chinese restaurateurs had either opened suburban restaurants or had resorted to operating '"take home" chop suey and chow mein establishments'.

> These are located at busy intersections, attracting many working wives who stop on their way to buy ready-cooked dinners, boxed in paper cartons. Soy sauce is placed in small glass vials and all the necessary items for dinner are conveniently packaged to take home.

She then discussed whether, as a result of these changes, Chinese food had become more or less popular in the United

States. She noted the competition from fast food, Italian food and the food of the south-western United States. She pointed out that Chinese restaurants were no longer found in cities with a population of less than 25,000, and that there were fewer Chinese restaurants in larger cities. Although Chinese restaurants had experienced a boom in the Second World War, immediately afterwards they had suffered a reversal because of the Korean War and the position of the 'two Chinas'. Now Americans patronized Chinese restaurants with less enthusiasm, while some shunned them entirely.[5]

In a survey of the role of the Chinese in American life, S. W. Kung estimated that in 1960 there were well over 6,000 Chinese restaurants in the United States and by that time Chinese employment in the restaurant business had far surpassed that of Chinese in laundry work. In New York City, Newark and the surrounding country there were 600 restaurants and in San Francisco and the Bay area there were even more. The average capital investment required to open a restaurant had risen sharply and he cited as an extreme example the recent opening of the Four Seas Restaurant in San Francisco by K. L. Woo, who headed a quarter-million dollar corporation. The restaurant accommodated 650 guests and offered Shanghai, Beijing and Guangzhouese cuisine. He added that more and more restaurateurs were becoming concerned with the problem of improving business management and that one New York restaurant had provided college scholarships for two Chinese-Americans to study food store management.[6]

In the 1960s the Chinese population of the United States increased by 84 per cent, mainly through new immigration. A significant proportion of these new immigrants found that the catering industry was the most accessible form of employment available to them. How this process occurred in 'Valley City', that is Sacramento, was studied by Melford S. Weiss. He noted that the Chinese population of Sacramento had risen from 1,508 in 1940 to 6,770 in 1960 and to about 10,000 in the early 1970s. By 1961 most Chinese had moved out of the old Chinatown district into residential areas and the Chinese community had become much more assimilated. More Chinese

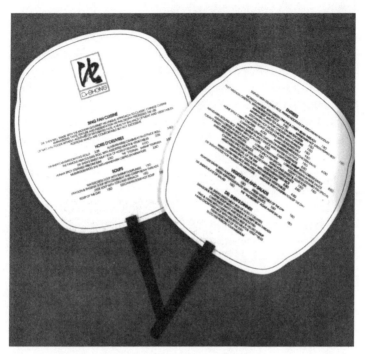

Menu from Dr Shen's Restaurant, Chicago, late 1970s.

could now speak English and an increasing proportion of young
Chinese could not speak or understand Chinese. Although
many young Chinese were moving into professional and technical jobs, catering was an important source of employment. In
new areas of settlement the Chinese opened supermarkets and
restaurants. These supermarkets, although still largely patronized by Chinese customers, now carried both Chinese and
American foodstuffs. By 1966 there were also at least 66
Chinese restaurants in Valley City. The larger establishments
served both Chinese and American food, and even those which
specialized in Chinese food did not cater to Chinese customers
exclusively.[7]

By 1980, according to Wilbur Zelinsky, the number of
Chinese restaurants in the United States and Canada had risen
to 7,796, 29 per cent of all the ethnic and regional restaurants
listed in telephone directories. These restaurants were to be
found in all but one of the major metropolitan areas he sur-

veyed. However, although Chinese restaurants in the United States were most numerous along the east coast and in Chicago, Los Angeles, San Francisco and Seattle, and in Canada around Vancouver and Toronto, they did not strongly dominate any region. In the early 1960s most Chinese restaurants were chop suey joints, with few pretensions beyond offering a cheap meal. Zelinsky's survey showed that by 1980 many Chinese restaurants were describing themselves as offering a regional cuisine, the most common choice being Guangzhouese, but 412 described themselves as Polynesian Chinese.[8] Harvey Levenstein offered an explanation for the pattern of the spread of Chinese food across America. He began by pointing out that the adoption of new food tastes 'is probably facilitated by an absence of low-status people from whose homelands they originate'. In the United States the concentration of the Chinese population in coastal cities probably helped, rather than hindered, the 'steady march of chop suey and chow mein through Middle America'. The white 'sophisticates' of the coastal cities were not drawn to the cuisine of local Chinese-Americans, most of whom were southerners from Guangzhou, but to the regional cuisines of Beijing, Shanghai, Sichuan and Hunan. It was only later that these sophisticates rediscovered the merits of Guangzhou cooking.[9]

A snapshot of the Chinese restaurant business as it had developed in New York by 1980 was provided by Bernard P. Wong, He estimated that in New York City Chinatown 5,000 Chinese were working in some 250 restaurants. In the past most of these restaurants had been content to serve chop suey dishes and after a Chinese meal American diners were entertained with fortune cookies containing 'Confucius sayings'. However, with the publication of the menu for the banquet given for President Nixon by Zhou Enlai in 1972, many Americans had become curious about things Chinese and wanted to try Chinese regional cuisines. The latest trend was for Hunanese cuisine, and many Chinese restaurants, seeking to meet customer demand, had gone Hunan style. He added other examples of how Chinese restaurants had sought to attract a steady flow of American customers. The décor had to be 'comfortably oriental', the restaurant had to have silverware as well as chopsticks and preferably have a bar. In China restaurants served only tea to their customers, but in America they also had to provide soft drinks, ice and cold water. As Americans were not used to hot spices, seasoning had to be toned down. For connoisseurs of Chinese food, specialty restaurants served dim sum and noodle dishes. Wong concluded 'it is the ability of the Chinese restaurant to heed the culinary needs, trends and tastes that make the restaurant business prosperous. Innovation, adaptation, and variety are essential parts of this ethnic business.' These words implied that to succeed Chinese restaurants should not only seek to respond to customers' preferences, but should also subscribe to the American business ethic.[10]

New York's Chinatown restaurants have also been discussed by Jan Lin in a recent book. He argued that in the mid-1990s Chinatown was experiencing a profound economic and cultural change, arising in part from internal forces, in part from the new global economy. He began by criticizing the voyeuristic nature of tourist visits to the neighbourhood.

> The typical American encounters Chinatown as part of a process of alimentary gratification. Aside from providing a break from normal culinary routine, the prospect of eating Chinese food in association with a journey into the central-city district of Chinatown also affords the diner the opportunity of experiencing the exotic Orient without undertaking transpacific travel.

He calculated that in Chinatown in 1995 there were 412 Chinese American (or Vietnamese American) full-service restaurants and 50 takeout or delicatessen-type eating places. He divided the restaurants into three categories: smaller noodle shop and dumpling house establishments; medium-sized and medium priced restaurants which offered more extensive menus, including regional cuisines; large banquet-style restaurants offering specialized dishes and extravagant meals for special occasions. The first two categories of restaurant might well be used by non-Chinese, and tourists or office workers on business might lunch at the banquet-style restaurants. But at other times these restaurants catered for the Chinatown community rather than outsiders. The largest of these restaurants, the Jing Fong, originally seated 300 guests. After obtaining a $3,000,000 loan from the Bank of China, it reopened in 1992 with seating for 1,100 guests.

Jan Lin also discussed labour disputes involving employees of Chinese restaurants. In 1993, 44 of the employees of theπ Silver Palace were locked out for refusing to sign a new contract. They picketed the restaurant and the management responded by offering a discount of up to 30 per cent on prices. In return the strikers displayed a coffin bearing the words 'No More Slavery, Justice for Workers'. After a seven-month lockout the strikers won a partial victory. A similar dispute broke out in 1995 between waiters and management at the Jing Fong. The Chinatown Chinese press favoured the management, but English-language newspapers sympathized with the workers. A local television channel raised the issue of alleged collusion between the management, tongs (criminal gangs) and the police. Some students connected with a group called Students for Workers' rights staged a one-week hunger strike and 5,000 signatures were collected in support of the hunger strikers. Once again the employees gained a partial victory. In both these disputes the employees received some support from the non-Chinese public, a remarkable progression from the indifference and suspicion which had formerly been directed at employees in Chinese restaurants.[11]

In the late 1970s the boom in the ethnic food market had led to the appearance of ethnic fast food restaurants which offered a version of Chinese food, although the restaurants were neither run by Chinese nor cooked the food according to Chinese techniques. The best-known, Charlie Chan's, derived its name from the detective in a series of racist Warner films. The food used was flash-frozen and microwavable, and featured egg rolls, fried chicken and shrimp and 'Chan fries'. Service was provided by teenagers working part-time, and the restaurants were brightly coloured and decorated with Chinese hieroglyphics and Chan props. Charlie Chan restaurants faltered in the 1980s, but TGI Friday's continued the ethnic theme, offering three potato skin selections: Mexican, Italian and Oriental, the last-named being filled with water chestnuts, shrimp and cabbage.[12] More from one's host's chopsticks and to watch a Chinaman eat was not a pretty sight. However, she concluded with 'a few simple recipes for dishes that are easy to prepare and very good'. Listeners were told that the ingredients could be obtained from the Shanghai Emporium in Greek Street.[52]

During the Second World War, when China was Britain's ally, the number of Chinese restaurants slowly increased. Before the war a number of men belonging to the Man lineage from San Tin village in the Hong Kong New Territories had jumped ship in London. Five of these ex-seamen now opened small restaurants.[53] In Liverpool, where up to 10,000 Chinese seamen were on shore at any one time, some of them profited from their time ashore by opening restaurants which served dishes from the regions from where they came, such as Ningbo, Fuzhou, Hainan, Shantou and Shanghai. These restaurants were probably the earliest regional Chinese restaurants in Britain. Perhaps the best of them was the Central Restaurant on the north side of Great George Square, where Kenneth Lo was given a twelve-course dinner in his honour in 1945. Nevertheless in the years after the war a Chinese restaurant distant from an area of Chinese settlement was a rare sight. There were *no* Chinese restaurants in Manchester and the Blue Barn restaurant in Cambridge had been destroyed by a German bomb.[54]

However the Second World War had affected British eating habits. Many British servicemen and women had travelled to Asia, and it is to their experience of eating Chinese food in various places that one can attribute, at least in part, the change in attitude which was to lead to the great uptake in the consumption of Chinese food a decade later. In Bombay, sailors from British naval ships, having failed to understand Indian food, and having grown tired of the English food served in Indian restaurants, sought out Chinese restaurants where they could eat American Chop Suey. In Bangalore the Victory Chinese Restaurant offered a menu which was remarkably similar to that of many Chinese restaurants in Britain today.[55] On the home front change was less apparent. Wartime rationing and food shortages led to the publication of a rash of books offering recipes using little meat. Some of these recipes were named

Menu of the Victory Chinese
Restaurant, Bangalore, 1946.

after wartime allies, and this may explain the origins of a dish
called Chinese Cake, which consisted of haricot beans, potatoes, fat boiled bacon, sugar, breadcrumbs and herbs, mixed
together and baked in the oven and served with Brussels sprouts
and brown gravy.[56]

SEVEN

The Globalization of Chinese Food since 1945

UNITED STATES AND CANADA: FROM CHOP SUEY TO REGIONAL CUISINES

In the years after the Second World War a number of factors encouraged the spread of Chinese food in the West, but it was not until the late 1950s that change gathered pace and the globalization of Chinese food became evident. By the 1960s Chinese restaurants could be found in Turkey, where one could get a plain Chinese meal or dine in style on Chinese food at the Istanbul Hilton. In Nairobi, Kenya, there was the Pagoda Restaurant and in Salisbury, Southern Rhodesia (now Harare, Zimbabwe) one could find the ornate Bamboo Chinese Restaurant and the noisier Golden Dragon. In Addis Ababa the China Bar had become a favourite with Ethiopian women.[1] On the other side of the world, in Lima, Peru, which had a Chinese community dating back to the mid-nineteenth century, the numerous Chinese restaurants known locally as *chifas* were patronized by a wide cross-section of the community. But the most dramatic examples of globalization were to be found in Western countries which had a long-established Chinese population, notably the United States and Canada, and in Western countries which had recently received an influx of Chinese people, particularly the United Kingdom.

In the immediate post-war years there was little indication that such a change was impending. In the United States, basic food tastes had changed little since before the war, although the methods, processes and products which delivered this kind of food had altered. Although on occasions an appreciation of the food of other peoples was advocated, a 'deep-rooted distaste for most foreign foods ... was still an integral part of American culture'. There were two exceptions to this rule. Bland versions of Italo-American food, such as pasta and tomato sauce, which had become popular during the war and, in the 1950s, pizza, which in any form resembling the authentic could not easily be made at home, began to gain wide acceptance. As for Chinese food, a wartime version of chop suey, which used ketchup and Worcester sauce, gave way to a post-war version of chow mein which was composed of canned bean sprouts, canned fried noodles and soy sauce. Heinz produced a version of this dish which used its cream of mushroom soup. For Americans to eat and like home-made chow mein has been described as a distinct step toward breaking out of a culinary straitjacket.[2] In Britain the austerity of wartime rationing had forced housewives to exercise some imagination in the preparation of food, but after the war a return had been made to traditional fare. However, a certain lack of confidence in the quality of Britain's cuisine left the door ajar for the introduction of ethnic cuisines, an early indication of this being the publication in 1950 of Elizabeth David's *A Book of Mediterranean Food*.[3]

It was under these circumstances that Chinese food began its dramatic advance in North America and Britain. Rhoads Murphey described the first stage of this expansion as it occurred in Boston, Massachusetts. Boston's Chinatown, which dated back to about 1890, was situated on reclaimed tidal flats which had previously been settled by Irish, Central European Jews and Italians. In 1899 the construction of an elevated railway through the northern part of Chinatown had further depressed land values. Then in 1941 the elevated railway was torn down for scrap, the war brought about an economic recovery and the land on which Chinatown was built rose in value. Within a decade a dozen restaurants had been built or remodelled, complete with neon signs to attract non-Chinese trade. Chinese restaurateurs estimated that whereas in the past three-quarters of their trade had come from their own people, now the balance was exactly reversed in favour of non-Chinese Americans. By 1952 in Chinatown itself, there were 26 restaurants and in Greater Boston alongside the 48 Chinese laundries there were 34 Chinese restaurants.[4]

Rose Hum Lee, writing in 1960, discussed how American attitudes towards the Chinese and Chinese food had changed since the 1940s. In small cities the cafés and restaurants run by Chinese but serving purely American food had virtually disappeared. The independent Chinese vegetable vendor was a figure from the past, and the small grocery stores run by Chinese were passing out of existence. Chinatowns had now become tourist attractions. On Sundays whites and Chinese converged on the Chinatowns of New York and San Francisco looking for Chinese food, relaxation, meetings, purchases and sociability. Along Grant Avenue in San Francisco the restaurants catered for tourists. But elsewhere in Chinatown there were older restaurants which only served banquets and old-world dishes to a discerning Chinese clientele. This Chinatown was the only source of authentic mooncakes, engagement cookies, and multi-course feasts for various occasions and its food shops sold a wide range of imported Chinese food.

Rose Hum Lee noted that the Chinese no longer had a monopoly of the dishes that they had introduced – some of the best Chinese dishes were procured from Japanese, Jewish and American establishments, which employed chefs trained to prepare Chinese dishes. These establishments spent more money on providing an exotic atmosphere and were more alert in experimenting with ingredients that appealed to the American palate. Whereas Chinese restaurants maintained a 'customer-seller' relationship, these new establishments adopted an 'intimate friendly' approach to their clientele. As a consequence many Chinese restaurateurs had either opened suburban restaurants or had resorted to operating '"take home" chop suey and chow mein establishments'.

> These are located at busy intersections, attracting many working wives who stop on their way to buy ready-cooked dinners, boxed in paper cartons. Soy sauce is placed in small glass vials and all the necessary items for dinner are conveniently packaged to take home.

She then discussed whether, as a result of these changes, Chinese food had become more or less popular in the United

States. She noted the competition from fast food, Italian food and the food of the south-western United States. She pointed out that Chinese restaurants were no longer found in cities with a population of less than 25,000, and that there were fewer Chinese restaurants in larger cities. Although Chinese restaurants had experienced a boom in the Second World War, immediately afterwards they had suffered a reversal because of the Korean War and the position of the 'two Chinas'. Now Americans patronized Chinese restaurants with less enthusiasm, while some shunned them entirely.[5]

In a survey of the role of the Chinese in American life, S. W. Kung estimated that in 1960 there were well over 6,000 Chinese restaurants in the United States and by that time Chinese employment in the restaurant business had far surpassed that of Chinese in laundry work. In New York City, Newark and the surrounding country there were 600 restaurants and in San Francisco and the Bay area there were even more. The average capital investment required to open a restaurant had risen sharply and he cited as an extreme example the recent opening of the Four Seas Restaurant in San Francisco by K. L. Woo, who headed a quarter-million dollar corporation. The restaurant accommodated 650 guests and offered Shanghai, Beijing and Guangzhouese cuisine. He added that more and more restaurateurs were becoming concerned with the problem of improving business management and that one New York restaurant had provided college scholarships for two Chinese-Americans to study food store management.[6]

In the 1960s the Chinese population of the United States increased by 84 per cent, mainly through new immigration. A significant proportion of these new immigrants found that the catering industry was the most accessible form of employment available to them. How this process occurred in 'Valley City', that is Sacramento, was studied by Melford S. Weiss. He noted that the Chinese population of Sacramento had risen from 1,508 in 1940 to 6,770 in 1960 and to about 10,000 in the early 1970s. By 1961 most Chinese had moved out of the old Chinatown district into residential areas and the Chinese community had become much more assimilated. More Chinese

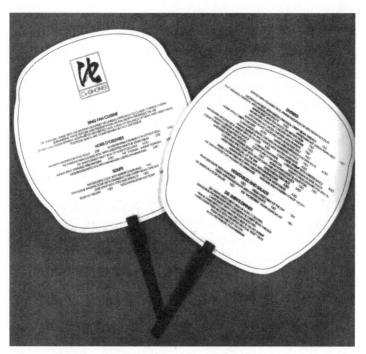

Menu from Dr Shen's Restaurant, Chicago, late 1970s.

could now speak English and an increasing proportion of young
Chinese could not speak or understand Chinese. Although
many young Chinese were moving into professional and technical jobs, catering was an important source of employment. In
new areas of settlement the Chinese opened supermarkets and
restaurants. These supermarkets, although still largely patronized by Chinese customers, now carried both Chinese and
American foodstuffs. By 1966 there were also at least 66
Chinese restaurants in Valley City. The larger establishments
served both Chinese and American food, and even those which
specialized in Chinese food did not cater to Chinese customers
exclusively.[7]

By 1980, according to Wilbur Zelinsky, the number of
Chinese restaurants in the United States and Canada had risen
to 7,796, 29 per cent of all the ethnic and regional restaurants
listed in telephone directories. These restaurants were to be
found in all but one of the major metropolitan areas he sur-

veyed. However, although Chinese restaurants in the United States were most numerous along the east coast and in Chicago, Los Angeles, San Francisco and Seattle, and in Canada around Vancouver and Toronto, they did not strongly dominate any region. In the early 1960s most Chinese restaurants were chop suey joints, with few pretensions beyond offering a cheap meal. Zelinsky's survey showed that by 1980 many Chinese restaurants were describing themselves as offering a regional cuisine, the most common choice being Guangzhouese, but 412 described themselves as Polynesian Chinese.[8] Harvey Levenstein offered an explanation for the pattern of the spread of Chinese food across America. He began by pointing out that the adoption of new food tastes 'is probably facilitated by an absence of low-status people from whose homelands they originate'. In the United States the concentration of the Chinese population in coastal cities probably helped, rather than hindered, the 'steady march of chop suey and chow mein through Middle America'. The white 'sophisticates' of the coastal cities were not drawn to the cuisine of local Chinese-Americans, most of whom were southerners from Guangzhou, but to the regional cuisines of Beijing, Shanghai, Sichuan and Hunan. It was only later that these sophisticates rediscovered the merits of Guangzhou cooking.[9]

A snapshot of the Chinese restaurant business as it had developed in New York by 1980 was provided by Bernard P. Wong, He estimated that in New York City Chinatown 5,000 Chinese were working in some 250 restaurants. In the past most of these restaurants had been content to serve chop suey dishes and after a Chinese meal American diners were entertained with fortune cookies containing 'Confucius sayings'. However, with the publication of the menu for the banquet given for President Nixon by Zhou Enlai in 1972, many Americans had become curious about things Chinese and wanted to try Chinese regional cuisines. The latest trend was for Hunanese cuisine, and many Chinese restaurants, seeking to meet customer demand, had gone Hunan style. He added other examples of how Chinese restaurants had sought to attract a steady flow of American customers. The décor had to be 'comfortably oriental', the restaurant had to have silverware as well as chopsticks and recently, greater success has been achieved in developing Chinese restaurant chains. For example Quik Wok in Boise, Idaho started a Chinese drive-through service in 1986 and then expanded to open several drive-though diners which offered 'authentic Chinese cuisine as well as American dishes at affordable prices'.[13]

Progress towards the acceptance of Chinese food followed a similar path in Canada. By the early 1950s restrictive immigration policies had reduced the Chinese population to under 35,000. Thereafter, with restrictions repealed, the Chinese population began to grow, reaching 58,197 by 1961. Further changes in immigration regulations then allowed Chinese to be admitted under the same criteria as other immigrants. Between 1971 and 1981 the Chinese population rose from 118,815 to 289,245, and by 1991 there were over 600,000 individuals of Chinese origin in Canada. Many of those who came in the first wave of immigration were the wives and children of those previously admitted. Many later immigrants came from urban environments, particular from Hong Kong and Taiwan and many were in their prime working years, that is between 15 and 34. Nearly half of the 241,046 Chinese who arrived in Canada between 1949 and 1994 to join the labour force had as their intended occupation managerial, professional and white-collar jobs. However 18 per cent came as service workers, probably intending to work in restaurants and the food service industry. Many of the new arrivals dispersed to suburbs and middle-class neighbourhoods. Others reinforced the population of Chinatowns which now exploited their appeal as a tourist attraction becoming, in Peter S. Li's words, 'a commercial district marketing ethnic goods'. One of the most important of the ethnic goods on offer was Chinese food.[14]

At first Chinese restaurants continued to be small family firms, where the staff worked long hours doing unpleasant work at low wages. However by the 1980s the injection of capital led to a transition of Chinese businesses and to the establishment of larger and more luxurious Chinese restaurants, which attracted the more affluent Chinese community as well as Westerners in search of an exotic experience. A notable example of this trend was the Top Gun restaurant in Richmond, BC, which opened in the late 1980s in a medium-sized mall on Westminster Highway, and which offered an expensive menu in a plush environment. Within two years it was so overbooked that its owner opened a second restaurant in the prestigious Aberdeen Mall, where it was equally well patronized by affluent Chinese and Caucasian customers.[15]

BRITAIN: FROM TAKEAWAYS TO *NOUVELLE* CHINESE CUISINE

The spread of Chinese restaurants and takeaways throughout the British Isles occurred under different circumstances from those prevailing in North America, and went through several distinct phases: a post-war period during which the Chinese concentration in the field of catering gradually increased, a period from the late 1950s to the mid 1960s when a boom occurred in Chinese catering, a period in the 1970s and 1980s when the consumption of Chinese food in various forms became entrenched in British eating habits, and from the late 1990s a period when substantial amounts of capital were invested into more sophisticated restaurants.

In the post-war years and until the late 1950s, the number of Chinese restaurants in central London increased slowly. Several of the restaurants which had been established before the war were still going strong. These included Ley On's, which was particularly popular with Westerners and the Shanghai Restaurant, which offered lunches from a rather shorter menu. Other central London Chinese restaurants included the Hong Kong on Shaftesbury Avenue which sprawled over three floors, the Freddie Mills Restaurant in Tottenham Court Road, a Chinese restaurant owned by the British boxer, and Choy's Chinese Restaurant in Frith Street, the proprietor of which practised judo at the nearby Japanese-run Budokwai judo club. Several new restaurants opened in the early 1950s, some owned by members of the staff from the former Nationalist Chinese embassy in London and Liverpool who had remained in Britain after the revolution and had became restaurateurs. As many of them came from North China, they extended the range of

Chinese cooking available in Britain. As I mentioned in Chapter six, during the war members of the Man lineage from the Hong Kong New Territories had opened small restaurants in London. Now wealthy, middle-aged members of the same lineage began to invest in London, transforming the Man foothold into a dozen large restaurants. By the mid-1950s the number of proprietors and managers of Chinese restaurants in Britain was estimated to be 36, a figure which probably refers largely to central London.[16]

Chinese restaurants began to appear in numbers in Britain when the wartime canteen culture was disappearing. They offered an element of consumer choice to those who may have been bored by the uniformity and egalitarianism fostered by rationing.[17] Some who chose to eat in Chinese restaurants explained that they had been introduced to Chinese food when they, their partners, or their parents had been working abroad. One *Saga Magazine* reader, who was stationed in Singapore between 1953 and 1955, remembered the 'marvellous taste of Mah Mee cooked in the open streets'. Another had accompanied her father, who was serving in the Royal Air Force, to Singapore. Because the Suez Canal was closed, their ship went via Capetown, and on the long voyage she learned to enjoy egg fried rice with prawns cooked by the Chinese cooks among the crew. In Singapore she discovered the open air food stalls. With scant regard for hygiene she enjoyed 'nasi goreng, mee hoon, chow siu fong, foo yong hai, oyster omelettes, chillie crab stalls on Changi beach after a swim'.

In the post-war period a few chop suey restaurants were still to be found in areas of Chinese settlement in Liverpool and London's East End. When the war ended many of the Chinese sailors who had lived for a time in Liverpool returned to China. However the Chinese community had grown and had begun to spread into the streets surrounding Pitt Street and Cleveland Square. By 1951 the number of Chinese restaurants had risen to 12. In the East End, where the area of Chinese settlement had been largely destroyed by bombing, at least one Chinese restaurant was still operating. In 1948 or 1949 two adventurous teenage English boys lighted on a restaurant in Dockland. The aroma of cooking bean sprouts wafted from the door. After some delay the boys plucked up courage to enter. The restaurant was small and bare, with scrappy wooden chairs. The waiters were not the white-jacketed waiters of today, but older and bent, wearing tunics and skull caps. The boys were served chow mein and given chopsticks, but as they had no idea how to use them they were given spoons instead. The whole meal, as much as they could eat, cost them sixpence each.[18] Modest establishments such as this, which served cheap and acceptable food to a largely working-class clientele, may have been the foundation on which the restaurant boom which was to follow was built.

A few enterprising Chinese had opened restaurants in fresh locations. In Edinburgh, by 1951, there was a restaurant on Chambers Street which served fried rice to intrepid young Scots couples. A Chinese restaurant in Petty Cury in Cambridge, open by 1954–5 and described as small and poorly furnished, offered half portions to students. In 1955, the Nanking Restaurant, situated in a side street in Brighton, served a meal for two for seven shillings and sixpence. The food was described as beautifully presented and the setting suited young courting couples. The 1955 *Good Food Guide* included that restaurant among the five Chinese restaurants it recorded. Two of these were in London and the other two in Liverpool and Manchester. A Chinese restaurant in Reading, operating from about 1956, offered an inclusive-price three-course lunch menu, which made it popular with working girls who would not have felt comfortable going into a public house. The same restaurant offered a three-course inclusive-price dinner which provided a popular venue for outings for girls on Friday nights.[19] By 1956 the number of Chinese restaurants in Britain had risen to about 300.[20]

The second phase, Britain's Chinese restaurant boom, started in the late 1950s and lasted for about a decade. This boom derived from two complementary impulses. On the one hand strong economic factors encouraged Chinese to migrate from the Hong Kong New Territories to Britain and to concentrate on catering for their subsistence. On the other hand a wide range of changes in British social attitudes created an expanding clientele for Chinese restaurants and takeaways.

The economic impulse promoting migration has been traced to factors affecting the livelihood of villagers in the Hong Kong New Territories. A typical example is that of the inhabitants of San Tin, a single-lineage village where virtually all the male inhabitants share the surname Man and recognize a common ancestor. The Man lineage was traditionally a rice-growing community, although some of its members did work away as sailors, sending back remittances to support their families with whom they hoped eventually to be reunited. In the 1950s this economic arrangement began to collapse. Enterprising immigrant farmers from mainland China who had settled in the locality began to grow vegetables for the Hong Kong urban market. The Man farmers were too proud to change from growing rice and this proved a grave disadvantage when the import of cheap rice from South-east Asia caused the price of rice to fall. However, the success of the members of the Man lineage who had settled and set up several restaurants in London now offered an economic lifeline to San Tin villagers: the prospect of well-paid employment in Britain. With assistance from the lineage, a system of chain migration was set up and many young male members of the Man lineage migrated to Britain to work in Man-owned establishments. Villagers from other New Territories' villages followed suit. Some belonged to lineages as strong as that of the Mans and received lineage support for making the move. Others lacking that support came to Britain as individuals.[21]

Chinese immigration from Hong Kong to the United Kingdom accelerated in the early 1960s because of the immigrants' anxiety to arrive before the Commonwealth Immigrants Act came into effect on 1 July 1962. This act restricted the admission of male holders of British Hong Kong passports to those who could demonstrate that they had a job waiting for them. Thereafter the Chinese population continued to grow through the admission of dependents, in particular wives and children. Until 1973 it also grew because a loophole in the law permitted Chinese aliens from mainland China to enter Britain as a separate category. This loophole allowed some 10,000 Chinese, many of whom were in their early twenties, to be admitted to Britain between 1962 and 1973. They provided a pool of cheap labour exploited by some of the larger Chinese restaurants. In addition, in the 1970s, 16,000 Vietnamese refugees, 70 per cent of whom were ethnic Chinese, arrived in Britain. As a result, by 1981 the Chinese population of Britain had risen to 154, 763.[22]

The great majority of these new arrivals looked to the catering industry for employment and as a consequence the number of Chinese restaurants, and then the number of Chinese takeaways began to rise sharply. According to figures given by James L. Watson, between 1957 and 1964 the number of Chinese restaurants rose from 300 to 800. In 1970 a card file held in the Hong Kong Government Office in London identified 1,400 Chinese restaurants, a figure which included some 400 takeaways and fish and chip shops. These figures were almost certainly under-reported and another estimate sets the figure at 4,000 Chinese eating establishments, twice the number of Indian and Pakistani restaurants, which had also begun to proliferate.[23] By 1977 Watson was writing 'It is now almost impossible to find a town in England (and increasingly in Scotland) with a population of 5000 or more that does not have at least one Chinese or take-away shop.' He estimated that the number of restaurants and takeaways was about 4,000, and suggested that saturation point had been reached.[24] Nevertheless the number of restaurants and takeaways continued to increase and by 1984 the total was estimated at 7,000. This dramatic expansion slowed in the 1980s, in part because the economic recession, rising costs and higher value-added tax rates were making such enterprises less profitable.[25] However the number of Chinese restaurants and takeaways has continued to rise, and a recent estimate puts the total at 8,000 outlets.[26]

As early as 1960 some of the sons and nephews of the earlier Chinese emigrants to Britain, anticipating that the British market would soon reach saturation point, had begun to open restaurants on the continent. By 1977 there were at least 10,000 Chinese living in Holland where they competed with Indonesian immigrants in the restaurant trade.[27] At that time the number of Chinese immigrants in other northern European countries was quite small, but that situation was to change in the 1970s when Chinese restaurants began to open in West

Germany, and then, after the reunification of Germany, Chinese from the west of the country were quick to seek opportunities in East Berlin and other cities of the former German Democratic Republic.

This proliferation of Chinese food outlets owed much to the desire of Chinese employees to have their own businesses. After a few years working in a restaurant, and having learned basic catering skills, Chinese families – wives playing a crucial role in this transition – were in a position to raise the modest capital required to open their own small restaurant or a takeaway. Such enterprises were usually family concerns with low overheads, which were able to withstand economic setbacks. The willingness of Chinese families to work long, anti-social hours enabled them to compete successfully with British proprietors of fish and chip shops. However Chinese takeaways could only succeed if set at a distance from other establishments selling identical food at identical prices and for many Chinese families this resulted in social isolation.[28] Few of these new proprietors, including the Man immigrants who at the start of the boom had opened about a hundred restaurants around the country, had any skills in cooking. Their establishments were 'chop suey' restaurants, which offered food judged to suit the palate of their British clientele. They were described as 'paddy farmers'. 'Half an hour's training is enough. Tell them to use plenty of ginger, bean sprouts and dried citrous peel, give them a *wok* and a bottle of soy sauce and they know all there is to know about "Chinese cooking".'[29] However in 1965 five superior Chinese restaurants were opened in Gerrard Street in Central London and this area began to develop as a centre for the Chinese community in Britain. These restaurants served authentic Chinese food and catered almost exclusively for the growing Chinese population. By 1975, Tong Yan Gai, Guangzhouese for Chinatown, had become the recreational centre of the Chinese all over Britain. In four of the 'authentic' Chinese restaurants outsiders were made to feel uncomfortable unless they were accompanied by a Chinese friend.[30]

The operation of a central London Chinese restaurant and the opening of a Chinese takeaway in Croydon provided the subject matter for *Sour Sweet* by Timothy Mo. Set in the 1960s, the novel describes how Chen, born in Hong Kong and with a limited command of English, saves enough from his job as a waiter in a restaurant just off Gerrard Street to open a takeaway. In several passages Mo refers sardonically to the food served in the restaurant and to that cooked by Chen at his own takeaway. The food served on the 'tourist' menu at the restaurant is described as 'total *lupsup*, fit only for foreign devils'. Whereas the waiters prefer serving Chinese food to Chinese customers, the proprietor's preference was for

> a preponderance of Westerners who consumed expensive and unsuitable wines as well as beer with their meal and did not share the irritating obsessions of the Chinese customers with their totally unreasonable insistence on a meal made up of fresh materials, authentically cooked, and presented at a highly competitive price.

Usually the two types of Chinese food were kept well apart, but when Chen's personal problems increase, he begins to confuse orders 'bringing lurid orange sweet and sour pork with pineapple chunks to outraged Chinese customers and white, bloody chicken and yellow duck's feet to appalled Westerners'.

The takeaway which Chen and his wife open in a converted terrace house is named the Dah Ling after his wife's home village. The only decoration is a Chinese calendar on the wall. As for the food,

> It bore no resemblance at all to Chinese cuisine. They served from a stereotyped menu, similar to that outside countless other establishments in the UK . . . 'Sweet and sour pork' was their staple, naturally: batter musket balls encasing a tiny core of meat, laced with a scarlet sauce that had an interesting effect on the urine of the customer the next day . . . 'Spare ribs' (whatever they were) also seemed popular. So were spring-rolls . . . parsimoniously filled mostly with bean-sprouts. All to be packed in the rectangular silver boxes, food coffins, to be removed and consumed statutorily off-premises.

Chen would willingly have discarded the last element of authenticity in the dishes he cooked and would have 'fried thick tombstone slabs of meat or entire splinters of bamboo, used clear sauces of pure Knorr stock or thickened with Bisto', but the recipes were constructed along 'cynical economic lines'. The meat-shavings went further and the thick cornflour sauce gave the illusion of substance. Even so the net profit of the take-away was no more than the wages Chen had earned as a waiter.[31]

Twenty years later, the writer Lynn Pan met a British-born Chinese who was helping her mother in a takeaway near Stockport prior to going up to Oxford to read English. Her rueful description of her duties caught the frustration and boredom of the long hours required to run such an enterprise.

Meal for one: steamed fish, vegetables and rice . . . The prime food is money. The recipe includes the following ingredients: forty grams effort or slavery; thirty grams cerebral power; the both seasoned ad lib with tolerance and other virtues. Method: work. [32]

If Chinese restaurants and takeaways were to succeed they had to attract British custom, and this required a major change in the eating habits of the British public. In the second half of the twentieth century many factors had initiated such a change. Growing affluence enabled people to eat out regularly or buy takeaway meals. Supermarkets offered an increasingly wide choice of convenience foods and of fruits and vegetables from overseas. Foreign travel encouraged the acceptance of different types of food. The growth of the Asian community led to the establishment of many Indian, Pakistani and Bangladeshi restaurants, which promoted the acceptance of ethnic food-stuffs and the expectation that inexpensive food outlets would be open in the late evening.

In British cities and towns in the 1950s the choice of places to eat out was restricted to hotels which served uninspired food, restaurants which tended to be expensive and pubs which might not be considered appropriate eating places for couples or young women on their own. A Chinese restaurant offered a cheap meal and table service in an acceptable environment. It also offered a kind of adventure. This combination was attractive to young people and in particular to students and so it is not surprising that some of the earliest Chinese restaurants in provincial Britain opened in university towns. Many of those who ate in Chinese restaurants in the 1950s were challenging parental opinions on what constituted an appropriate diet and were supposedly risking their health by eating in such establishments. These attitudes were recalled 40 years later by *Saga Magazine* correspondents. One wrote that his mother firmly believed that chicken served in Chinese restaurants came from dead cats. She would not, under any circumstances, accept an invitation to eat in such a place. Another had heard the rumours that 'Kit Kat' cat food was served in Chinese restaurants, but was determined not to be influenced by them. A third remembered that in 1960, while still in bed after the birth of her third child, her husband had volunteered to get a Chinese takeaway, even though at that time tales were rife of people who ate Chinese food getting bones stuck in their throats which were later identified not as chicken bones, but cats' or even rats' bones.

The shift in British attitudes towards Chinese food came in the early 1960s. By 1965 Smethurst's National Catering Enquiry was reporting that 31 per cent of those who ate out regularly had visited Chinese restaurants, a figure which rose to 48 per cent for respondents in Liverpool. The corresponding figures for Indian restaurants were 8 per cent and for Italian and French restaurants 5 per cent each. In the same period Chinese restaurants began to figure in *The Good Food Guide*. The 1963–4 edition listed eight Chinese restaurants in a total of 164 restaurants in London which had satisfied the examiners.[33]

How Chinese restaurants and takeaways gained a foothold in localities which had no Chinese community may be illustrated by reference to developments in Manchester and Huddersfield in northern England. The first Chinese restaurant in Manchester, the Ping Hong, opened in Moseley Street in 1948, and two other Chinese restaurants opened in the city in the next few years. For reasons unknown, all three restaurants closed before the end of the 1950s. Between 1960 and 1964 fourteen new Chinese restaurants opened and a Chinatown began to develop in central Manchester. Five more restaurants started up in the 1970s and a further fourteen in the 1980s. By 1992 the number of Chinese restaurants in central Manchester had levelled out at 21. In 1970 Chinese supermarkets began to trade in the same area, and soon afterwards Chinese restaurants and takeaways opened across Greater Manchester, with a boom period in the 1970s and 1980s. By 1992 there were at least 400 Chinese takeaways and 60 restaurants in the area, which meant that there was at least one takeaway to every three square kilometres in the entire conurbation and at least one takeaway to every square kilometre in the central area. In some places three or four Chinese takeaways might be found along the same street, but the more common pattern was for takeaways to be scattered to cater for an essentially local market in 'low order' food. More than half of these takeaways were in premises formerly used as fish and chip shops. The most favoured locations were in areas with a high concentration of single households and students.[34]

In the 1950s Huddersfield, in West Yorkshire, was an important but declining textile manufacturing town. Its textile industry had received a temporary boost through the introduction of cheap labour from the Indian subcontinent, and the presence of Indian and Pakistani communities led to the opening of a few Asian shops and food outlets. It was in this context that Huddersfield's first Chinese restaurant, the Rice Bowl, opened its doors in 1957 or 1958. The premises, which had previously been used as a café, were in the town centre, near the railway station. The proprietor, who originated from Hong Kong, and his English wife, had come from Liverpool where there was already a range of established Chinese restaurants. From the start the owners encouraged English people to eat in the restaurant. On the opening day patrons were offered a steak lunch costing two shillings and sixpence. The restaurant followed the pattern already established in Chinese restaurants elsewhere in Britain of serving a three-course meal. The first course was soup, which came in various colours but always tasted the same. The main course might be the Rice Bowl 'special', which consisted of fried rice with mushrooms, bamboo shoots, water chestnuts, topped by a fried egg. This was followed by a 'pudding', usually ice cream or banana or jam fritters, served with custard made with water not milk. Later tinned lychees were added to the menu. Guests normally ate with knives and forks. The restaurant was licensed: one informant recalled that he took his fiancée to the Rice Bowl on Saturday nights and they always drank a bottle of Mateus Rosé with their meal. Patronage was also secured by accepting luncheon vouchers from local firms. The women employed by a company manufacturing dental equipment regularly ate their midday meal at the Rice Bowl, and apprentices from an engineering firm went to the Rice Bowl for a business lunch, which in the 1970s cost two shillings and sixpence. The successful opening of the Rice Bowl was followed shortly by the establishment of two other Chinese restaurants in the town centre. The Wah Yan restaurant, sited near the bus station, offered similar food and attracted a similar clientele to the Rice Bowl. In another part of the town the Hong Kong restaurant had a wider menu and was more expensive. Soon after these restaurants had become established, two Chinese takeaways opened on suburban streets.[35]

Why should Yorkshire people who had, and still have, a reputation for conservatism in many matters including food, have decided to risk eating Chinese food? Some of those who went first to the Rice Bowl had tried Chinese food during the war, when serving in the armed forces. Others had eaten their first Chinese meals at Chinese restaurants in neighbouring cities, notably Bradford and Leeds. For many of the clients, however, eating at the Rice Bowl was their first experience of Chinese food. The novelty of eating in such an establishment, and the opportunity to taste different sorts of food and different cooking methods were the main attractions. In northern towns, where in the past the usual choice of food when eating out was fish and chips, a Chinese restaurant offering a cheap and acceptable meal was an intriguing option.

The description of the food served in the Rice Bowl illustrates how Chinese restaurants and takeaways in Britain developed a stylized adaptation of Chinese cooking to suit British tastes and British purses. Prominent on the menu of many restaurants and most takeaways are chop suey dishes and chow mein dishes, which are Chinese American dishes. Other common dishes to be found on menus are 'char siu' (roast pork), sweet and sour meat and prawns and egg foo yung (omelettes). 'Egg foo yung' derives from a Guangzhouese dish in which the whites of eggs are used to create a delicate texture, *foo yung* meaning 'white lotus petals'. In Britain the yolks are also used and the result is an omelette. Dishes other than chow mein and fried rice are served with a choice of boiled rice or chips. Frozen peas, and the types of carrots and celery commonly available in Britain are substituted for authentic Chinese ingredients. Takeaway menus also offer 'special combination meals', set meals for two to four persons, which comprised appetizers, usually chicken and sweetcorn soup, spare ribs and prawn crackers and a selection of main dishes. Alongside the Chinese menu there is usually a range of curry dishes (thereby competing with Indian takeaways) and a limited choice of Western dishes.

Since the initial boom period, efforts have been made to attract a more discriminating Western custom to Chinese restaurants by improving the range and quality of food on offer. In 1966 the Beijing chef of an east London restaurant opened his own restaurant on Willesden High Road and began to serve north Chinese food there, an event which *The Good Food Guide* was later to describe as 'the most important cultural defection since Nureyev'.[36] In the 1970s Kenneth Lo attempted to encourage this tendency by organizing a Chinese Gourmet Club. In 1983 the Yang Sing in Manchester became the first ethnic restaurant to win the coveted *Good Food Guide* restaurant of the year award. In the 1980s, although most Chinese restaurants and takeaways continued to serve a Guangzhou-style cuisine, the number of restaurants serving regional Chinese food, notably Beijing-style or other north Chinese-style food increased. The majority of their customers were said to be European, not Chinese. Takeaways took the hint and their menus now included dishes such as Beijingese Chow Mein and Beijingese Chop Suey.

In the 1990s, in response to urban development, increasing affluence, and greater mobility, more sophisticated and more expensive Chinese restaurants began to be opened. This change began in London and Manchester and then spread to other large cities and towns. Maxi's Chinese Restaurant, which

Kenneth Lo at the Memories of China restaurant, London, in the late 1980s.

opened on the outskirts of Leeds in 1989, assumed that its customers would arrive by car and provided parking. Its proprietor, Raymond Wong, later opened similar establishments in York and Ripponden. These restaurants set out to provide quality food in a comfortable setting. They did not offer any specific Chinese cuisine, but in other ways claimed a degree of authenticity by expecting clients to use chopsticks and by not offering Western dishes alongside the Chinese menu.[37] Mr Pangs in Stamford offered dishes of lobster and monkfish and a vegetarian set dinner, a response to the growth of vegetarianism, particularly among young people. Another trend evident in the 1990s was an explicit rejection of the stereotype of Chinese food which had dominated the scene for the previous 30 years. The Yming in Greek Street, London, whose proprietress had played a leading role in the establishment of the school of Chinese cookery at Westminster College, set new standards of cooking and presentation of North Chinese food. Elsewhere noodles were hailed as the new universal food, and Chinese noodle houses offering soup noodles and fried noodles in either cheap or chic surroundings began to appear. At the chic end of the market, Jenny Lo's Tea House in Eccleston Street in Belgravia offered not only noodles, but also 'classy dumplings'. To accompany this food a 'Chinese medicine guru' had produced some bespoke teas.[38] The range of ethnic choice was extended, with restaurants describing themselves as Vietnamese, Malaysian and Singaporean. These offered the standard Chinese-restaurant menu, with the inclusion of dishes such as satay. Expensive restaurants, which aspired to cater for more sophisticated tastes and the desire for novelty, produced dishes which employed Chinese cooking methods and materials in an innovative fashion. Diners at The Orient at the China House, on Piccadilly in London, ate in an environment that was 'meditative and elegant'. They were offered dim sum and other

Chinese New Year Banquet for the Manchester Chamber of Commerce, Yang Sing Restaurant, Manchester, 2002.

dishes of which the 'primary cooking influences' might be Chinese, but the presentation and sometimes the structure of the dishes was more reminiscent of Japanese cuisine.[39]

New levels of investment were achieved in the late 1990s with the opening of a string of restaurants and cafés in London and southern England owned by the Oriental Restaurant Group PLC, a company quoted on the London Stock Exchange. The restaurants served menus designed by Ken Hom, referred to as 'our consulting chef', which included dishes of Chinese, Malay, Thai and Japanese origin. The Oriental Restaurant Group also owned Yellow River Cafés, the first two branches of which were opened in late 1999 in Chiswick and Canary Wharf, with other branches opening later in Guildford, Reading and Portsmouth. The food served was described as 'high quality, healthy, accessible, modern Oriental food with tastes from China, Malaysia, Thailand and Singapore'. Each café was decorated in the distinctive Yellow River interior design, with dark woods, bamboo, tea house booths, silk lanterns and Chinese pigments. A children's menu was provided with Ken Hom stressing his belief that children should learn healthy eating habits from an early age. The sale of a range of Yellow River merchandise, including T-shirts, baseball caps and mini-footballs, was a further inducement to bring children to the café. A takeaway and delivery service was available, the food being packaged in 'reheatable oriental-style bento boxes' despatched by uniformed members of staff riding Japanese motorcycles.[40] The idea that a Chinese restaurant in the West should be a family restaurant was still a novelty in England, although it has long been the practice in the United States and has also been used in Japan, for example in Chinese restaurants in Yokohama.[41]

Substantial investment has also led to the opening in Britain and elsewhere of Chinese restaurants which emphasize conspicuous consumption and fashion trends and which offer a *nouvelle* Chinese cuisine. A significant part of the capital investment and culinary influence in this new development derives from Hong Kong. A notable example of this trend was the opening in London in 1998 of the Jen Restaurant which proclaimed that its objective was to serve the best Hong Kong style food available.

The phrase 'Hong Kong style' requires some explanation. According to Sidney Cheung, a Hong Kong identity began to emerge in the late 1960s and by the late 1970s not only had Hong Kong society become visibly cosmopolitan, but also a modified Guangzhouese cuisine had emerged which 'combined exotic or expensive ingredients and western catering'.[42] It is this cuisine which is now offered to a cosmopolitan customer base in Britain. The most up-market of this new generation of Chinese restaurants in central London is the Hakkasan Restaurant which opened in April 2001. Many aspects of the Hakkasan, from its design to its menu, were planned to contrast with the stereotype of the Chinese restaurant in the West. Entry to the restaurant is down two flights of green slate stairs, which lead to a large reception hall illuminated by floating candles and decorated with lilies in tall glass vases. The restaurant itself is inside a carved wooden cage. Every attention is paid to image: brightly coloured food is served on large white platters, the piped music is modern soul or pop, the clientele is young, besuited and upbeat. Many of the staff and the majority of the customers are not Chinese. As for the food, it combines elements derived from traditional Hakka Chinese cooking – which is distinguished by its use of greater quantities of meat and ingredients such as pickled vegetables – with food items derived from the West, a combination exemplified by dishes such as 'Bird's nest and foie gras soup with wolfberry'. An appeal is made to the organic market with a claim that organic pork is used. [43]

The extent to which Chinese food in Britain has been modified to suit British tastes and eating habits may also be gauged by brief reference to Chinese food in Western Europe. A few Chinese restaurants had opened in France after the First World War, and between 1954 and 1975 more were opened in the Latin Quarter and other central Paris locations. It was not until between 1975 and 1987, when over 145,000 refugees arrived from Indochina, of whom between 50 and 60 per cent were ethnic Chinese, that a substantial Chinese food industry began to develop. By 1992 there were 728 Chinese restaurants in Paris and catering had become the dominant Chinese economic activity in the capital.[44] France, of course, takes a deep pride in its *patrimoine culinaire* and for a foreign cuisine to make significant inroads into French eating habits some concessions had to be made to that pride. As it happened the 1980s was the decade when fast-food establishments began to spread rapidly in France. Many of these were American, or copies of American fast-food outlets, and were viewed as a threat to France's traditional culinary practices. This issue distracted attention from the spread of Vietnamese-Chinese food, which in some respects conformed more closely to French eating habits, for example in terms of family restaurants offering a *menu à prix fixe*. The range of dishes served also showed some modification to suit French tastes. That of La Couronne Royale, a restaurant and takeaway in Chalon-sur-Saône, listed '*rouleau de printemps*', spring rolls, sweet and sour prawns and chop suey, and the desserts included banana fritters. But it also offered frogs' legs cooked with ginger and chives, and there was a gesture towards healthy eating with the inclusion of salads. It is often said that Chinese restaurateurs in France are aware that the French have higher expectations of food than do the British, and some support is given to this view by the inclusion on the menu of a range of '*specialités à la vapeur*', that is dim sum.

The acceptance of Chinese food in the Netherlands was influenced by Dutch colonialism in South-east Asia. A number of Chinese-Indonesian restaurants had opened in the 1930s, but after the independence of Indonesia in 1949, and the return to Holland of members of the Dutch colonial élite and demobilized Dutch soldiers who had acquired a taste for eastern cooking, the number of Chinese restaurants rose spectacularly. They offered Chinese food – or Chinese food adapted to suit the Dutch taste and varied according to the price of ingredients – and added Indonesian dishes to the menu, or offered *rijsttafel*, a selection of dishes accompanied by hot sauces. As the Netherlands had no tradition of affordable restaurants for ordinary people and there was no competition from other ethnic groups, Chinese-Indonesian restaurants soon acquired a monopoly of the ethnic food market. Then in the late 1950s and early 1960s Hong Kong Chinese, anticipating that the British catering market was getting saturated, began to move to the Netherlands. By 1982 there were 1,916 Chinese-Indonesian restaurants, one for every 7,500 inhabitants. But in the 1980s the Netherlands suffered a general economic crisis, and the restaurant boom collapsed. By now Chinese-Indonesian restaurants had so adjusted to Dutch tastes that spring rolls, fried rice and noodles practically counted as Dutch food. The catering business was subject to scandals about hygiene and allegations of connections with organized crime. Non-Chinese foreign restaurants, which offered a novel and therefore more attractive option for 'eating out', gained ground. Only in the 1990s when a younger generation of Chinese entrepreneurs set out to improve the quality of Chinese food and to present it in a more attractive environment, did recovery begin.[45]

In Germany modification to suit German preferences is more evident in the types of food outlets than in the food served. In Berlin three types of Chinese food outlets may be found: restaurants, snack bars and takeaways often described as 'China Imbiss' and fast-food self-service outlets. In German Chinese restaurants there is an emphasis on an attractive environment, nearly always with an aquarium as a feature, on efficient service and on generous quantities of food. Meals invariably conclude with a complimentary glass of *pflaumenwein*, plum wine. A China Imbiss resembles a hamburger stall, but the food sold is Chinese food served in foil cartons, while the Chinese fast-food cafés are organized like other fast-food outlets, offering a range of Chinese dishes at self-service counters.[46]

HOW TO COOK AND EAT IN CHINESE

The spread of Chinese food through the Western world has occurred not only through the opening of Chinese restaurants and takeaways but also through attempts by Westerners to cook Chinese food for themselves. These attempts have been facilitated by the publication of recipe books, the broadcast of radio and television programmes giving instructions on the techniques of Chinese cooking and by the greater availability of Chinese foodstuff in various forms in shops and supermarkets.

The first recipe books for Chinese food written in English appeared in the United States in the 1920s and 1930s. *Chinese Recipes* by A. Moore was published in New York in 1923 and the

Mandarin Chop Suey Cookbook, author unknown, was published in Chicago in 1928. Corinne Lamb's *The Chinese Festive Board*, previously discussed, was published in Shanghai in 1935. Perhaps the first Chinese recipe books aimed at a wider Western audience were Buwei Yang Chao, *How to Cook and Eat in Chinese*, the first edition of which was not dated, but which probably appeared in 1945, and M. P. Lee, *Chinese Cookery*, published in New York in 1945. Lee's book, which contained 'practical recipes', was illustrated by Chiang Yee, author of the popular *Silent Traveller* books, which described the artist's impressions of the West.

In 1949 Agnes Ingle, in a talk on Woman's Hour on the BBC, struck a positive note on the subject of Chinese food. She began by comparing food preferences. A Chinese friend had told her that his most difficult adjustment to English life was eating pieces of cold meat. Her bugbear at Chinese dinners had been 'boiling hot sea-slugs'. She then suggested that 'In our present meat-starved menus, the Chinese way with food can give use some practical and interesting ideas.' In China meat was always sliced in the kitchen and used in savoury vegetable stews. Sometimes, when she had only a little 'off the ration' cold meat she copied this idea. She chopped up the meat, put it into a prepared gravy, added some onions or sliced greens previously fried with a morsel of bacon and boiled some rice or macaroni to eat with it. 'It's very tasty, and can almost make a Chinese homesick!' This mixture could also be put into cases of noodle dough and boiled in salted water. She then gave an enthusiastic account of Chinese ways of cooking fish, of how to prepare Peking Duck, known to foreigners as 'ducks and d'oyleys', and how to make the traditional sweet called the 'Eight Precious Things'. She concluded by saying that a good Chinese cook grudged neither his time nor his labour. The common Chinese greeting was not 'Lovely day,' or 'Good afternoon,' but 'Have you eaten food?' 'They know that food has a lot to do with the making of a good day and if you've had the luck to be greeted like this, you will remember how the warmth of it curls right round your heart.'[47]

Two books published in 1952 indicate the persistence of contrasting attitudes towards cooking Chinese food. *Chinese Cookery Secrets* by Esther Chan contained a foreword by

Front cover of Esther Chan, *Chinese Cookery Secrets* (Singapore, 1953).

Malcolm MacDonald, the British Commissioner General of South East Asia, and son of Britain's first Labour Prime Minister. MacDonald wrote 'To eat a Chinese dinner is to enjoy one of the truly delicious pleasures of life.' He referred to the Chinese as artists, and said that they displayed 'their noble creative gift as truly in the cooking of food as in carving jade, casting bronze, shaping porcelain, fashioning calligraphy and painting pictures.' The compiler of the recipe book, Esther Chan, had previously been employed by the United States Military Advisory Group in Nanjing, where she had held a cookery class. After the Communist victory in 1949 she moved to Singapore and some of her recipes appeared in the *Straits Times*. She claimed that it was in response to readers' requests that she had decided to publish her recipes. Her book began with information on cooking utensils, foodstuffs, seasoning, cooking methods and suggested menus. There followed some 300 recipes, many of which used readily available ingredients and which were simply prepared. Some, however, were more demanding. The recipe for Steamed Turtle began 'Kill the

Three types of Chinese kitchen, from Chan, *Chinese Cookery Secrets*.

turtle', that for Sea Blubber Skin with Turnip Shreds stated that the blubber skins should be washed in hot water and the red stuff on the skin should be pulled off. Mrs Chan was aware of Western tastes and included a section on chop suey, which she conceded was probably a dish invented in America, commenting 'The reason for its popularity is that probably it has no strong flavour or taste of any kind, and is, therefore, more easily acceptable to Western palates.' She added that the dish 'gives Westerners an idea of novelty and a kind of exotic experience although it is not a genuine Chinese dish, yet being quite distinct from Western food'. Other comments echoed such colonial attitudes towards Chinese food. 'Nowadays,' she wrote, 'in modern Chinese homes, some of the utensils employed for cooking are almost the same as in any Western home, but many are still bereft of modern cooking equipment.'[48]

Chinese cooking utensils, from Chan, *Chinese Cookery Secrets*.

On the other hand Doreen Yen Hung Feng's book, *The Joy of Chinese Cooking*, published in London and New York, set out to introduce Westerners to the joys of 'preparing and indulging in the tastiness of Chinese dishes'. She assured her readers that there was 'no mystery involved in Chinese cooking' unless knowing what ingredients to use and where to buy them might be termed a mystery. That was merely a matter of information which her book, she hoped, would reveal and so 'bring joy, excitement, and a little bit of China' into her readers' kitchens, homes and lives. She explained Chinese methods of cooking and illustrated her points with her own illustrations. She stressed the need for maximum preparation, neatness and systematic arrangement, for these would 'smooth the road toward the joy of Chinese cooking'. The pleasure of cooking came from training oneself to dispense with the measuring spoon and eventually to

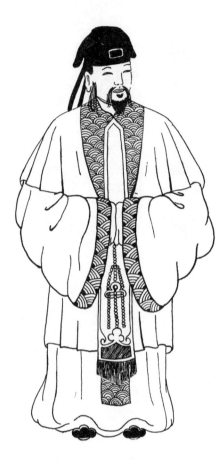

The God of the Kitchen, from the *Joy of Chinese Cooking*.

How to hold chopsticks, from Doreen Yen Hung Feng, *Joy of Chinese Cooking* (London, 1966).

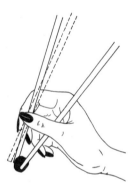

be able to cook with 'dabs and pinches and indulge in your own gifts of ingenious inventiveness'. The recipes which followed were demanding and their authenticity appeared assured because each dish was given its Chinese name with a romanization of the Guangzhouese pronunciation. The recipe for Casserole of Mushroom Squabs sounded straightforward, assuming that squabs could be obtained. However her cook, a man of great importance, had tried in vain to teach her to recognize 'a certain squeal of rawness issuing from the sizzling hot oil', which indicated that the birds were cooked to a juicy tender finish on the inside. Despite these considerable challenges to the amateur cook, Doreen Yen Hung Feng's book was well received and was reissued by the Cookery Book Club in 1966.[49]

However, Mary Mather, who gave a talk on BBC radio in 1953, was not convinced that genuine Chinese meals could be reproduced by Westerners in the West. It seemed as much out of place as 'those pathetic parties in Hong Kong where English people stand round in one another's drawing rooms, eating fish and chips with their fingers out of the South China Morning newspaper'. For the Chinese, food was not only something to satisfy hunger, it had a social and ritual position as well. Her own Chinese guests, most of whom were students, never expected much of English food and often brought something of their own to supplement it. On one occasion a girl student had brought a very lively hen in a carrier bag. She had taken it into the yard, cut its throat, plucked and cleaned it. She had then given instructions how it should be cooked: first rubbed with a mixture of spring onions, ginger, sugar and soy sauce, then steamed, glazed and finally deep fried. 'As you may imagine, though the flesh was tender and piquant, it was the skin, crisp and golden, which was the most delicious.'[50]

Notwithstanding the alleged demands and difficulties associated with cooking Chinese food, by 1966 at least another twenty Chinese cookbooks had been published in English in the United States and other parts of the world. They included Yep Yung Hee, *Chinese Recipes for Home Cooking* (Sydney, 1953), which contained a foreword from the Consul-General of the Republic of China, who assured readers that eating Chinese food was not necessarily an expression of sympathy for the Communist regime in China. In London in 1955 Kenneth Lo, who was to become one of the most prolific writers on Chinese food, published, *Cooking the Chinese Way*. Three years later, in New York, Calvin Lee's *Chinese Cooking for American Kitchens* appeared. This contained 150 'easy recipes' with instructions on how to buy the ingredients required. Many Chinese cookbooks referred to the 'art' and 'secrets' of Chinese cooking and both terms appeared in the title *The Art and Secrets of Chinese Cooking*, published in the United States in 1959, which came with the compliments of La Choy foods, an indication of the growing importance of the Chinese food industry. In the meantime the appeal of cooking Chinese food had been extended in other directions. Lee Su Jan's *The Fine Art of Chinese Cooking*

(New York, 1961) was said to cover 'the philosophy and art of over twenty-two centuries of oriental cooking written in practical terms for the American kitchen'. These recipes were a combination of 'pure Chinese', American dishes with 'a Chinese flavor', and 'Chinese treats adapted to the American palate'. Two years later the first Chinese kosher cookbook was published.

Until the late 1960s Western enthusiasm for things Chinese was restrained by political considerations. After the Cultural Revolution had abated, attitudes began to change, an alteration which coincided with changing lifestyles in the West and increasing affluence. This was marked by the publication of coffee-table books such as *Chinese Cooking* by Emily Hahn, whose autobiography about her life in China, *China to Me*, has already been quoted. She prefaced her cookbook by explaining how she had first encountered Chinese food in the 1930s.

> I grew up in the Mid-West with the firm conviction that it was wrong to take an interest in food . . . There was I, nourished on steak, pot roast, apple pie à la mode, banana split, and (on football days) waffles with a heathen mixture of sausages and syrup. There was I, suddenly face to face with the ancient, honourable and superlative cuisine of the world's oldest civilization. Inevitably the result of the confrontation was a complete transformation of one opinionated Mid-Westerner to whom all food, but especially Chinese food, suddenly became a brilliant revelation.

Emily Hahn was anxious to make a political point about Chinese cooking. Before the Communist revolution, she declared, 'Chinese cooking had always been something understood and loved by all classes. It made something good and healthful of ordinary ingredients, and the poorest man, though he rarely had enough, could have something that tasted good when he did have food.' In the Cultural Revolution the Red Guards had 'attacked every symbol of what they regarded as bourgeois culture'. They had forced restaurants to burn their menu cards and substitute 'standardized lists of commune food'. Her recipe book was based on 'the old dishes and methods', and was intended to preserve the best of Chinese cooking, which she described as 'a triumphant blending of inventiveness, flavour and economy'. Chinese and French cuisines were widely regarded as the two greatest cuisines, but she – and many other former devotees of French cooking – had concluded that Chinese was better.[51]

After Richard Nixon's visit to China in February 1972 there was a surge in the publication of books about Chinese cookery. In the next two years at least 26 new Chinese recipe books appeared in the United States and Britain. Some of these emphasized that Chinese cooking was quick and easy and could be tackled by anyone. Others claimed that the recipes printed were authentic, that they revealed secrets of Chinese cooking and that a gourmet would be satisfied with the results. Two introduced Chinese vegetarian cooking and others described Chinese regional cooking. Well-known chefs and food critics appeared in the media and published their own recipe books. Craig Claiborne, the food editor of *The New York Times*, and Virginia Lee produced *The Chinese Cookbook*, which for long was to be regarded as the most accurate and authentic Chinese cookery book available in the United States. Claiborne's description of how he began cooking Chinese food resembled a religious conversion. During the Depression he had been taken to a big city where he had eaten a memorable Chinese meal. The food he ate on that occasion, he now realized, was probably 'quite spurious, adapted to the southern palate, and dreadful'. But it had 'kindled a flame'. After the war he had trained in French cookery at a Swiss hotel. French cookery, though without end in its variations, had techniques which could be mastered. On the other hand, the Chinese kitchen was 'as involved and interwoven as a bucket of boiling noodles'. But then he met Virginia Lee, who had taught him that Chinese cooking was by no means an impossible art. From her, 'one of the great natural cooking experts of this age', he had been afforded a glimpse into China's culture and philosophy through its cuisine.[52]

After the interest engendered by Nixon's visit to China had died down, the output of books on Chinese cooking slowed. In 1989, the year of the Tiananmen Square massacre, only two new titles appeared. The body of published literature was by now extensive, and new authors had to find fresh angles on the subject. One such angle was to link Chinese food with healthy eating. Perhaps the first book to exploit this connection was Ruth Rodale Spira, *Naturally Chinese: Healthful Cooking from China*, published in 1972. Over the next few years other titles were to offer low-calorie and low-cholesterol Chinese recipes. By the 1980s doubts about the efficacy of Western medicine led to an interest in alternative treatments. The long-established connection in Chinese thought between diet and health came into its own. In 1983 Bob Flaws and Honora Lee Wolfe published *Prince Wen Hui's Cook: Chinese Dietary Therapy* which set diet in the context of Chinese classical medicine. Cecilia Tan in *Family Herbal Cookbook: A Guide to the Ancient Chinese Philosophy of Food and Health*, 1995, pursued a similar theme. *Selected Ancient Chinese Recipes*, translated from the Chinese and published in Beijing in 1997 contained an extensive list of recipes divided into various disease categories.

The therapeutic and philosophical implications of eating were explored further in two books both published in 1999. In *Feng Shui Food* Steven Saunders and Simon Brown explained 'how to create dishes that not only taste sensational but can also bring about positive changes in your life.' In *The Tao of Food* Richard Craze and Roni Jay declared their intention to be to look at ways of improving our diet according to the principles of Chinese Daoist philosophy. These principles included the concept of *qi*, or energy, and the classifying of foodstuffs as *yin* or *yang* according to the type of energy each type of food contains. Daoism, they wrote, was about simplicity. In the ideal Daoist kitchen one would cook on a log fire using timber one had felled oneself. Such a return to nature was not practical, but what was simple and natural should always be preferred. Food should be fresh, cooked plainly and served simply with due regard to texture and colour. The recipes which followed were accompanied by frequent references to the *yin* or *yang* qualities of the dishes and employed Chinese cooking practices, but the resultant dishes were far removed from traditional Chinese food.

In the meantime other trends had emerged in the continuing output of Chinese cookery books. So Yan-kit, a food historian, combined academic rigour with a flair for cooking in her *Classic Chinese Cookbook* (1984). Celebrity chefs published recipes they had devised which brought together the ingredients and techniques of Asia and the West, a practice known as 'cross-cultural cooking'. Ken Hom started this in *East Meets West* (1987), which he dedicated to 'my Chinese mother and my French family'. A recent example of this genre is *Blue Ginger: East Meets West* (1999), by Ming Tsai, the proprietor of the Blue Ginger restaurant in Massachusetts. Another trend, initiated in 1970 by Kenneth Lo in *Chinese Regional Cooking*, was to write cookery books based on a single cuisine.[53] A recent example of this genre is Fuchsia Dunlop's *Sichuan Cookery* (2001), which she describes as 'one of the great unknown cuisines of the world'. 'These dishes,' she wrote, 'are simply so different from any Chinese food most people in Europe have ever tasted.'[54]

THE AVAILABILITY OF CHINESE FOOD IN THE WEST

When Westerners began to try cooking Chinese food, their first problem was how to obtain the correct ingredients. Chinese grocery stores, an obvious source for imported Chinese foodstuffs, had existed in areas of Chinese settlement in the United States and Canada from the nineteenth century onwards and by the 1930s a Chinese grocery could be found in many American towns and cities. But it was still difficult for Westerners to use these stores to buy the ingredients to cook Chinese food. In *The Joy of Chinese Cooking* Doreen Yen Hung Feng made light of this difficulty, claiming that wherever there was more than one Chinese family in a city or town abroad, there was almost inevitably a Chinese restaurant or grocery shop in the vicinity. From the grocery shop, she advised, one could get what one wanted by pointing. If the certain cuts of meat and varieties of fresh vegetables could not be obtained, substitutes could often be found without too much difficulty or harm to the recipe. Bean sprouts could be grown in one's own kitchen. Many Chinese sauces, including soy sauce, oyster sauce, black and red bean sauce, could be bought in bottles or cans.

'Jan-U-Wine' recipe book, Los Angeles, *c*. 1955.

In the 1930s a few Chinese stores might be found in London and Liverpool, and Asian foodstuffs might also be bought at the Bombay Emporium in Grafton Way, London W1, but it was not until the 1960s that the ingredients of Chinese food began to become more widely available in Britain. The change, when it came, was rapid. By 1969 Chinese provision stores could be found in Liverpool, Birmingham, Bradford, Middlesborough and Leeds. The main importer of Chinese food from the People's Republic of China was Biddle Sawyer of Fitzroy Street, London. In the same year Emily Hahn claimed that only two

Chinese ingredients - winter melon and *sao ma* (meat dumpling wrappers) could not be bought in Britain.[55] By 1972 all the utensils and ingredients for cooking Chinese food were obtainable at Loon Fung's in Gerrard Street in London, but outside London it was still extremely difficult to buy Chinese ingredients, even in canned or bottled form. In the late 1970s British stores such as Marks & Spencer began to recognize the potential of the ethnic food market and introduced Chinese food to their shelves, and this move was soon copied by the major supermarket chains.

The great engine which was to expand the consumption of Chinese food was its industrial production. Two of the first companies to move into this field in the United States were Jan-U-Wine in Los Angeles and La Choy in Archbold, Ohio. In a recipe booklet published in 1955 to advertise its products, Jan-U-Wine claimed to have been producing 'America's finest Chinese foods' for over half a century, at first by supplying food to Chinese restaurants. It had recently completed construction of a new million-dollar plant in Los Angeles, which incorporated extensive laboratory facilities for food research and product development. Visitors to its plant, the booklet remarked, were amazed at the sight of its hydroponic farm which could produce 100 tons of bean sprouts a day. Among the tinned goods the firm sold were ready-made meals including Chicken Chow Mein and Beef Chop Suey and ingredients for Chinese cooking, including water chestnuts and bamboo shoots. It also marketed a 'triple-pac' of three tins of Chinese food for a 'Mandarin Banquet'.[56] La Choy Food traced its history back to 1920, when its co-founders began to grow bean sprouts for sale at a grocery store. In 1937 the firm bought its own plant in Detroit, but this was requisitioned during the war for the manufacture of rifles. The firm moved to Archbold and expanded its operations to the point that in 2001 its hydroponic gardens were producing 1.5 million pounds of fresh bean sprouts. The company now describes itself as 'America's Taste of Asia Since 1920'. Chun King, another brand name well known in the United States, was producing canned chop suey in the 1950s. In Britain much of the manufactured Chinese food consumed was produced by the Amoy Canning Corporation, founded in Xiamen (Amoy) China in 1908. By the 1950s the company was marketing a wide range of soy sauces and tinned vegetables and fruit, and by the 1980s its products, which included 34 sauces, had their biggest markets in the United States, Britain and Japan. By then it had also moved into convenience foods in the form of prepared meals such as Crispy Wontons filled with Prawn and Bamboo Shoots, which were sold alongside Marks & Spencer's chilled foods. In 1977 G. Costa and Co. Ltd, originally an importer of speciality foods from India, introduced the Blue Dragon brand in Britain, which in time covered 400 oriental products, including noodles and a variety of cooking sauces and bottled sauces. Blue Dragon's most popular innovation was the introduction, in 1986, of stir-fry sauces in sachets.

In the 1970s, when women's magazines in the North America and the United Kingdom started to print recipes for Chinese meals, large food stores and supermarkets began to stock the ingredients for cooking Chinese meals, for example tinned water chestnuts and bamboo shoots. At about the same time mainstream food manufacturers began to move into the field of Chinese food, a lead which was followed shortly by supermarket chains with their own brands of Chinese food. In so doing they were following a path already trodden by manufacturers of ready-to-eat Indian meals. Vesta curries – to which

Chinese cooking is . . .

SIMPLE The Chinese are a nation of epicures who have always regarded the preparation of food as being worthy of serious study, and in the course of centuries of experiment they have evolved a method of cooking which is quite unique in its subtle use of contrast and harmony of flavour to please the palate and stimulate the appetite. But in spite of all this Chinese cooking is not complicated. NO SPECIAL UTENSILS ARE NEEDED and if you use the high quality carefully prepared ingredients supplied by the AMOY CANNING CORPORATION and follow the simple instructions contained in this booklet, you will quickly become expert in the preparation of delicious Chinese dishes which will be popular with your family and establish your reputation for originality as a hostess.

'Chinese Cooking is . . . SIMPLE', from an *Introduction to Chinese Cooking* published by Amoy Canning Corporation (Hong Kong) in the 1950s.

one just had to add water – were introduced by Batchelor's in 1961. A decade later Homepride Foods began to manufacture their own versions of Chinese food, including a tinned cook-in sweet and sour sauce. In the early 1980s, by which time the demand for Chinese food ingredients had begun to rise sharply, enterprising British vegetable growers realized that British supermarkets could now sell bean sprouts. A dual market developed, with Chinese growers supplying Chinese restaurants with bulk supplies of bean sprouts, and British growers selling small packages of bean sprouts to supermarkets. As a result bean sprouts lost their direct connection with Chinese food.[57]

By 1990 the *British Food Journal* was remarking on the rapidity of the growth in the ethnic food market in the United Kingdom and discussing reasons for this. The rate of growth far outstripped the increase in the Indian or Chinese population, so rising demand from either community was not the explanation. The increase in foreign travel, which gave many people the opportunity to try new foods, might well be a factor though the premise had yet to be tested. The attention paid to Indian and Chinese food, by media 'stars' such as Madhur Jaffrey and Kenneth Lo undoubtedly encouraged people to experiment with flavours perhaps first encountered in a restaurant, and this tendency was reinforced by the growth in the cookery book market, with expenditure on Indian and Chinese cookery books now estimated at 30 per cent of the market. In addition the rise in consumers' disposable incomes and leisure time enabled them to eat out more and to experiment more freely with home cooking. These reasons, the journal noted were consumer led but 'the most significant influences on penetration may well be those which are "push" or producer led'. In 1984 the imposition of value-added tax on hot takeaway foods had curtailed the sale of Chinese and Indian food, but the increase of disposable incomes had overcome this and media promotion and improved manufacturing, distributing and retailing practices had all contributed to the increase in sales of ethnic foods. The article concluded by relating the growth of ethnic foods to marketing theory. Traditional sources of diffusion assumed that an innovation only existed in one or a small number of formats. However ethnic food existed in five formats simultaneously:

restaurant, takeaway, total meal, precursor and commodity, formats differentiated by levels of added value. Total diffusion would only be reached when 100 per cent of potential customers had used the product in one or more of the five basic formats.[58]

This confident assessment of the potential for growth of the ethnic food market was vindicated in the 1990s. By 1993 *The Grocer* was reporting that 'Indian, Chinese, Italian, Mexican and other foods now figure in the daily diet of consumers,' who were progressing from using cooking sauces to preparing their own exotic meals. Indian food remained the most popular ethnic food, but the sale of Chinese cuisine, which 'could not be more suited to today's consumer' as it was healthy as well as quick and easy to cook, was increasing at a rate of 20 per cent year on year. In 1998, although growth in the ethnic food market remained buoyant, that of Chinese food had slowed, with expenditure on liquid sauces and noodles, the largest areas within the sector, both declining. But by 2001 sales of Chinese food, in particular sales of ready meals, were again rising, perhaps because of an association with healthy eating. At the same time 'authenticity' as a selling point was being replaced by 'regionality', which in Chinese food meant reference to provinces such as Sichuan, or to Singaporean or Malaysian food.[59] The estimated value of the Chinese food market in the United Kingdom in 2001 was £348 million, an increase of 71 per cent over five years. A *Market Intelligence* report on the ethnic food boom commented:

> All sectors are expanding, driven by changing consumer eating habits, more disposable income and continuing desire for quick meal preparation. Consumers are looking for more variety in their main meal occasions but want to spend less time cooking meals – particularly during the week.

The increased consumption of Chinese food was aided by 'a growing preference for fresh or freshly prepared food which has given a boost to stir-frying and the use of woks'. Consumers were demanding more authentic flavours in their ethnic meals and were moving away from basic recipes such as Sweet and

Sour towards a wider range of authentic regional flavours and recipes.

The same report gave the results of consumer research conducted in March 2001 concerning Chinese food. This showed that 59 per cent of adults surveyed had stated that Chinese food was among their favourite types of food, which placed it ahead of Indian and Italian food and second only in order of preference to British food. The Chinese food consumer profile had a more female bias than that of Indian food and consumers were most likely to live in London and the Midlands and least likely to live in the South, in Scotland and in the North West. By now 65 per cent of British households owned a wok, and this, coupled with the greater availability of cooking sauces, noodles and accompaniments (for example, prawn crackers) allowed customers to create a Chinese meal at home more easily and more successfully. The fastest growing sector of the market was Chinese chilled ready-meals sold in supermarkets, which raised the question whether the Chinese takeaway sector, which had hitherto acted as a brake on the expansion of the retail sector, was under threat. In future Chinese takeaways might be used more as a replacement for restaurants, for example on special meal occasions, rather than a source of food on ordinary occasions. More encouragingly for Chinese working in the food industry, the survey showed that whereas the customers for Indian food tended to be younger and more concentrated in the better-off sub-groups, the consumers of Chinese food were spread across all ages under 65 and across all socio-economic groups.[60]

EIGHT

On the Globalization of Chinese Food

This survey of how and when Chinese food spread throughout the Western world has raised many questions on why, and in what manner, this has occurred. In this chapter some of these questions will be discussed, for the most part, on the grounds of space and familiarity, with reference to the British experience. An attempt will then be made to locate the acceptance of Chinese food in the Western world in the wider discussion of globalization.

One theme that can only be touched on in a study of this length is the comparison of the spread of Chinese food with that of other national or ethnic cuisines. In the Western world the cuisine which first and most influentially spread beyond national borders was of course that of France. In Britain in the eighteenth century the attractions and repulsions of French cooking were already commonplace topics of comment. The British aristocracy employed French cooks, but chauvinistic comments about French food abounded. In 1748 William Hogarth published a popular print, *The Gate of Calais*, which depicted a massive joint of beef as a symbol of English freedom amid the misery of French enslavement.[1] Samuel Johnson was also critical. After a visit to France in 1775 he observed that the meat in the markets of Paris was such as would be sent to gaol in England, and he quoted with approval his friend the brewer Henry Thrale, who had observed that 'The cookery of the French was forced upon them by necessity; for they could not eat their meat, unless they added some taste to it.'[2] Despite such disparaging remarks, which included objections to what the French ate, notably snails' and frogs' legs, as well as criticisms of French standards of hygiene, French cuisine remained a synonym for sophisticated eating through the nineteenth century and into the modern age.

A closer comparison to the record of the globalization of Chinese food may be found in the introduction of Indian food to the West and in particular to Britain, where it has achieved a remarkable level of acceptance. This acceptance had its origins in the establishment of the British presence in India and the experience of eating Indian food by employees of the British East India Company resident there. When they arrived in India in the seventeenth century, English cooking was still heavily reliant on spices, and as a consequence they found spiced Indian food readily acceptable. Chillies had been introduced into India from South America in the sixteenth century, but it was not until some time later that Indian food became characteristically hot. At first this too was congenial to the British who ate heavy meals with large quantities of curried meat and poultry. By the eighteenth century the British in India had developed 'indian-ized habits', eating a version of Indian food, chewing betel nut as an aid to digestion and wearing Indian clothes. These habits were brought to England by East India Company employees on leave or after retirement. Curry is said to have appeared on the menu of the Norris Street Coffee House in the Haymarket as early as 1773. The most celebrated eater of curry in literature, the Collector of Boggley Wallah in William Makepeace Thackeray's novel *Vanity Fair* (1847–8), thought it amusing to ply his unsuspecting guests with hot curries.[3]

However in the nineteenth century the atmosphere of heightened imperialism and racial superiority led the British in India increasingly to reject Indian food. French cuisine became fashionable and curries were relegated to luncheon rather than dinner fare. Indian cooks were called upon to produce elaborate versions of Western cooking, and meals were served *à la russe*, that is to say as a sequence of courses, rather than all dishes being placed on the table at the same time, as was the Indian custom. Foods imported from Europe figured increasingly in the British diet. As early as 1830 tinned hare pâté from Perigord was available in Simla, and by 1891 the Army & Navy Stores in Bombay could supply a wide variety of preserved foods by mail order.

In India and in Britain, from quite an early date, the Western menu included hybrid dishes which could claim an Indian origin, but which had been modified to suit the British taste. Kedgeree, a dish originally composed of daal, rice and spices, had by the eighteenth century been transformed by the addition of hard-boiled eggs and fish, which when served in Britain was smoked haddock. Mulligatawny, which in Tamil means 'pepper water', had been introduced into Britain as a soup in the early nineteenth century and by the middle of the century tins of 'mulligatawny paste' were on sale. Worcester sauce derived from an Indian recipe and piccalilli was an imitation of Indian chutney, the English word deriving from the Hindi *chatni*. That elements of Indian cookery had become acceptable to the English palate was demonstrated most clearly by the inclusion of a recipe for chicken curry and chickpeas in Mrs Beeton's *The Book of Household Management*, first published in 1861.[4]

The popularization of Indian food in Britain and to a lesser extent in countries throughout the world was still a long way ahead. The oldest surviving Indian restaurant in Britain, Veeraswamy's, was opened in Regent Street in 1926 by Edward Palmer, whose family had lived in India for four generations. According to a customer who ate at the restaurant in the 1950s, 'There seemed nothing authentic about the food. I thought it was specially prepared for the British palate.' By 1938 there was a well-established restaurant, the Kohinoor, in Cambridge. At about the same time recipe books directed at a domestic British audience and containing instructions on how to cook authentic Indian food – that is, going further than adding a pinch of curry powder to a dish – began to be published. A new style of Indian restaurants emerged in the 1950s. In 1954 Shamsuddin Khan acquired an Italian restaurant in Clapham. At first he continued with the Italian menu and then gradually added a few curries.[5] By the late 1950s Indian restaurants offering cheap and substantial meals to a largely student clientele were to be found in Oxford and Cambridge and some other university cities. In 1964 Tassaduq Ahmed, a key figure in the Bengali language movement, which was to play a part in the creation of Bangladesh in 1971, opened the Ganges Restaurant in Gerrard Street. By 1970 there were some 2,000 Indian restaurants in

Britain and in the next decade restaurants and takeaways offering Indian food spread rapidly to all parts of the country, the great majority of them being run by Bangladeshis from Sylhet. Indian food, like Chinese, was adapted to suit Western palates and to economize in terms of costs. The most famous example of this adaptation, the dish known as chicken tikka masala, is said to date from the mid-1970s and to be a response to an English demand for chicken tikka to be served with 'gravy'. It was not long before tins of tikka masala cooking sauce were being produced, and in 1999 Burger King launched a Masala Burger. Balti cooking, in which the food is cooked and served in small metal dishes, may have originated in Birmingham in the 1980s. As with Chinese food, Indian food was promoted through the publication of recipe books and the appearance of media personalities, the best known being Madhur Jaffrey. Indian food was also taken up on a large scale by supermarkets, with Waitrose leading the way with the introduction of chilled Indian ready-meals in 1987. In the 1980s, and increasingly in the 1990s, some Indian restaurateurs made a determined effort to break away from the 'curry and beer' image attached to Indian food in Britain and opened up-market restaurants in London and other cities. Nevertheless most Indian food outlets continued to appeal to the popular end of the market and in 1997 a Gallup survey showed that curry was Britain's favourite ethnic food, with a quarter of the population eating curry at least once a week. By 1999 the number of Indian restaurants in Britain was estimated to be 8,000.[6]

The British reaction to Indian food in India and its subsequent acceptance in Britain has many parallels with the reception of Chinese food in the Western world. At various times Indian food was regarded by the British as an exotic experience, as the product of a despised society, and as a source of cheap and convenient meals. The Bangladeshi communities established in Britain identified and exploited an economic niche in the catering trade. This expansion came soon after the explosion in the growth of Chinese restaurants and takeaways and reflected on the one hand the entrepreneurial drive of the immigrants and on the other a substantial change in the eating habits and food preferences of the majority population. Other than in cities with a large Asian population, for example in Bradford, Indian restaurants and takeaways, like their Chinese counterparts, tended to be distributed thinly throughout the British Isles.

However, there are significant differences between the way in which Chinese and South Asians have been perceived in Britain, and this has had its effect on how the Chinese and Indian foodways have been accepted. Indians, Pakistanis and Bangladeshis have achieved a position in British society which is more integrated than that of the Chinese. They form sizeable ethnic communities, they have made a major contribution to the labour force, both to the professions and on the shop floor, and they have developed a range of services which sustain their own communities and, in the case of grocery and general stores, the wider population. The operation of restaurants and take-aways, though a significant source of employment, is not nearly as important to the South Asian communities as it is to the Chinese in Britain. Whereas India was part of the British empire, China, with the important exception of Hong Kong, was not, and elements of this colonial past are evident. In an interesting article Uma Narayan pointed out that curry powder, which one might suppose was the basis of authentic Indian cooking, was in fact a British fabrication, and she linked this with what she described as the 'colonial fabrication of India'. She considered the proliferation of 'ethnic cuisines' in the post-colonial Western context, and suggested that Westerners' attitudes to 'ethnic foods' involved forms of 'food colonialism' and 'culinary imperialism'.[7] One has only to glance at an early and popular recipe book for Indian food, Harvey Day's *The Complete Book of Curries*, published in 1966 – a 'book written by a white Englishman on how to cook "proper" curries', to find evidence to support her statement. Day likened the sprouting of Indian and Pakistani restaurants in Britain to 'mushrooms in a midden' and sneered at the competence of the cooks they employed and their exploitation of the gullible British public.[8] In the light of these comments, it is not surprising that when Dharamjit Singh wrote the preface to *Indian Cookery* (1970), he found it necessary to warn that although Indian cookery like French and Chinese cookery had a system, an architecture, of its own, it was little known outside India. Even in India the tradition had never been recorded and now, with the decay of the princely states, it was no longer being preserved by the master cooks and great chefs of the past and was in danger of being lost forever.[9]

Do Uma Narayan's remarks relating to Indian food in Britain apply equally to Chinese food? The first part of this book has shown that colonial attitudes played an important part in shaping British attitudes towards, and later acceptance of, Chinese food in China. When the first Chinese restaurants catering for Westerners opened in Britain they offered something of an exotic or aesthetic experience, but much of this was to be lost with the proliferation of 'chop suey' restaurants and takeaways that offered inexpensive dishes which had been modified to suit Western tastes. The very cheapness of Chinese food in such places, the boorish behaviour of a minority of customers, the ignorance and indifference of many customers not only on the subject of Chinese food, but also on many if not all aspects of Chinese culture, certainly betrayed colonialist attitudes. However the distinctive features of Chinese culture and of the Chinese cuisine or cuisines prevented Chinese food from becoming colonialized to the same extent as Indian food. The defined techniques of Chinese cooking, the use of characteristic vegetables and sauces, the claims for benefits to health, may have enabled Chinese food to retain a status somewhat higher than that of Indian food.

The continuing suspicion and at times hostility towards Chinese food may be a consequence of this persistent independence. Since China as a country, and the Chinese people as a race, have often evinced negative responses in the West this is not surprising. Hostile remarks relating to Chinese food – as evidenced over the last few years – fall into three categories. The first is the revulsion expressed over the Chinese use of certain animals for food or medicine. The eating of animals treated as pets in the West and the exploitation of endangered species promote outrage among some Westerners. Visitors to Guangzhou often comment adversely on seeing snakes, rare birds, puppies, and other animals offered for sale as food. Horrifying photographs of cats and dogs displayed on market stalls in Guangzhou and Xi'an may be found on the internet. Recent newspaper and magazine articles support this condemnation. In April 2000 it was reported that 7,000 caged bears were undergoing agonizing treatment in 'bile farms' in China. The World Society for the Protection of Animals had discovered that untrained workers were surgically mutilating the animals to 'milk' the bile from gall bladders to be used as a tonic for fevers and stomach complaints.[10] On July 2001 the *New York Times* reported that the biggest dog breeder in Peixian, Jiangsu was raising 100,000 dogs a year for slaughter at six months old for human consumption. The report commented that whereas eating dog had nearly died out during the Cultural Revolution, when keeping dogs was condemned as a bourgeois extravagance, dog meat was now back on the menu and was one of the most expensive meats available. As one of the breeds most often reared for food was the Saint Bernard, SOS Saint Bernard Dogs International presented a petition signed by 11,000 people to the Swiss government asking it to intervene to stop China's use of the 'most faithful friend of humans' for food. Also published was a recipe for 'Dog Stir-fry' taken from Calvin Schwabe, *Unmentionable Cuisine* (Charlottesville, VA, 1979). The magazine which reprinted this article for a British audience added 'that we do not support the killing or eating of puppies but are printing this recipe in the spirit of culinary toleration'.[11]

Chinese restaurants (like other ethnic restaurants) have often been the scene of abusive and racist behaviour. In Britain the most serious confrontation occurred in 1963 at a Chinese restaurant in St Helen's, Lancashire. Several British youths refused to pay their bill and a fight broke out between them and six Hakka waiters, in which a British youth was killed. Local residents held a protest march and three Chinese restaurants and laundries were damaged. At the subsequent trial one waiter was acquitted and the other five were sentenced to three years imprisonment.[12] In 1988, at the Diamond Chinese restaurant in the West End of London when five white customers, including one employee of the British diplomatic service, were asked to pay their bill they attacked the waiter. Three of his colleagues came to his rescue and a fight ensued. When the police arrived the white customers were taken to hospital but the waiters were taken to the police station and charged. Subsequently they were convicted of affray and sentenced to two years imprisonment. Chinese groups throughout Britain campaigned on behalf of the 'Diamond Four'. A campaign leaflet said 'The necessity to defend themselves from racist customers is now an everyday experience for waiters in Chinatown.'[13] This situation continues: in Gloucester, in April 2000, racially aggravated harassment in Indian and Chinese restaurants was sufficiently common to warrant a police operation, named Operation Napkin, which arranged for plainclothes police to eat in ethnic restaurants on Friday and Saturday nights.[14] Despite the limited success of Operation Napkin – only one person was cautioned – the Metropolitan Police in London conducted a similar operation in April, 2001. Chinese restaurateurs told them that some groups of men and women, predominantly between the ages of 35 and 45, would say that everything was fine during the meal, but when they had finished would complain about the service and food and refuse to pay. In cases of refusal to pay, Chinese managers would usually call the police, but racist remarks were so common that they had forbidden their staff to respond to insults.[15]

Although the good service provided in Chinese restaurants has been quoted as one reason for the acceptance of Chinese food, the rudeness of the Chinese waiter has become something of a cliché. Jeffrey Bernard, a journalist writing for the *Spectator*, listed his expenses as follows:

> Chicken in lemon, beef with spring onions and ginger, mixed vegetables in Jubilee Dragon . . . £6.50. Iodine, sticking plaster and bandages for wounds inflicted by Chinese waiters £1.75.[16]

The relationship between English customers and Chinese staff was studied by Chung Yuen Kay, who worked as a waitress in a Chinese restaurant in Manchester in the early 1980s. The customers, who assumed that Chinese staff would have a language problem, were surprised to find a Chinese waitress speaking good English. She noted a transaction between Koo, a colleague who spoke English with a very heavy accent, and some customers.

Offensive people at T[able] 2. Koo was serving them and they kept making fun of his pronunciation. They ordered Crab and Sweetcorn Soup, and when Koo repeated their order back to them they imitated the way he had said 'crab' which had sounded like 'crap', and they kept saying to him, "yea, that's right sunshine, Chinese food is crap, eh?", and they laughed among themselves. Poor Koo was bewildered as he did not know what they meant.

However one of the waitresses, Fey, was adept at gaining revenge for this sort of abuse.

Rather drunk man at Table 17 was being difficult over his order which Fey was trying to take. I went over to see if I could help. As I neared her, I heard her saying softly but audibly, in Cantonese, "why don't you drop dead!" She then proceeded to consign the souls of his ancestors to hell![17]

This relationship was determined more by race than by food. A white waitress, who worked in a Chinese restaurant in West Yorkshire for several years in the late 1990s, could recall no examples of offensive behaviour of this sort directed at her or at the food which she served.[18]

Another type of negative reaction concerns health worries associated with eating Chinese food. A long-standing criticism relates to the use of MSG, monosodium glutamate, or 'taste powder' to enhance the flavour of dishes. According to Emily Hahn, writing in 1969, 'no self-respecting chef in China would use even a small amount; to do so not only would be regarded as an admission of the inadequacy of his skill, but might also obscure the more subtle taste sensations of his dishes and reduce their variety.'[19] However many writers of recipe books for Western audiences – for example Craig Claiborne and Kenneth Lo – have recommended the use of small quantities of MSG in their recipes. The excessive use of MSG to compensate for the use of cheap and flavourless ingredients remains a common criticism of Chinese restaurants. If consumed in quantity it may cause a brief episode of sweating and numbness.[20] Another concern was identified in June 2001 when the British Food

Standards Agency found that 22 out of 100 samples of soy sauce products contained worryingly high levels of potentially cancer-causing chemicals. These samples, from brands which formed a very small proportion of the UK market, were imported from Thailand, China, Hong Kong and Taiwan. Rather defensively the Food Standards Agency remarked that there was no reason to avoid Chinese food and it had never advised people to do so.

Other, more serious complaints about Chinese restaurants refer to low standards of hygiene and the serving of food unfit for human consumption, a complaint also levelled against Indian restaurants. It has often been alleged that pet food is served in these establishments, or that domestic animals, most frequently cats, are cooked and served as food. Most of these allegations have no foundation other than sub-racist attitudes towards ethnic minorities. Occasionally some evidence has been produced to support these charges, which at times may have been initiated by rival Chinese establishments. Undoubtedly there have been cases of poor hygiene. In September 2000, after an outbreak of 37 cases of *salmonella enteriditis* in Scotland, Chinese restaurants were cited as a 'possible link between a large number of the cases'. In April 2001, soon after the onset of the worst outbreak of foot-and-mouth in the British Isles, reports circulated that meat smuggled into Britain from Asia and destined for the Chinese catering trade might be responsible for the outbreak, the suggested link being restaurant leftovers sold to farms as pigswill. Restaurateurs in the infected regions and in London reported a downturn in trade amounting to 40 per cent. Jabez Lam, a Chinese community leader in London and a member of the National Civil Rights Monitoring Group, condemned the widespread reporting of this unsubstantiated link between foot-and-mouth and the Chinese food industry and said that it had the potential to incite hate crime. On 8 April some 500 demonstrators from Gerrard Street in the heart of London's Chinatown marched to the headquarters of the Ministry of Agriculture, Food and Fisheries demanding justice for the Chinese on this issue. Chinese restaurants closed for two hours as owners showed their anger at being blamed for the crisis.[21]

A third negative response relates to alleged links between Chinese restaurants and criminal gangs. At various times in the past it has been stated that Triad societies exert a powerful influence in the Chinese community. That issue was raised again in most tragic circumstances at Dover in June 2000 when 58 illegal Chinese immigrants suffocated in the trailer of a lorry which had come through the Channel tunnel. Their journey was traced back to South China and to the 'snakeheads' who, at a price, had made the travel arrangements for the immigrants. The reporting of these events linked the activities of Triad gangs, the operation of Chinese restaurants and the promotion of prostitution. It was assumed that many of the illegal Chinese immigrants would have to work in Chinese restaurants, or resort to prostitution, to pay off their debts.[22] A year later, newspapers reported that the owner of the Wong Chu restaurant in Manchester, his wife and his two-year-old son, had died in a fire at their home in Droylsden. The police announced that they had been stabbed, and that were victims of a murder which could be linked to the Triads.[23]

On the other hand, the image of Chinese food has benefited from lifestyle changes in the West, notably in the growing interest in the relationship between food and health. An authoritative explanation of the relationship appeared in 1983 in *Prince Wen Hui's Cook* by Bob Flaws and Honora Lee Wolfe, who described themselves as 'American practitioners of Classical Chinese Medicine'. The book began by explaining that diet was the third of the Eight Limbs of Classical Chinese Medicine. Two other limbs, acupuncture and herbal therapy, were better known in the West, but neither would have a satisfactory effect unless supported by proper dietary therapy. The writers' aim was to 'translate Oriental principles of eating into contemporary, delicious, and nutritious American cuisine without undue dependence on, or fascination with, exotic Eastern ingredients'. As the leitmotifs of the oriental life-arts were naturalness, unpretentiousness, and adaptability (qualities which the writers did not associate with the American lifestyle), it was inappropriate to suggest that Americans should eat Chinese, Japanese or Korean foods as staples. However the principles of Chinese dietary therapy could be incorporated into American eating habits. There followed a description of the three levels of diet therapy: yogic, preventive and remedial. The remedial level concerned the diagnosis of the patient's condition and the formulation of a dietary prescription that would balance or cancel any imbalance or syndrome. For example the diagnosis might reveal a Damp Bi Syndrome, indicated by the patient being overweight, the flesh feeling flabby and the stools loose. The dietary therapy would involve eating more warming *yang*-supporting foods, and a list of recipes to achieve this was appended. One recipe was for Stir-fried Daikon (radish) with Scallion and Carrot. This dish, it was stated, could be listed with either American or Chinese recipes since turnips could be substituted for daikon. In either case it would benefit a Deficient and Damp Spleen.[24]

A popular response on the same theme appeared in an article in the *Independent on Sunday* by Michael Bateman, in which he discussed the high sales figures of Nina Simonds' *A Spoonful of Ginger* which had been published in the United States in 1999. He attributed this success to the current interest in the notion of functional foods, food products which treated specific conditions such as high blood pressure, cholesterol, ulcers etc. According to Simonds, Chinese medicine had practised this for 5,000 years. Through trial and error, China had developed a holistic, balanced and harmonious approach to healthy eating. But in the West, when at last the connection between food and health was recognized, the tendency was merely to 'nail the bad guys – fat bad, fruit and veg good'. Bateman described a visit he had made to the Imperial Herbal Restaurant in Singapore. The restaurant, which was a showcase for Chinese medicine, featured a consulting counter and a wall of 100 drawers containing dried foods with various health-giving properties. The menu claimed to have a cure for most human ills from cancer to bedwetting. Although Bateman was sceptical about this claim, and the assertions made by Nina Simonds in her book, he was sufficiently impressed to include a recipe from the restaurant for Yin-yang prawns which, if a sachet of hawthorn were added to the sauce, was said to improve digestion, dissolve cholesterol deposit and relieve blood pressure. He also quoted Simonds' tips for perfect balance in food by paying attention to their *yin* and *yang* qualities. Ginger was a *yang* force, which pumped energy into mild-mannered *yin* foods. It also helped to sweat out colds and flu, prevented travel sickness and cleaned toxins out of the blood stream.[25]

GLOBALIZATION, CULTURAL CAPITAL AND THE BEST OF EAST AND WEST

The spread of Chinese food throughout the world is undoubtedly one of the most remarkable examples of the globalization of food. Though remarkable it is by no means unique, as the evidence of the inexorable rise of McDonald's and the consumption of hamburgers testifies.

In several respects McDonald's and other fast food chains which have their origin in the West and the lower half of the ethnic food market have things in common. They both provide cheap takeaway food at outlets which stay open until late. In nineteenth-century Britain this need was met by fish and chip shops and in the north by pie and peas shops and stalls. In the latter half of the twentieth century the increasing affluence of young people, less formal eating habits, the rise of restaurant eating, admiration for American culture and curiosity about other cultures as experienced through food, and a host of other factors, led to the proliferation of food outlets which served these needs. Ethnic cuisines, and in particular Chinese food, gained a niche in this market. In Britain the break with past food habits was made explicit when Chinese takeaways took over fish and chip businesses.

Although cheapness and convenience are important reasons for the spread of fast food including Chinese food across North America and Britain, over a much longer period changes in middle-class dietary habits have been influenced less by economic factors and more by 'the transformation of individual tastes under the influence of a greater awareness of the rules of nutrition'.[26] The recent and rapid increase in the habit of eating out, coupled with the explosion in the number of ethnic restaurants in the West has been the subject of a number of studies. A connection has been found between the development of travel and the growing popularity of ethnic food. Tourists, having experimented with new eating experiences abroad, seek to repeat that experience in their home country. 'External tourism' has been compared with 'internal tourism', whereby foreign-ness can be experienced by eating in ethnic restaurants, without the need to travel abroad.

Claims about the globalization of culinary cultures were discussed by Ian Cook and Philip Crang. They pointed out that in the 1990s, when use of the term 'globalization' had become commonplace, it appeared that the long record of interconnections between peoples and places had greatly intensified over the previous 30 years, producing an increasingly compressed economic, political and cultural world. Greater awareness of these compressions had given rise to the concept of the globalization of the food system. They used a quotation from the London publication *Time Out* as a starting point for an analysis of these claims. *Time Out* had stated that in London one could find 'The world on a plate,' and it had urged its readers to 'Give your tongue a holiday and treat yourself to the best meals in the world – all without setting foot outside our fair capital.' The implication of this claim was that the culinary culture to be found in London had not submitted to the homogenization promoted by a monolithic transnational capitalism (in other words 'McDonaldization'), but had staged, and perhaps reconstructed, cultural differences to create a 'globalization of diversity'. Cook and Crang pointed out that cultural diversity sells and that the touristic quality of food was now being exploited. What was being sold purported to be an authentic example of an exotic dish, and this was being reinforced by messages imparted by the décor and other features of the location in which the food was served. However, they said, it was simplistic to think of food cultures as spatially defined and unchanging. Ethnic cuisines should be seen as contemporary fabrications – the example given was that of chilli con carne, a Texan construction of a Mexican dish. Regional cuisines, moreover, were invented traditions, inventions in which cookery books had played an important role.[27]

Adopting a different perspective, Jack Goody related the globalization of Chinese food to the globalization of world cultures.

He pointed out that there were two aspects of globalization, which proceeded concurrently. On the one hand there was homogenization – he cited the example of Coca-Cola – whereby one product came to dominate the world market in non-alcoholic drinks. On the other hand there was global differentiation, which consisted in the adoption or spread of local products, for example forms of cooking, which led to multiculturalism. Goody argued that in terms of sociocultural systems, which included the culture of food, there were continuities within Eurasia and that the cultural flow in the past had been more from East to West than the other way round. The assumption that globalization implied homogenization dominated by American influence could be gainsaid by the evidence of the globalization of Chinese food which had enriched the industrial cultures of the West by giving them a global dimension.[28]

A related argument was expressed in a recent essay by David Wu. Basing his discussion on the cuisine offered in Chinese restaurants in Papua New Guinea and Hawaii from the early 1970s, he suggested that the globalization of Chinese cuisine overseas 'did not follow the rules suggested by current globalization theories'. These theories assumed 'a direct flow of cultural traditions from the centre to the periphery,' and 'the diffusion of capitalized cooking industry pushed from the Chinese homeland by professional chefs and restaurateurs'. His evidence suggested, however, that Chinese cuisine in these territories had evolved, and was continuing to evolve, through the actions of self-taught cooks who improvised both cooking materials and how to present their dishes to satisfy a clientele comprising both Chinese immigrants and non-Chinese host populations. Whereas Western political economists had interpreted the globalization of Chinese food in the context of 'multi-national capitalistic domination, industrialization, and international trade', the dishes and cooking styles he had studied continued to be subject to 'local invention, adaptation, advertising and popular imagery about what Chinese food and culture are supposed to be'.[29]

Another concept relevant to the acceptance of Chinese food by Westerners is that of 'cultural capital', a phrase coined by the French sociologist Pierre Bourdieu to describe the social status acquired through the ability to make cultural distinctions. This idea was applied by A. Warde, L. Martens and W. Olsen to the consumption of food. They used the term 'omnivorousness' to denote what was described as the recent phenomenon of gaining cultural distinction through the consumption of a wide variety of foods. Cultural capital could be accumulated by acquiring the capacity 'to behave properly and knowledgeably in public, to exercise discriminating taste when selecting places to go and things to eat, and to facilitate conversation about and evaluation of culinary matters'.[30]

How do these theoretical approaches illuminate our understanding of the ways in which Chinese food has become accepted in the West? On the theme of the 'globalization of diversity', much can be said in support of the points made by Ian Cook and Philip Crang. 'Chinese food' in the multivarious forms in which it appears in the West, is not the food that the Chinese eat in China. Nor is it consistent in its appearance in various Western states. One might pause to consider the validity of terms such as 'Anglo-Chinese food', or 'Franco-Chinese food', which draw attention to the different ways Chinese food is presented in different national settings. Moreover there are wide variations between Chinese food outlets which stress cultural differences and those which minimize those differences in the interests of unobtrusive occupation of an economic niche. One might well question whether any Chinese food prepared outside China is 'authentic' – but the question soon loses its clarity when it is recognized that Chinese food, like the food of any other culture, varies according to its region of origin, the social class of those who produce it, and that, even within China, it is subject to continuous change. Chinese food in the West has been adapted to suit the circumstances under which it has been received, but this adaptation has not gone so far as 'creolization', the term coined to denote cultural mixing to the extent of dissociation with any one particular culture.

On the question of whether the consumption of Chinese food leads to the accrual of cultural capital, this study suggests that for a long time Westerners regarded eating Chinese food as causing a *loss*, not a gain, of cultural capital. In the nineteenth century, Chinese food was rejected or derided by almost all

Westerners who held status in treaty port society. Missionaries from the China Inland Mission, enlisted from humble backgrounds by Hudson Taylor, compounded their shortage of cultural capital by making it a principle to eat Chinese food. Subsequently the idea that social capital might be accrued by eating Chinese food did begin to be recognized, but for different reasons from those described by Bourdieu. In the 1930s a some aesthetes expressed their appreciation of things Chinese and extended that appreciation to Chinese food, but they were few in number and they self-consciously separated themselves from the majority view among Westerners of appropriate behaviour. The same was true of the journalists and political sympathizers who during the Sino-Japanese War elected to eat the food of ordinary Chinese as an expression of their support for the Chinese cause. Later, as the struggle narrowed to one between Communists and Nationalists, a willingness to eat peasant food was a passport for acceptance on the Communist side.

Another way of locating the position that Chinese food occupies in Western society at present is to follow up the ideas put forward by David Bell and Gill Valentine in *Consuming Geographies: We Are Where We Eat*. Bell and Valentine began by remarking that food in postmodern Western societies had ceased to be merely about sustenance and nutrition, it was packed with social cultural and symbolic meanings. They commented, 'what we eat (and where and why) signals . . . who we are'. To develop that statement they adopted, as a structuring device, the spatial scale suggested by Neil Smith of *body-home-community-city-region-nation-global*. The first location refers to our perception of the relationship between the food we eat and our bodies. Chinese food may include foodstuffs which in the West have been regarded as offensive to ingest, or which flout ethical or conservationist principles. It may include too much MSG and it may be subject to allegations about poor hygiene. But these are minor issues when placed in the context of other features of Chinese food which involve the body. As indicated above, Chinese views on dietary therapy have received some recognition in the West. Claims have been made that to eat Chinese food is to eat healthily, and this is supported by recipes and diets which are low-fat, or low-meat, or low-cholesterol. The cooking and eating of Chinese food has been presented as a way of maintaining a vital internal balance. The introduction to a Western audience of philosophical concepts, particularly those of Daoism, concerning the preparation and consumption of food has given a comforting spiritual significance to the process of eating which contrasts sharply with the food anxieties prevalent in the West.

As long as eating Chinese food implied eating away from the house, the next location, the home, had little relevance to Chinese food. The introduction of Chinese takeaway food increased choice from fish and chips but did not impinge on domestic cooking. But from the 1960s in the United States and perhaps a decade later in the United Kingdom, the domestic preparation and consumption of Chinese food began to be represented as an attractive option, particularly when entertaining guests, a form of recreation very much on the increase. At first the appeal was directed at women and guidance was given to them in women's magazines. In 1970 *Women's Own* carried an article captioned 'Jane Beaton's Chinese Feast' which claimed

> More and more people are enjoying Chinese food when they eat out, but many cooks believe that Chinese dishes are too complicated to make at home. Well, they're not, and on these three pages Jane Beaton proves it. She shows you how to make a traditional Chinese feast with crispy noodles, pancake rolls, fried rice and all. Exotic fruits make a perfect finish to the meal.[31]

The cooking of Chinese food was now represented as a relatively straightforward task, which required no special equipment. Kenneth Lo's *The Chinese Cookery Encyclopedia* (1974) contained illustrations of a hot pot, bamboo steamers, a whisk, a wok, a pestle and mortar and other utensils, but nowhere did it refer to the wok as an essential acquisition – a frying pan was all that was needed.

The idea of cooking Chinese food as a form of domestic recreation and as an encouragement to family harmony was promoted by Ken Hom. In the introduction to the book which accompanied his 1984 television series *Chinese Cookery* he explained how, by planning a meal which combined a cold dish, a braised dish and a stir-fried dish, the beginner could avoid arriving at the table hot and flustered. He emphasized the healthiness of the Chinese diet and, having referred to the '*yin yang* theory of food science', he pointed out that a sensible mixture of *yin* and *yang* foods could complement an individual's personality type. He remarked that for the Chinese eating was a communal experience and that a shared meal was regarded as 'the visible manifestation of the harmony which should exist between family and friends'.[32]

Bell and Valentine pointed out that since industrialization most food activities in the Western world have been ascribed to women. Man's role was that of the provider, woman's that of the nourisher. By the 1980s this distinction was breaking down, and the cooking of Chinese food may have played a minor role in that change. Men's forays into the kitchen often include trying out new recipes and experimenting with ethnic food, activities that may require new equipment. In this context the most obvious addition to a household's *batterie de cuisine* is the wok.

The location of community refers in particular to the extent to which food habits are used to shore up a sense of an ethnic minority's community identity. When overseas Chinese communities became established in North America, Chinese food habits, insofar as that was possible, were preserved by importing Chinese foodstuffs. Nevertheless compromises had to be made and local fruit and vegetables were substituted as required. Still the sense of community continued to be reinforced through the medium of food and this was particularly apparent on special occasions such as Chinese New Year. The Chinese involvement in fruit and vegetable production helped the community to maintain its identity through food. However when catering for non-Chinese became an important part of the economy of the Chinese community, a rift emerged between producing food for Chinese consumers and retailing what was represented as Chinese food to a Western clientele. This rift may be observed within other ethnic communities in North America, notably among Italian-Americans, who have sought to maintain clearly defined food habits at home, while at

the same time marketing an acceptable form of Italian food to the majority community. Some of the stratagems devised by Overseas Chinese to deal with this dilemma have already been mentioned, for example the production of hybrid dishes such as chop suey, and the segregation of customers by presenting a menu on which dishes deemed to be more acceptable to Chinese customers are listed in Chinese and dishes for Westerners described in English. As the production of industrial food has increased, so has the output of canned foods described as Chinese but intended mainly for the non-Chinese market. In countries like the United Kingdom, which did not have a long-established Chinese community, the catering industry concentrated on serving a Western clientele. As a consequence the adaptation of Chinese food to satisfy that clientele was apparent early on.

Once Chinese restaurants had become commonplace sights in North American and European towns and cities, their proprietors had to choose between emphasising or playing down their exoticism. Restaurants which depend on Chinese custom, or which sell not only food but also an exotic experience, have catered to these expectations by serving food regarded as typically Chinese, for example Beijing duck, by insisting on the use of chopsticks and bowls, and by creating an ambience, through pictures, music and other means which give the impression of authenticity. On the other hand many local Chinese takeaways have played down exotic references, partly for reasons of economy, their function being to provide a cheap source of convenience food, and partly to minimize the appearance of intrusion in the neighbourhood. British Chinese takeaways usually deal with their customers in an utilitarian, plainly furnished outer room. Only the name of the establishment and a calendar on the wall may confirm its Chinese identity. The kitchen, the kitchen staff, and the whole process of food preparation are invisible. The menus are stereotyped and the food is served in neat, anonymous foil packages.

The next two points on Smith's spatial scale are the city and the region. It was in an urban environment that Chinese food acquired many of its characteristics, and it was in Western cities that Chinese food was first made available to Westerners.

Chinese entrepreneurs played a major role in widening the eating choices available in town or city beyond indigenous food habits, perhaps varied with the occasional French restaurant, to include an exotic option, at times in a Chinatown, more commonly along a high street. These entrepreneurs were quick to respond to changes in urban lifestyle, pioneering inexpensive eating options in restaurants and later in takeaways. From there Chinese food infiltrated other lifestyle choices, for example convenience foods, fast-food home delivery and leisure cooking. In so doing it extended its penetration to suburban and small town locations.

As for the region, perhaps because of ignorance, perhaps because of an assumption that Chinese society was monolithic, the first Westerners to describe Chinese food did not refer to regional cuisines. It was not until the 1920s, when aesthetes like Richard Wilhelm extolled the sophistication of Chinese food, that regional differences began to gain Western recognition, and it was not until much later that regional cuisines were treated in Chinese cookery books. Kenneth Lo, writing in 1972, listed his recipes under four geographical divisions, South, North, East, and West and West-Central China, the last division including the province of Sichuan. Lo was at pains to explain that he and his colleagues had known scarcely anything about the last-named division until they had been forced to move there during the Japanese War. Then they had been so starved that they had eaten everything that came their way without appreciating the quality of the food. To make a balanced assessment of the cooking of the region he had re-examined some recipes and had identified some seasonal dishes from the area. Craig Claiborne, writing at about the same time, was also cautious on the subject of the regional cookery of China. He pointed out that whereas one could easily distinguish the cookery of North and South Italy – the former for its refined dishes with rice as a staple, and the latter for earthy dishes with tomatoes and garlic and pasta – in China regional dishes had been adopted and adapted in other regions, and new dishes and ingredients had constantly been incorporated. Nevertheless he identified three regions, Northern, Yangzi Valley and Southern and then remarked that the Western region of the Yangzi Valley, which included the cooking of Yunnan and Sichuan, was different because of the sharpness of its flavours and the sting of its spices. Sichuan food, he noted, had suddenly become popular in the United States and the 'wildest phenomenon of recent years' had been the proliferation of Sichuan restaurants from one end of Manhattan to another.[33] Since Kenneth Lo and Craig Claiborne wrote, many Chinese restaurants and many Chinese cookbooks have laid claim to a regional cuisine, which in Western eyes seems to imply a more sophisticated and more authentic version of Chinese food.

The penultimate point on Neil Smith's spatial scale, the nation, provides some contradictory reflections. As pointed out above, in recent years the more sophisticated version of Chinese food, as presented in the West, has disowned a national identity in favour of a regional location. On the other hand at a more general level, Chinese food is treated as if it were the product of a single culture, if not of a single nation. When David Bell and Gill Valentine interviewed British people asking for their definition of British food, one interviewee responded:

> British is your sausage and your, your joints of beef or – just your traditional meat and two veg, I would have thought as British, or stews, pies, that type of thing. Maybe chilli, or lasagne, or spaghetti bolognese is foreign, Chinese I'd say was foreign.[34]

The implication was that some dishes, like chilli or lasagne, had become so widely accepted in Britain that their foreignness was no longer evident. Chinese food, however, had not reached that level of acceptance, although the widespread adoption of stir-fry cooking and the easy availability of stir-fry sauces implied that that in some respects the foreign stigma was disappearing.

As for globalization, this study suggests that the ugly neologism 'glocalization' may capture a feature of the way in which Chinese food has been accepted in the West. 'Glocalizing' is defined as 'succumbing to the twin forces of universalism (McDonald's again) and particularism (the authentic exotic)'. The global spread of Chinese food has not been greeted with the combination of eager acceptance and resentment which the threat of American cultural hegemony has received, although at times the perception of China in the West has affected the reception of Chinese food. Although Chinese food, as known in the West, shows many modifications from the food eaten by Chinese in their native land, it is not packaged or homogenized to the extent which marks off American food outlets. The 'authentic exotic' component, which may vary from marked to barely perceptible, has to date prevented the complete absorption of the materials and techniques of Chinese food into the consumption patterns of the Western world.

The note of caution expressed in the previous paragraph about where the future of Chinese food lies in the perceptions and habits of the Western world leads to one final theme: how Chinese food in the West will fare alongside the widening range of ethnic food choices. In recent years the choice of ethnic foods deriving from outside Europe has expanded significantly, and this has challenged the dominant position hitherto occupied in the North American market of Italian, Mexican and Chinese food and in the United Kingdom market of Indian and Chinese food. In Britain the increase in the number of restaurants offering Mexican, Thai, Vietnamese and Japanese food, and the increase in the sale of prepared food from these cuisines, has influenced attitudes towards Indian and Chinese food. A study of the eating habits of students at Bristol University – a university which attracts an above-average proportion of students from middle-class families – showed that in the year 2000 students gained the greatest amount of cultural capital by being seen eating at these new ethnic restaurants and by displaying knowledge of these new cuisines. Students commented that for one of their number to be seen consuming Indian food, presumably after drinking a lot of alcohol, was potentially damaging in terms of cultural capital. To be seen eating Chinese food was less undesirable, but in terms of omnivorousness it was of little advantage, as consuming a Chinese takeaway was regarded as as unadventurous as eating fish and chips.[35]

As long as the ethnic food market continues to expand, the implications for the Chinese food industry may not be severe. However there are limits how far any cuisine – even one as rich and varied as that of China – can respond to the demands for novelty. One should remember that the origin of the Chinese food industry in the West lay in the need of a minority community to find an economic niche. Although food is a very important part of Chinese life, the Chinese by instinct are no more cooks than they were once laundrymen. In recent years, many Chinese Americans and Chinese Canadians have abandoned catering in favour of higher-status employment. Many young Chinese in Britain have ambitions which far exceed the choice of following their parents in the restaurant business. These considerations cast doubt on the continuation of the present pattern of the supply and consumption of Chinese food in the Western world. At the same time Western perceptions of Chinese food cannot be expected to remain unchanged. Present-day attitudes are the product of a particular era, the first phase in a major revision of the eating habits of the Western world resultant from the twentieth-century experience of imperialism, war, mass tourism, social change and increasing affluence. Eating habits will continue to evolve through the twenty-first century. One inevitable change will be the passing of the age group which never tried Chinese food, and then of the age group which pioneered the consumption of ethnic food out of a spirit of adventure, and their replacement by generations for whom ethnic foods are part of the accepted diet.

Another change, which is already well-established and may be expected to go further, is increasing eclecticism in matters concerning food, in this context through the application of Chinese cooking techniques to foodstuffs which are not typically Chinese, and through the wider use of typically Chinese foods, for example bean curd, Chinese vegetables and Chinese sauces, all now readily available in the West. This approach was pioneered by Ken Hom, who related it to the influence of *la nouvelle cuisine*, which shortened cooking times and emphasized the freshness and lightness of food, and to the burst of interest in cooking and food which he had witnessed in the San Francisco Bay area in the 1970s. He claimed that the recipes in his 1987 cookery book, *East Meets West*, were 'an unforced, natural blending of ingredients and techniques borrowed mainly from China, France and America'. His goal was to accentuate 'the best of both East and West, and to assist in the creation of new and palatable foods'. The recipes which followed contained some surprising combinations, for example Goat's Cheese Wonton Soup.[36] Even further removed from traditional Chinese food was the cuisine which the Los Angeles chef Wolfgang Puck promoted in the late 1980s, which was described as an example of 'postmodern American foodways'. His Chinois Restaurant in Santa Monica featured a French-Asian cuisine, which represented no single identity but 'an accretion and proliferation of ingredients and identities'. The menu juxtaposed Crab with Bean Sauce (a straightforward Chinese dish), with Ginger Crème Brûlée (a French dish with Asian seasoning). The restaurant itself, which had an exposed kitchen, and its staff, who wore unisex black jackets with toggle ties, were a pastiche of the usual presentation of Chinese food. By rejecting any claim to ethnic authenticity, and by denying any intention of presenting foreign food, Puck implied that the Chinese food tradition could be wholly subsumed into American foodways, thereby completing the circle of the acceptance of Chinese food.[37]

References

INTRODUCTION

1 For a recent discussion of some other aspects of the global spread
of Chinese food see David Y. H. Wu and Sidney C. H. Cheung,
The Globalization of Chinese Food (Richmond, 2002).
2 Kenneth Lo, *Chinese Food* (Harmondsworth, 1972), p. 69.
3 Harold Isaacs, *Images of Asia: American Views of China and India* (New
York, 1972), pp. 70–2. See also Colin Mackerras, *Western Images of China*
(Hong Kong, 1989) and J.A.G. Roberts, *China Through Western Eyes:
The Nineteenth Century* and *China Through Western Eyes: The Twentieth
Century* (Stroud, 1991, 1992).

PART I: WEST TO EAST

ONE · CHINESE FOOD

1 Unless otherwise indicated, the material for this chapter is derived from
K. C. Chang, ed., *Food in Chinese Culture: Anthropological and Historical
Perspectives* (New Haven, CT, 1977); E. N. Anderson, *The Food of China*
(New Haven, CT, 1988) and Frederick J. Simoons, *Food in China:
A Cultural and Historical Enquiry* (Boca Raton, FL, 1991).
2 Chang, *Food in Chinese Culture*, p. 338.
3 D. C. Lau, trans. and ed., *Mencius* (Harmondsworth, 1970), pp. 51, 59.
4 Robert Darnton, 'The workers' revolt: the great cat massacre of the rue
Saint-Séverin', in Robert Darnton, *The Great Cat Massacre and Other
Episodes in French Cultural History* (London, 1988), pp. 93–4.
5 The terms used are those employed by Kenneth Lo in *Chinese Food*
(Harmondsworth, 1972), pp. 10–26.
6 R. Dawson, ed., *The Legacy of China* (Oxford, 1971), p. 342.
7 Peking United Famine Relief Committee, 1922, quoted in J. Spence,
'Food', in Chang, *Food in Chinese Culture*, p. 261.
8 Jack Goody, *Cooking, Cuisine and Class: A Study in Comparative Sociology*
(Cambridge, 1982), pp. 97–114.
9 Ken Hom, *Ken Hom's Chinese Cookery* (London, 1984), p. 8.
10 Chang, *Food in Chinese Culture*, p. 9.
11 Doreen Yen Hung Feng, *The Joy of Chinese Cooking* (1952, reprinted
London, 1966), p. 11.

1 Ronald Lytham, trans. and ed., *The Travels of Marco Polo* (Harmondsworth, 1958), pp. 152, 156, 178–9, 214–15, 218, 220, 231.

2 Henry Yule and Henri Cordier, trans and eds, *Cathay and the Way Thither: Being a Collection of Medieval Notices of China*, 3 vols (London, Hakluyt Society, 1915) II, pp. 182, 211.

3 C. R. Boxer, ed., *South China in the Sixteenth Century: Being the Narratives of Galeote Pereira, Fr. Gaspar da Cruz, O. P., Fr. Martin de Rada, O.E.S.A.*, (London, Hakluyt Society, 1953), pp. 8–9, 14, 121, 133–4.

4 Quoted in J. H. Parry, ed., *The European Reconnaissance* (New York, 1968), pp. 269–72.

5 Yule and Cordier, *Cathay and the Way Thither*, I, p. 292.

6 Sir Richard Carnac Temple, ed., *The Travels of Peter Mundy in Europe and Asia 1608–1667*, 3 vols (London, Hakluyt Society, 1914), III, pp. 190–1, 194, Plate XV.

7 J. S. Cummins, ed., *The Travels and Controversies of Friar Domingo Navarrete 1618–1686*, 2 vols (Cambridge, Hakluyt Society, 1962), I, pp. 92–3, 137–8, 148–51; II, pp. 192, 195–8, 216.

8 J. B. Du Halde, *A Description of the Empire of China and Chinese-Tartary*, 2 vols (London, 1738), I, pp. 277, 301–3, 314–17.

9 D. Diderot and J. d'Alembert, eds, *Encyclopédie, ou dictionnaire raisonné des sciences, des arts et des métiers*, 17 vols (Paris, 1751–65), VII, pp. 664a–667a, VIII, p. 888b, XIV, pp. 261a–262b, 306b–308b, XV, pp. 403b, 484b–485b, XVI, pp. 223b–226b.

10 Daniel Defoe, *Robinson Crusoe* (London, 1906), p. 410.

11 Captain Alexander Hamilton, *A New Account of the East Indies*, 2 vols (Edinburgh, 1727), II, p. 236.

12 Richard Walter, *A Voyage Round the World in the Years MDCCXL, I, II, III, IV by George Anson Esq.*, (London, 1748), pp. 361, 397–8.

13 John Lockman, ed., *Travels of the Jesuits into Various Parts of the World: Particularly China and the East-Indies*, 2 vols (2nd edition, London, 1762), I, pp. 57, 145–6.

14 J. L. Cranmer-Byng, ed., *An Embassy to China: Being the Journal Kept by Lord Macartney during His Embassy to the Emperor Ch'ien-lung 1793–1794*, (London, 1962), pp. 71, 123, 163, 215, 225.

15 Aeneas Anderson, *A Narrative of the British Embassy to China in the Years 1792, 1793, and 1794*, (London, 1795), pp. 63–4, 93, 105, 142, 153.

16 Sir George Staunton, *An Authentic Account of an Embassy from the King of Great Britain to the Emperor of China*, 2 vols (London, 1797), II, pp. 399–400.

17 William Jardine Proudfoot, *Biographical Memoir of James Dinwiddie, L.L.D., Astronomer to the British Embassy to China, 1792, '3, '4* (Liverpool, 1868), pp. 33, 35.

18 John Barrow, *Travels in China, Containing Descriptions, Observations, and Comparisons, Made and Collected in the Course of a Short Residence at the Imperial Palace of Yuen-min-yuen and on a Subsequent Journey through the Country from Pekin to Canton* (London, 1804), pp. 67, 89, 109, 546–7.

19 C. Toogood Downing, *The Fan-Qui in China in 1836–7*, 3 vols (London,

1838, 1972), I, pp. 88, 306–10, III, pp. 83–5, 118–20, 147–62, 238, 316–17.

20 W. C Hunter, *The 'Fan Kwae' at Canton Before Treaty Days 1825–1844* (London, 1882, Taipei, 1970), pp. 40–2, 97, 144.

THREE · NINETEENTH-CENTURY REACTIONS TO
CHINESE FOOD

 1 George Wingrove Cooke, *China: Being 'The Times' Special Correspondence from China in the Years 1857–8* (London, 1858), p. 389.

 2 Sir John Francis Davis, *The Chinese: A General Description of China and Its Inhabitants*, new edition (London, 1840), pp. 145–51.

 3 P.G.L., *A Reminiscence of Canton 1863* (London, 1866), quoted in Frances Wood, *No Dogs and Not Many Chinese: Treaty Port Life in China 1843–1943* (London, 1998), p. 45.

 4 D. F. Rennie M.D., *Peking and the Pekingese During the First Years of the British Embassy at Peking*, 2 vols (London, 1865), II, p. 28.

 5 J. H. Gray, *China: A History of the Laws, Manners and Customs of the People*, 2 vols (London, 1878), II, pp. 64–77.

 6 S. Wells Williams, *The Middle Kingdom: A Survey of the Geography, Government, Literature, Social Life, Arts and History of the Chinese Empire and Its Inhabitants*, 2 vols (New York, 1883), I, pp. 771–81.

 7 Arthur H. Smith, *Chinese Characteristics*, (New York, 1894), p. 22.

 8 W. H. Medhurst, *The Foreigner in Far Cathay* (London, 1872), pp. 3, 96–100.

 9 Davis, *The Chinese*, pp. 373–4.

10 Robert Fortune, *A Journey to the Tea Countries of China; Including Sung-lo and the Bohea Hills* (London, 1852), pp. 93–4.

11 Henry Hobhouse, *Seeds of Change: Five Plants that Transformed Mankind* (London, 1985), pp. 93–137; Robert Gardella, *Harvesting Mountains: Fujian and the China Tea Trade, 1757–1937* (Berkeley, 1994), p. 111.

12 Katherine F. Bruner, John K. Fairbank and Richard J. Smith, eds, *Entering China's Service: Robert Hart's Journals 1854–63* (Cambridge, 1986), pp. 63–4, 270.

13 Laurence Oliphant, *Narrative of the Earl of Elgin's Mission to China and Japan in the Years 1857, '58, '59*, 2 vols (Edinburgh, 1859), I, pp. 67–8, 165, 215, 408.

14 Quoted in Wood, *No Dogs*, pp. 115–16.

15 Charles Drage, *Servants of the Dragon Throne: Being the Lives of Edward and Cecil Bowra* (London, 1966), pp. 76–7.

16 Stanley Lane-Poole, *Sir Harry Parkes in China* (London, 1901), pp. 76, 99, 118.

17 Bruner, Fairbank and Smith, *Entering China's Service*, p. 89.

18 Stuart Creighton Miller, *The Unwelcome Immigrant: The American Image of the Chinese, 1785–1882* (Berkeley, CA, 1969), p. 161.

19 P. D. Coates, *The China Consuls: British Consular Officers, 1843–1943* (Hong Kong, 1988), pp. 286, 389.

20 Oliver G. Ready, *Life and Sport in China* (London, 1903), quoted in Wood, *No Dogs*, p. 132.

21 James Henderson, *Shanghai Hygiene or Hints for the Preservation of Health in China* (Shanghai, 1863), quoted in Wood, *No Dogs*, pp. 29–30.

22 John Gavin, Letter book, British Library, quoted in Wood, *No Dogs*, p. 112.

23 Edward Barrington de Fonblanque, *Niphon and Pe-che-li; or Two Years in Japan and Northern China* (London, second edition, 1863), pp. 228–9.

24 Coates, *The China Consuls*, p. 205.

25 The process of tinning food had been invented at the time of the Napoleonic Wars. Initially food preserved in this way was largely for naval use, but a wide variety of tinned foods intended for civilian consumption was displayed at the Great Exhibition in 1851. Until the 1860s tinned food was overcooked, did not smell or taste appetising, and was not cheap. See Sue Shephard, *Pickled, Potted and Canned: The Story of Food Preserving* (London, 2000), pp. 221–50.

26 Paul King, *In the Chinese Customs Service: A Personal Record of Forty-Seven Years* (London, 1924), pp. 28–9.

27 Coates, *The China Consuls*, p. 307.

28 Bruner, Fairbank and Smith, *Entering China's Service*, p. 96.

29 Ready, quoted in Wood, *No Dogs*, p. 122.

30 M. Huc [Évariste Régis Huc], *The Chinese Empire*, 2 vols (London, 1855), I, pp. 168–9, 195–8; II, pp. 368–9.

31 Fortune, *A Journey to the Tea Countries of China*, pp. 190, 207.

32 T. T. Cooper, *Travels of a Pioneer of Commerce in Pigtail and Petticoats: Or, An Overland Journey from China towards India* (London, 1871), pp. 41–2, 181–3.

33 Archibald R. Colquhoun, *Across Chrysê: Being the Narrative of a Journey of Exploration Through the South China Border Lands*, 2 vols (London, third edition, 1883), I, p. 77; II, pp. 38, 354.

34 Isabella Bird, *The Yangtze Valley and Beyond: An Account of Journeys in China, Chiefly in the Province of Sze Chuan and Among the Man-tze of the Somo Territory* (London, 1899), pp. 191, 294–8. See also Isabella Bird, *Unbeaten Tracks in Japan* (London, 1880) 1984 edn, p. 23.

35 Pat Barr, *To China with Love: The Lives and Times of Protestant Missionaries in China 1860–1900* (Newton Abbot, 1973), pp. 124–5.

36 John L. Nevius, *China and the Chinese: A General Description of the Country and Its Inhabitants* (London, 1869), p. 317.

37 Irwin T. Hyatt, *Our Ordered Lives Confess: Three Nineteenth-Century American Missionaries in East Shantung* (Cambridge, MA, 1976), pp. 15–16, 69.

38 Rev. R. H. Cobbold, *The Chinese at Home: Pictures of the Chinese Drawn by Themselves* (London, 1860), p. 202.

39 Dr and Mrs Howard Taylor, *Hudson Taylor in Early Years: The Growth of a Soul* (London, 1911), pp. 215, 376, 390.

40 Barr, *To China With Love*, p. 26.

41 Timothy Richard, *Forty-Five Years in China* (London, 1916), p. 83.

42 Paul Richard Bohr, *Famine in China and the Missionary: Timothy Richard as Relief Administrator and Advocate of National Reform 1876–1884* (Cambridge, MA, 1972), pp. 16b, 19.

43 Claude Rhea, comp., *Lottie Moon Cookbook: Recipes Used by Lottie Moon*

1875–1912 (Waco, 1969), p. 26.

44 Hyatt, *Our Ordered Lives Confess*, pp. 107, 123, 129, 136.

45 Archibald E. Glover, *A Thousand Miles of Miracle in China: A Personal Record of God's Delivering Power from the Hands of the Imperial Boxers of Shan-si*, (London, 1908), pp. 162, 323, 357.

46 Susanna Hoe, *Women at the Siege, Peking 1900* (Oxford, 2000), pp. 151, 153.

47 Peter Fleming, *The Siege at Peking* (London, 1962), p. 148.

48 Mary Hooker [Polly Condit Smith], *Behind the Scenes in Peking* (London, 1910), pp. 86, 162.

FOUR · 1900–49: WESTERN IMPRESSIONS OF CHINESE FOOD IN CHINA

1 Daniele Varè, *Laughing Diplomat* (London, 1941), pp. 106–7, 305–6. 'The Bill of Supper' also amused G. E. Morrison, correspondent of *The Times*, Cyril Pearl, *Morrison of Peking* (Harmondsworth, 1970), p. 288.

2 Christopher Cook, *The Lion and the Dragon: British Voices from the China Coast* (London, 1985), p. 23.

3 W. Somerset Maugham, *On A Chinese Screen* (London, 1922), pp. 31–2.

4 Robert Bickers, *Britain in China: Community, Culture and Colonialism 1900–1949* (Manchester, 1999), p. 174.

5 Cook, *Lion and the Dragon*, p. 56.

6 Carl Crow, *Handbook for China* (Shanghai, 1933), pp. 32, 35. The prevalence of disease in the Chinese population explains why Crow felt it necessary to warn newcomers to safeguard their health. A study of faecal-borne diseases published in 1937 suggested that 60 million people were infected with amoebic dysentery and approximately 80 per cent of the population had ascarid or round-worm infestation. G. F. Winfield, 'Studies on the control of faecal-borne diseases in North China', *Chinese Medical Journal*, LI, (1937), pp. 221–3.

7 Frances Wood, *No Dogs and Not Many Chinese: Treaty Port Life in China 1843–1943* (London, 1998), plate 41, between pp. 176–7.

8 Cook, *Lion and the Dragon*, pp. 23, 37, 44–5.

9 Alice Tisdale Hobart, *Oil for the Lamps of China* (New York, 1933), pp. 24–6, 33–4, 228, 333.

10 Fay Angus, *The White Pagoda* (Wheaton, IL, 1978), p. 70.

11 Averil Mackenzie-Grieve, *A Race of Green Ginger* (London, 1959), p. 56.

12 Sir Meyrick Hewlett, *Forty Years in China* (London, 1944), pp. 205, 218.

13 Bickers, *Britain in China*, pp. 206, 212.

14 Richard Wilhelm, *The Soul of China* (London, 1928), pp. 331–41, 353.

15 Hermann Keyserling, trans. J. Holroyd Reece, *The Travel Diary of a Philosopher* (n.p., n.d.,) quoted in Hsiao Ch'ien, comp., *A Harp with a Thousand Strings* (London, 1944), pp. 165–8.

16 Osbert Sitwell, *Escape With Me! An Oriental Sketchbook* (London, 1939), pp. 171, 236–40, 330–1.

17 George N. Kates, *The Years That Were Fat: The Last of Old China* (Cambridge, MA, 1967), pp. 134–6.

18 Nora Waln, *The House of Exile* (Harmondsworth, 1939), pp. 26, 42–3.

19 Emily Hahn, *China to Me* (Philadelphia, 1944), pp. 9, 43.
20 Corrinne Lamb, *The Chinese Festive Board* (Shanghai, 1935), *passim*.
   J. Dyer Ball, in *Things Chinese: Or, Notes Connected with China* (1892, fifth
   edition, London, 1926), p. 250, gave three 'Chinese receipts' translated
   from a Chinese cookery book. These were for Steamed Shark's Fins,
   Chicken with the Liquor of Fermented Rice and Genii Duck. He did not
   expect his readers to attempt these recipes.
21 Between 1928 and 1949, while Nanjing was the capital of China, Beijing
   was known as Beiping.
22 Pearl S. Buck, *The Good Earth* (London, 1931) 1994 edn, pp. 22, 83, 271.
23 Agnes Smedley, *Chinese Destinies* (London, 1934), pp. 31–7.
24 Edgar Snow, *Red Star Over China* (London, 1937), pp. 375–6.
25 Joshua S. Horn, *Away with All Pests . . . : An English Surgeon in People's
   China* (London, 1969), pp. 17, 23.
26 Bernard Llewellyn, *I Left My Roots in China* (London, 1953), pp. 92–3,
   133–4, 166–7. Another member of the Unit, George W. Parsons, had
   similarly warm memories of the food at roadside restaurants. He wrote,
   'Like Bernard [Llewellyn] I think I came to feel I was part of the scene
   and to identify with the people along the road.' Correspondence
   following the publication of a letter in *Saga Magazine*, June 2001.
27 W. H Auden and Christopher Isherwood, *Journey to a War* (London,
   1939), pp. 40–1, 46–7, 56, 76, 176–9, 230–1.
28 Harold B. Rattenbury, *China-Burma Vagabond* (London, 1946),
   pp. 103–6.
29 Harold B. Rattenbury, *Face to Face with China* (London, 1945),
   pp. 5, 100–3.
30 Eve Curie, *Journey Among Warriors* (London, 1943), pp. 373, 376.
31 Robert Payne, *Chungking Diary* (London, 1945), pp. 388, 487.
32 Graham Peck, *Two Kinds of Time*, second edition (Boston, 1967),
   pp. 277–81.
33 Theodore H. White and Annalee Jacoby, *Thunder Out of China* (New
   York, 1946), pp. 8, 169, 176–7.
34 Ilona Ralf Sues, *Shark's Fins and Millet*, (London, 1944), pp. 10, 37, 222,
   235, 251–2, 256.
35 Agnes Smedley, *China Fights Back* (London, 1938), p. 113; *China
   Correspondent* (London, 1984), pp. 318–20.
36 Clare and William Band, *Dragon Fangs: Two Years with the Chinese
   Guerrillas* (London, 1947), pp. 151–2.
37 Harrison Forman, *Report from Red China* (New York, 1945, 1975), pp. 66,
   178.
38 Angus, *White Pagoda*, pp. 117, 131.
39 Robert Payne, *Journey to Red China* (London, 1947), p. 53.
40 Jack Belden, *China Shakes the World* (1949, London, 1973), pp. 53, 142,
   290, 318–19, 350, 481.
41 William Hinton, *Fanshen: A Documentary of Revolution in a Chinese Village*
   (Harmondsworth, 1972), pp. 340–3.

1 Joshua Horn, *Away with All Pests: An English Surgeon in People's China* (London, 1969), pp. 50, 61.
2 James Cameron, *Mandarin Red: A Journey Behind the 'Bamboo Curtain'* (London, 1955), pp. 44–50, 186.
3 Robert Guillain, *The Blue Ants: 600 Million Chinese Under the Red Flag* (London, 1957), pp. 6–7, 20–1, 31–2, 42.
4 Felix Greene, *The Wall Has Two Sides: A Portrait of China Today* (London, 1962), pp. 31–6, 183–4.
5 Sven Lindqvist, *China in Crisis* (London, 1965), pp. 13–16, 23, 41.
6 Colette Modiano, *Twenty Snobs and Mao* (London, 1970), pp. 11, 29–30.
7 Ross Terrill, *800,000,000: The Real China* (London, 1972), pp. 41–2, 115–16.
8 Paul Hollander, *Political Pilgrims: Travels of Western Intellectuals to the Soviet Union, China, and Cuba 1928–1978* (New York, 1981), p. 366.
9 Henry Kissinger, *The White House Years* (London, 1979), pp. 743, 750, 1068–9.
10 John Kenneth Galbraith, *A China Passage* (Boston, 1973), pp. xi, 19, 22, 31, 56, 62, 66, 115.
11 Simon Leys [Pierre Ryckmans], *Chinese Shadows* (Harmondsworth, 1978), pp. 7, 28–9, 74–5.
12 Simon Leys [Pierre Ryckmans], *The Burning Forest* (London, 1988), pp. 188–97.
13 Orville Schell, *China: In the People's Republic* (London, 1978), pp. 136, 147–8, 169.
14 Frances Wood, *Hand-Grenade Practice in Peking: My Part in the Cultural Revolution* (London, 2000), pp. 27, 44, 83–4, 90, 135–7.
15 Steven W. Mosher, *Broken Earth: The Rural Chinese* (London, 1984), pp. 48, 97–9, 299.
16 Rosemary Mahoney, *The Early Arrival of Dreams* (London, 1991), pp. 41, 131–3, 192–4.
17 Justin Hill, *A Bend in the Yellow River* (London, 1998), pp. 56–9, 120–1, 223–4, 256.
18 Fredric M. Kaplan and Arne J. de Keijzer, eds, *The China Guidebook*, fifth edition (New York, 1984), pp. 65–6, 122–5.
19 The Embassy of the United States of America, Beijing, *Beijing Guidebook* (Beijing, 1985), pp. 100–115.
20 Joe Cummings, Robert Storey, Robert Strauss, Michael Buckley, Alan Samalgalski, eds, *Lonely Planet Travel Survival Kit: China*, third edition (Hawthorn, Victoria, Australia, 1991), pp. 131–5.
21 Colin Thubron, *Behind the Wall: A Journey Through China* (London, 1988), pp. 9, 71, 117, 133, 148, 182–6, 191–226, 233.
22 *The National Geographic Traveller* (Washington, DC, 2001), p. 363.
23 Cummings et al., *Lonely Planet: China*, seventh edition (Footscray, Victoria, Australia, 2000), p. 146.
24 George McDonald, *China* (Peterborough, 2002), p. 165.

PART II: EAST TO WEST

SIX · THE GLOBALIZATION OF CHINESE FOOD – THE
EARLY STAGES

1 Gunther Barth, *Bitter Strength: A History of the Chinese in the United States*
   1850–1870 (Cambridge, MA, 1964), pp. 82, 181.
2 William Shaw, *Golden Dreams and Waking Realities* (1851), quoted in Jack
   Chen, *The Chinese of America* (San Francisco, 1980) p. 57.
3 Joseph R. Conlin, *Bacon, Beans and Galantines: Food and Foodways on the
   Western Mining Frontier* (Reno, 1986), pp. 190–2.
4 William C. Milne, *Life in China* (London, 1859), p. 28.
5 Atwell Whitney, *Almond-Eyed: The Great Agitator; a Story of the Day* (San
   Francisco, 1878) quoted in William F. Wu, *The Yellow Peril: Chinese
   Americans in American Fiction 1850–1940* (Hamden, CT, 1982), pp. 31–2.
6 Yong Chen, *Chinese San Francisco, 1850–1943: A Trans-Pacific Community*
   (Stanford, CA, 2000), p. 65.
7 Mark Twain, *Roughing It* (Berkeley, CA, 1972), pp. 353–5.
8 Betty Lee Sung, *Mountain of Gold: The Story of the Chinese in America*
   (New York, 1967), pp. 202–3. The 'invention' of chop suey was also said
   to have occurred in San Francisco, but Li Hongzhang did not visit the
   city. The Americanizing of the origin of chop suey may have led to a
   sharp increase in the number of Chinese restaurants in New York. See
   Lynn Pan, *Sons of the Yellow Emperor: The Story of the Overseas Chinese*
   (London, 1990), pp. 333–4.
9 Quoted in Harry Con, Ronald J. Con, Graham Johnson, Edgar
   Wickberg, and William E. Willmott, *From China to Canada: A History of
   the Chinese Communities in Canada* (Toronto, 1982), pp. 16–17.
10 Quoted in James Morton, *In the Sea of Sterile Mountains: The Chinese in
   British Columbia* (Vancouver, BC, 1974), p. 9.
11 Anthony Shang, *The Chinese in Britain* (London, 1984), p. 10.
12 P. J. Waller, 'Immigration into Britain: The Chinese', *History Today*,
   XXXV (1985), pp. 8–15.
13 *The I. G. in Peking: Letters of Robert Hart Chinese Maritime Customs
   1868–1907* edited by John King Fairbank, Katherine Frost Bruner
   and Elizabeth MacLeod Matheson, 2 vols (Cambridge, MA, 1975), I,
   pp. 516–9, 532.
14 *Pall Mall Budget*, 11 July, 1884.
15 *Punch, Or the London Charivari*, 26 July, 1884.
16 John Dudgeon, 'Diet, dress, and dwellings of the Chinese', *The Health
   Exhibition Literature*, 19 vols (London, 1884), XIX, pp. 253–495.
17 Vincent M. Holt, *Why Not Eat Insects?* (London, 1885, reprinted with
   an introduction by Laurence Mound, London, 1988), pp. 23–30.
18 Judy Yung, *Unbound Feet: A Social History of Chinese Women in San
   Francisco* (Berkeley, CA, 1995), p. 68.
19 *Who's Who of the Chinese in New York* (New York, 1918), quoted in
   Chunshing Chow, 'Immigration and immigrant settlements: The
   Chinese in New York City', University of Hawaii dissertation, 1984, p. 88.
20 Ivan Light, 'From vice district to tourist attraction: The moral career of
   American Chinatowns, 1880–1940', *Pacific Historical Review*, XLIII

(1974), pp. 367–94.

21 Xinyang Wang, *Surviving the City: The Chinese Immigrant Experience in New York City, 1890–1970* (New York, 2001), pp. 52–3, 73–6.

22 Rose Hum Lee, *The Chinese in the United States of America* (Hong Kong, 1960), pp. 59, 261.

23 Ibid., pp. 361–2.

24 H. J. Lethbridge, Introduction to Carl Crow, *Handbook for China* (Shanghai, 1933, reprint Hong Kong, 1984), p. xv.

25 Edgar Snow, *Journey to the Beginning* (London, 1959), pp. 28, 148.

26 Light, 'From vice district to tourist attraction', p. 385.

27 Wilbur Zelinsky, 'The roving palate: North America's ethnic cuisines', *Geoforum* XVI/1, 1985, pp. 51–72.

28 Judy Yung, *Unbound Feet*, p. 187, 201–4.

29 Light, 'From vice district to tourist attraction', p. 391.

30 Judy Yung, *Unbound Feet*, p. 175–6.

31 Ivan H. Light, *Ethnic Enterprise in America: Business and Welfare Among Chinese, Japanese, and Blacks* (Berkeley CA, 1972), pp. 1–18.

32 Yong Chen, *Chinese San Francisco*, pp. 197–8.

33 www.billlees.com/history.html.

34 H. Carr, *Los Angeles: City of Dreams* (New York, 1935), quoted in Roberta S. Greenwood, *Down by the Station: Los Angeles Chinatown, 1880–1933* (Los Angeles, 1996), p. 26.

35 Julia Chen, 'The Chinese community in New York: A study in their cultural adjustment, 1920–1940', American University dissertation, 1941, quoted in Chunshing Chow, 'Immigration and immigrant settlements', pp. 88–92.

36 Yong Chen, *Chinese San Francisco, 1850–1943*, p. 242.

37 Pearl S. Buck, preface to first edition of Buwei Yang Chao, *How to Cook and Eat in Chinese*, quoted in Harvey Levenstein, *Paradox of Plenty: A Social History of Eating in Modern America* (New York, 1993), p. 87.

38 Judy Yung, *Unbound Feet*, p. 269.

39 Kay J. Anderson, *Vancouver's Chinatown: Racial Discourse in Canada, 1875–1980* (Montreal, 1991), pp. 116–8.

40 Peter S. Li, 'Chinese immigrants on the Canadian prairie, 1910–47', *Canadian Review of Sociology and Anthropology*, XIX (1982), pp. 527–40.

41 Quoted in Con et al., *From China to Canada*, p. 154.

42 Anderson, *Vancouver's Chinatown* pp. 158–64.

43 Ibid., pp. 175–7.

44 Maria Lin Wong, *Chinese-Liverpudlians: A History of the Chinese Community in Liverpool* (Birkenhead, 1989), pp. 14–21, 45–7, 91, 96.

45 Kwee Choo Ng, *The Chinese in London* (London, 1958), p. 27.

46 Kenneth Lo, *The Feast of My Life* (London, 1993), p. 17.

47 Harold Acton, *Memoirs of an Aesthete* (London, 1948), pp.190, 194–8, 211.

48 Information provided by a reader of *Saga Magazine* in response to a letter published in June 2001. In 1942 a three-course meal at Ley On's cost 3s 6d. Later in the war rice became unobtainable and the restaurant served chips with its meals.

49 Ng, *The Chinese in London*, p. 27.

50 Jack Goody, *Food and Love* (London, 1998), p. 161.

51 Lo, *The Feast of My Life*, pp. 110, 122. Kenneth Lo attended the 1936 Berlin Olympics and ate a Chinese meal at a restaurant in Kant Strasse.

52 Jean Sterling, 'Foreign fare: Some typical dishes from China', 13 June 1939.

53 James L. Watson, *Emigration and the Chinese Lineage: The Mans in Hong Kong and London* (Berkeley, CA, 1975), pp. 67–9.

54 Lo, *The Feast of My Life*, pp. 128, 139, 142.

55 Information provided by readers of *Saga Magazine*.

56 Marguerite Patten, *We'll Eat Again: A Collection of Recipes from the War Years* (London, 1990), p. 27.

SEVEN · THE GLOBALIZATION OF CHINESE FOOD SINCE 1945

1 Emily Hahn and the editors of Time-Life Books, *The Cooking of China* (New York, 1969), p. 182.

2 Harvey Levenstein, *Paradox of Plenty: A Social History of Eating in Modern America* (New York, 1993), pp. 119–23.

3 Christopher Driver, *The British at Table* (London, 1983), pp. 38–57.

4 Rhoads Murphey, 'Boston's Chinatown', *Economic Geography*, XXVIII (1952), pp. 244–55.

5 Rose Hum Lee, *The Chinese in the United States of America* (Hong Kong, 1960), pp. 61–2, 261–8.

6 S. W. Kung, *Chinese in American Life: Some Aspects of their History, Status, Problems, and Contributions* (Seattle, 1962), pp. 181–3.

7 Melford S. Weiss, *Valley City: A Chinese Community in America* (Cambridge, MA, 1974), pp. 106–7, 118–21, 138–40.

8 Wilbur Zelinsky, 'The roving palate: North America's ethnic restaurant cuisines', *Geoforum*, XVI/1 (1985), pp. 51–72.

9 Levenstein, *Paradox of Plenty*, p. 216.

10 Bernard P. Wong, *Chinatown: Economic Adaptation and Ethnic Identity of the Chinese* (Fort Worth, 1982), pp. 37–43. Wong claimed that there were 4,500 Chinese restaurants in the greater New York area, presumably an error for 450 restaurants.

11 Jan Lin, *Reconstructing Chinatown: Ethnic Enclave, Global Change* (Minneapolis, 1998), pp. 68–76, 171.

12 Warren J. Belasco, 'Ethnic fast foods: The corporate melting pot', *Food and Foodways*, II (1987), pp. 1–30.

13 www.quikwok.com.

14 Peter S. Li, *The Chinese in Canada*, second edition (Toronto, 1998), pp. 89–101, 115, 134, 151.

15 Peter S. Li, 'Ethnic enterprise in transition: Chinese business in Richmond, BC, 1980–1990', *Canadian Ethnic Studies*, XXIV/1 (1992), pp. 120–38.

16 Hugh D. R. Baker, 'Nor good red herring: The Chinese in Britain', Paper prepared for the Second Sino–European Conference, Oxford, 1985, p. 3.

17 Jack Goody, *Food and Love* (London, 1998), p. 165.

18 This anecdote, and the information in the following paragraph and

elsewhere in this chapter, was supplied by readers of *Saga Magazine* in response to a letter published in June 2001.

19 James L. Watson, 'The Chinese: Hong Kong villagers in the British catering trade', in James L. Watson ed., *Between Two Cultures: Migrants and Minorities in Britain* (Oxford, 1977), pp. 181–213.

20 James L. Watson, *Emigration and the Chinese Lineage: The Mans in Hong Kong and London* (Berkeley, CA, 1975), p. 73.

21 Watson, *Emigration*, pp. 30–54. A similar chain migration occurred from the island of Ap Chau to Edinburgh.

22 1981 Census. This figure did not include heads of households born in Britain and other parts of the world.

23 Driver, *The British at Table*, p. 80.

24 Watson, 'The Chinese', *Between Two Cultures*, pp. 181, 183.

25 Anthony Shang, *The Chinese In Britain* (London, 1984), pp. 22, 27, 63–4.

26 *The Grocer*, 9 June 2001. The same article estimated that there were 10,000 Indian restaurants in the United Kingdom.

27 Watson, 'The Chinese', *Between Two Cultures*, p. 183.

28 The dispersal of Chinese restaurants and takeaways in Britain, and the social consequences of that dispersal, may be compared with the history of Chinese laundries in Chicago. See Paul C. Siu, *The Chinese Laundryman: A Study in Social Isolation* (New York, 1987).

29 A Chinese proprietor, quoted by Hugh D. R. Baker in 'Nor good red herring', p. 3.

30 Kwee Choo Ng, *The Chinese in London* (London, 1968), 29–31, 37; Watson, *Emigration*, pp. 28–30, 50–3, 60–9, 73, 104–6, 116–18.

31 Timothy Mo, *Sour Sweet* (London, 1982), pp. 17, 29, 61, 105–6, 138–9.

32 Lynn Pan, *Sons of the Yellow Emperor: The Story of the Overseas Chinese* (London, 1991), p. 327.

33 Driver, *The British at Table*, pp. 81–2.

34 Yi Liao, 'The Chinese community in Greater Manchester: The role of the catering trade', unpublished M. Phil. dissertation, University of Manchester, 1992, pp. 62–9, 120, 137–8, 178–80.

35 The above paragraphs are based on conversations with respondents to an article in the *Huddersfield Daily Examiner*, 1 August 2001.

36 Driver, *The British at Table*, p. 82.

37 Interview with Mr Raymond Wong, 26 September 2001.

38 *The Guardian*, 24 November 2000.

39 *The Guardian*, 8 April, 2000.

40 www.yellowriver.co.uk.

41 Sidney C. H. Cheung, 'The invention of delicacy: Cantonese food in Yokohama Chinatown', in David H. Wu and Sidney C. H. Cheung, eds, *The Globalization of Chinese Food* (Richmond, 2002), pp. 170–82.

42 Sidney C. H. Cheung, 'Food and Cuisine in a changing society: Hong Kong', in Wu and Cheung, op. cit., pp. 100–12.

43 Charles Campion, *The Rough Guide To London Restaurants*, fourth edition (London, 2001), p. 10.

44 Yu–sion Live, 'The Chinese community in France: Immigration, economic activity, cultural organization and representations', in Gregor Benton and Frank N. Pieke, eds, *The Chinese in Europe* (Basingstoke,

1998), pp. 96–124.

45 Frank N. Pieke and Gregor Benton, 'The Chinese in the Netherlands', in Benton and Pieke, op. cit., pp. 125–67.

46 Information supplied by Mr Norman Watson.

47 Agnes Ingle, 'Good cooking: Ways with food in China', BBC Woman's Hour, 21 November 1949.

48 Esther Chan, *Chinese Cookery Secrets*, second edition (Singapore, 1953), Foreword and pp. 1, 44, 83, 150.

49 Doreen Yen Hung Feng, *The Joy of Chinese Cooking* (1952, reprinted London, 1966), pp. 12, 16, 18, 123.

50 Mary Mather, 'Eating abroad – Hong Kong', BBC Radio 4, Woman's Hour, 10 July 1953.

51 Hahn, *The Cooking of China*, pp 6–7, 186.

52 Craig Claiborne, *The Food of China* (Aylesbury, 1973), pp. xiii–xxi.

53 Christopher Driver associated this trend with the rise of regional consciousness in Britain and Europe. Driver, *The British at Table*, p. 82.

54 The above paragraphs are based on an analysis of 173 books in English on Chinese cooking and related subjects published between 1928 and 1999.

55 Hahn, *The Cooking of China*, pp. 60–1.

56 *Jan-U-Wine Recipe Book* (Los Angeles, 1955).

57 Information from Ingle's Dawndew Salad Ltd, Poulton-le-Fylde, Lancashire.

58 Elaine Paulson-Box and Peter Williamson, 'The development of the ethnic food market in the UK', *British Food Journal* XCII/2 (1990), pp. 10–15.

59 *The Grocer*, 7 August, 1993, 28 August, 1998, 9 June, 2001.

60 *Market Intelligence*, May 2001.

EIGHT · ON THE GLOBALIZATION OF CHINESE FOOD

1 Derek Jarrett, *England in the Age of Hogarth* (St Albans, 1974), p. 22.

2 James Boswell, *Life of Johnson* (London, 1791), 1957 edn, pp. 658–9.

3 W. M. Thackeray, *Vanity Fair* (London, 1847), 1954 edn, pp. 38–9.

4 David Burton, *The Raj at Table: A Culinary History of the British in India* (London, 1993), pp. 1–12, 40, 70–2, 83, 94, 118.

5 Quoted in Christina Hardyment, *Slice of Life: The British Way of Eating Since 1945* (London, 1995), pp. 134–5.

6 Shrabani Basu, *Curry in the Crown: The Story of Britain's Favourite Dish* (New Delhi, 1999), p. 120.

7 Uma Narayan, 'Eating cultures: Incorporation, identity and Indian food', *Social Identities* I/1 (1995), pp. 63–86.

8 Quoted in David Bell and Gill Valentine, *Consuming Geographies: We Are Where We Eat* (London, 1997), pp. 174–5.

9 Dharamjit Singh, *Indian Cookery* (Harmondsworth, 1970), p. 9.

10 *The Big Issue in the North*, 10–16 April, 2000.

11 *The Guardian*, 21 July 2001.

12 Kwee Choo Ng, *The Chinese in London*, (London, 1968), pp. 58–9.

13 Jenny Clegg, *Fu Manchu and the 'Yellow Peril': The Making of a Racist Myth* (Stoke-on-Trent, 1994), p. 47.

14 *The Guardian*, 26 April 2000.
15 *Caterer and Hotelkeeper*, 12 April 2001.
16 Jeffrey Bernard, *Low Life* (London, 1987), pp. 82–3, quoted in Lynn Pan, *Sons of the Yellow Emperor* (London, 1991), pp. 328–9.
17 Yuen Kay Chung, 'At the Palace: Ethnography of a Chinese restaurant', unpublished dissertation, University of Manchester, 1981, pp. 44–55.
18 Information supplied by Ms Aimée Laycock.
19 Emily Hahn and the editors of Time-Life Books, *The Cooking of China* (New York, 1969), p. 77.
20 Report in the *New England Journal of Medicine* by Dr Robert Ho Man Kwok, discussed by Magnus Pyke, BBC Radio 3, 19 August 1969.
21 *The Guardian*, 27 March, 2 and 9 April, 2001.
22 *The Guardian*, 20 June 2000.
23 *The Guardian*, 30 June 2001.
24 Bob Flaws and Honora Lee Wolfe, *Prince Wen Hui's Cook: Chinese Dietary Therapy* (Brookline, MA, 1983), pp. 2–3, 64–5, 123.
25 *The Independent on Sunday*, 2 July 2000.
26 Marguerite Perrot, *Le mode de vie des familles bourgeoises, 1873–1953* (Paris, 1961), p. 292, quoted in Roland Barthes, 'Toward a psychosociology of contemporary food consumption', in Carole Counihan and Penny Van Esterik, eds, *Food and Culture: A Reader* (New York, 1997), pp. 20–5.
27 Ian Cook and Philip Crang, 'The world on a plate: Culinary culture, displacement and geographical knowledges', *Journal of Material Culture*, I/2 (1996), pp. 131–53.
28 Jack Goody, *Food and Love* (London, 1998), pp. 166–7.
29 David Y. H. Wu, 'Improvising Chinese cuisine overseas', in David Y. H. Wu and Sidney C. H. Cheung, eds, *The Globalization of Chinese Food* (Richmond, 2002), pp. 56–66.
30 A. Warde, L. Martens and W. Olsen, 'Consumption and the problem of variety: Cultural omnivorousness, social distinction and dining out', *Sociology*, XXXIII/1 (1999), pp. 105–27.
31 *Women's Own*, 25 April 1970.
32 *Ken Hom's Chinese Cookery* (London, 1984), pp. 12–14.
33 Kenneth Lo, *Chinese Food* (Harmondsworth, 1972), pp. 195–7; Craig Claiborne and Virginia Lee, *The Chinese Cookbook* (Aylesbury, 1973), pp. xix–xx.
34 Bell and Valentine, *Consuming Geographies*, p. 170.
35 Beth Mallinson, 'A study of the meanings associated with contemporary ethnic food trends among Bristol students', unpublished dissertation, School of Geographical Sciences, University of Bristol, December 2000.
36 Ken Hom, *Ken Hom's Cuisine: East Meets West* (London, 1988), pp. 1–20, 74.
37 Elizabeth Miles, 'Adventures in the postmodernist kitchen: The cuisine of Wolfgang Puck', *Journal of Popular Culture*, XXVII (1993), pp. 191–203.

Selected Further Reading

GENERAL WORKS

E. N. Anderson, *The Food of China* (New Haven, CT, 1988)
K. C. Chang, ed., *Food in Chinese Culture: Anthropological and Historical Perspectives* (New Haven, CT, 1977)
C. Claiborne, *The Food of China* (Aylesbury, 1973)
D. Burton, *The Raj at Table: A Culinary History of the British in India* (London, 1993)
J. Goody, *Cooking, Cuisine and Class: A Study in Comparative Sociology* (Cambridge, 1982)
K. Lo, *Chinese Food* (Harmondsworth, 1972)
F. J. Simoons, *Food in China: A Cultural and Historical Enquiry* (Boca Raton, FL, 1991)
R. L. Spang, *The Invention of the Restaurant: Paris and Modern Gastronomic Culture* (Cambridge, MA, 2000)
J. D. Spence, *Chinese Roundabout: Essays in History and Culture* (New York, 1992)
David Y. H. Wu and Sidney C. H. Cheung, eds, *The Globalization of Chinese Food* (Richmond, 2002)

WESTERNERS IN CHINA

R. Bickers, *Britain in China: Community, Culture and Colonialism 1900–1949* (Manchester, 1999)
J. F. Davis, *The Chinese: A General Description of China and Its Inhabitants*, new edn, (London, 1840)
J. B. Du Halde, *A Description of the Empire of China and Chinese-Tartary*, 2 vols, (London, 1738)
P. Hollander, *Political Pilgrims: Travels of Western Intellectuals to the Soviet Union, China, and Cuba 1928–1978* (New York, 1981)
M. Huc, *The Chinese Empire*, 2 vols (London, 1855)
C. Mackerras, *Western Images of China* (Hong Kong, 1989)
S. Wells Williams, *The Middle Kingdom: A Survey of the Geography, Government, Literature, Social Life, Arts and History of the Chinese Empire and Its Inhabitants*, 2 vols (New York, 1883)
F. Wood, *No Dogs and Not Many Chinese: Treaty Port Life in China 1843–1943* (London, 1998)

CHINESE FOOD IN NORTH AMERICA

K. J. Anderson, *Vancouver's Chinatown: Racial Discourse in Canada, 1875–1980* (Montreal, 1991)

Yong Chen, *Chinese San Francisco, 1850–1943: A Transpacific Community* (Stanford, CA, 2000)

R. H. Lee, *The Chinese in the United States of America* (Hong Kong, 1960)

H. Levenstein, *Paradox of Plenty: A Social History of Eating in Modern America* (New York, 1993)

P. S. Li, *The Chinese in Canada*, 2nd edn (Toronto, 1998)

S. C. Miller, *The Unwelcome Immigrant: The American Image of the Chinese, 1785–1882* (Berkeley, CA, 1969)

L. Pan, *Sons of the Yellow Emperor: The Story of the Overseas Chinese* (London, 1991)

B. L. Sung, *Mountain of Gold: The Story of the Chinese in America* (New York, 1967)

Xinyang Wang, *Surviving the City: The Chinese Immigrant Experience in New York City, 1890–1970* (New York, 2001)

CHINESE FOOD IN THE UNITED KINGDOM

G. Benton and F. N. Pieke, eds, *The Chinese in Europe* (Basingstoke, 1998)

C. Driver, *The British at Table 1940–1980* (London, 1983)

C. Hardyment, *Slice of Life: The British Way of Eating Since 1945* (London, 1995)

K. Lo, *The Feast of My Life* (London, 1993)

T. Mo, *Sour Sweet* (London, 1982)

K. C. Ng, *The Chinese in London* (London, 1958)

A. Shang, *The Chinese in Britain* (London, 1984)

J. L. Watson, *Emigration and the Chinese Lineage: The Mans in Hong Kong and London* (Berkeley, CA, 1975)

THE GLOBALIZATION OF CHINESE FOOD

W. J. Belasco, 'Ethnic fast foods: The corporate melting pot', *Food and Foodways*, II (1987)

D. Bell and G. Valentine, *Consuming Geographies: We Are Where We Eat* (London, 1997)

I. Cook and P. Crang, 'The world on a plate: Culinary culture, displacement and geographical knowledges', *Journal of Material Culture*, I/2 (1996)

C. Counihan and P. van Esterik, eds, *Food and Culture: A Reader* (New York, 1997)

J. Goody, *Food and Love* (London, 1998)

Uma Narayan, 'Eating cultures: Incorporation, identity and Indian food', *Social Identities* I/1 (1995)

Diva Sanjur, *Social and Cultural Perspectives in Nutrition* (Englewood Cliffs, NJ, 1982)

A. Warde, L. Martens and W. Olsen, 'Consumption and the problem of variety: Cultural omnivorousness, social distinction and dining out',

Sociology, XXXIII/1 (1999)

W. Zelinsky, 'The roving palate: North America's ethnic cuisines', *Geoforum* XVI/1 (1985)

Index

47, 72, 87, 91, 144, 182, 195
vitamins, vitamin deficiency 122, 130

waiters, waitresses 55, 94, 102, 123,
    142, 151, 153–4, 172, 176–7,
    210–12, 228
Waley, Arthur 157
Waln, Nora 90–1
Wang Xinyang 146
wars 227
    Opium (1839–42) 51, 53, 56
    'Arrow' (1856–60) 64
    First World 62, 146, 185
    Sino–Japanese (1937–45) 97–106,
        220, 224
    Second World 152, 155–6, 159,
        161, 164, 171
    civil (1946–9) 106–9
Warde, A. et al 219 *see also*
    'omnivorousness'
water chestnuts 17, 56, 168, 179,
    199–200
Watson, James L. 174
Wedemeyer, General Albert C. 113
Weiss, Melford S. 164–5
wheat 15, 23, 80, 92, 108, 110
White, Theodore H. 103
Wilhelm, Richard 87–8, 224
Williams, S. Wells 57–9
wine, Chinese 16, 21, 26, 29, 31, 34,
    36–7, 44, 46, 49, 51, 55–6, 66, 71,
    73, 86, 93, 108, 113, 115, 141–3
wok 22, 25, 101, 175, 202–3, 221–2
women 57, 74, 76, 80–1, 94, 101, 139,
    152, 172, 180, 188, 200, 203,
    221–2
Wong, Bernard P. 166–7
Wong, Raymond 182
wonton 25, 199–200 *see also*
    dumplings
Wood, Frances 121–2
Wu, David 218

Xiamen 53, 69, 200

Yan'an 96, 104–7
Yang Sing restaurant 181, 183
Yangzi river 23, 35, 70, 74
Yellow River Cafés 184
Yi Yin 87
yin and *yang* 26, 196, 215–16, 222
Yung, Judy 149

Zelinsky, Wilbur 165–6
Zhengzhou 99, 103
Zhou dynasty (1122–256 BC) 16, 18,
    21
Zhou Enlai 113, 117, 119, 166